The Evolution of Photography

John Werge

Copyright © BiblioLife, LLC

This book represents a historical reproduction of a work originally published before 1923 that is part of a unique project which provides opportunities for readers, educators and researchers by bringing hard-to-find original publications back into print at reasonable prices. Because this and other works are culturally important, we have made them available as part of our commitment to protecting, preserving and promoting the world's literature. These books are in the "public domain" and were digitized and made available in cooperation with libraries, archives, and open source initiatives around the world dedicated to this important mission.

We believe that when we undertake the difficult task of re-creating these works as attractive, readable and affordable books, we further the goal of sharing these works with a global audience, and preserving a vanishing wealth of human knowledge.

Many historical books were originally published in small fonts, which can make them very difficult to read. Accordingly, in order to improve the reading experience of these books, we have created "enlarged print" versions of our books. Because of font size variation in the original books, some of these may not technically qualify as "large print" books, as that term is generally defined; however, we believe these versions provide an overall improved reading experience for many.

THE EVOLUTION

OF

PHOTOGRAPHY.

WITH A

CHRONOLOGICAL RECORD

OF

DISCOVERIES, INVENTIONS, ETC.,

CONTRIBUTIONS TO PHOTOGRAPHIC LITERATURE,

AND

PERSONAL REMINISCENCES EXTENDING OVER FORTY YEARS.

BY

JOHN WERGE.

ILLUSTRATED.

LONDON:
PIPER & CARTER, 5, FURNIVAL STREET, HOLBORN, E.C.;
AND
JOHN WERGE, 11A, BERNERS STREET, OXFORD STREET, W.

1890.
[ALL RIGHTS RESERVED.]

Printed by Piper & Carter, 5, Furnival Street, Holborn, London, E.C.

PREFACE.

No previous history of photography, that I am aware of, has ever assumed the form of a reminiscence, nor have I met with a photographic work, of any description, that is so strictly built upon a chronological foundation as the one now placed in the hands of the reader. I therefore think, and trust, that it will prove to be an acceptable and readable addition to photographic literature.

It was never intended that this volume should be a text-book, so I have not entered into elaborate descriptions of the manipulations of this or that process, but have endeavoured to make it a comprehensive and agreeable summary of all that has been done in the past, and yet convey a perfect knowledge of all the processes as they have appeared and effected radical changes in the practice of photography.

The chronological record of discoveries, inventions, appliances, and publications connected with the art will, it is hoped, be received and considered as a useful and interesting table of reference; while the reminiscences, extending over forty years of unbroken contact with every phase of photography, and some of its pioneers, will form a vital link between the long past and immediate present, which may awaken pleasing recollections in some, and give encouragement to others to enter the field of experiment, and endeavour to continue the work of evolution.

At page 10 it is stated, on the authority of the late Robert Hunt, that some of Niepce's early pictures may be seen at the British Museum. That was so, but unfortunately it is not so now. On making application, very recently, to examine these pictures, I ascertained that they were never placed in the care of the curator of the British Museum, but were the private property of the late Dr. Robert Brown, who left them to his colleague, John Joseph Bennett, and that at the latter's death they passed into the possession of his widow. I wrote to the lady making enquiries about them, but have not been able to trace them further; there are, however, two very interesting examples of Niepce's heliographs, and one photo-etched plate and print, lent by Mr. H. P. Robinson, on view at South Kensington, in the Western Gallery of the Science Collection.

For the portrait of Thomas Wedgwood, I am indebted to Mr. Godfrey Wedgwood; for that of Joseph Nicephore Niepce, to the Mayor of Chalons-sur-Soane; for the Rev. J. B. Reade's, to Mr. Fox; for Sir John Herschel's, to Mr. H. H. Cameron; for John Frederick Goddard's, to Dr. Jabez Hogg; and for Frederick Scott Archer's, to Mr. Alfred Cade; and to all those gentlemen I tender my most grateful acknowledgments. Also to the Autotype Company, for their care and attention in carrying out my wishes in the reproduction of all the illustrations by their beautiful Collotype Process.

JOHN WERGE.

London, June, 1890.

CONTENTS.

INTRODUCTION 1

FIRST PERIOD.
THE DARK AGES 3

SECOND PERIOD.
PUBLICITY AND PROGRESS 27

THIRD PERIOD.
COLLODION TRIUMPHANT 58

FOURTH PERIOD.
GELATINE SUCCESSFUL 95

CHRONOLOGICAL RECORD.
INVENTIONS, DISCOVERIES, ETC. 126

CONTRIBUTIONS TO PHOTOGRAPHIC LITERATURE. ... 140

LIST OF ILLUSTRATIONS.

FRONTISPIECE	...	...	...	PORTRAIT OF THOMAS WEDGWOOD.
,,	...	...	...	PORTRAIT OF JOSEPH NICEPHORE NIEPCE.
,,	...	...	...	PORTRAIT OF REV. J. B. READE.
,,	...	...	...	PORTRAIT OF HENRY FOX TALBOT.
,,	...	...	...	PORTRAIT OF SIR JOHN HERSCHEL.
27	...	...	..	... PORTRAIT OF L. J. M. DAGUERRE.
27	...	...	...	... PORTRAIT OF JOHN FREDERICK GODDARD.
27	...	...	...	... COPY OF INSTANTANEOUS DAGUERREOTYPE.
58	...	...	...	... PORTRAIT OF FREDERICK SCOTT ARCHER.
58	...	...	...	... HEVER CASTLE, KENT.
95	...	...	...	... PORTRAIT OF DR. R. L. MADDOX.
95	...	...	...	... PORTRAIT OF RICHARD KENNETT.

INDEX.

Archer, Frederick Scott, 58-69
Argentic Gelatino-Bromide Paper, 106
Abney's Translation of Pizzighelli and Hubl's Booklet, 109
A String of Old Beads, 309

Bacon, Roger, 3
Bennett, Charles, 102
Boston, 51
Bromine Accelerator, 29
Bingham, Robert J, 87
Burgess, J., 93

Cabinet Portraits, 84
Camera Obscura, 3
Chronological Record, 126-139
Convention of 1889, 122
Claudet, A. F. J., 29, 86
Chlorine Accelerator, 29
Collodion Process (Archer's), 68
Collodio-Chloride Printing Process, 81

Davy, Sir H., 9
Daguerre, L. J M., 9, 43
Daguerreotype Process, 23, 24, 25
—— Apparatus Imported, 29
Diaphanotypes, 71
Dolland, J., 4
Donkin, W. F., 120
Draper, Dr., 107
Dublin Exhibition, 205-226

Eburneum Process, 82
Elliott & Fry, 96
Eosine, &c, 109
Errors in Pictorial Backgrounds, 231

First Photographic Portrait, 107
Fizeau, M., 6, 28
Flash-light Pictures, 118

Gelatino-Bromide Experiments, 91
Globe Lens, 78
Goddard, John Frederick, 28, 79

Harrison, W H., 87
Heliographic Process, 11, 12, 13
Heliochromy, 88
Herschel, Dr., 6
Herschel, Sir John, 94
Hillotypes, 71
Hughes, Jabez, 55, 75
Hunt, Robert, 117

International Exhibitions, 42, 77, 82, 111

Johnson, J. R , 107

Kennett, R , 96

Lambert, Leon, 93
Laroche, Sylvester, 116
Lea, Carey, 101
"Lux Graphicus" on the Wing, 273-299
Lights and Lighting, 311

Maddox, Dr R. L., 91
Magic Photographs, 83
Mawson, John, 85
Mayall, J E , 54
Macbeth, Norman, 120
Montreal, 51
Morgan and Kidd, 106

Newton, Sir Isaac, 3
New York, 48, 71
Niagara, 50
Niepce, J. Nicephore, 9, 11
Niepce de St Victor, 88
Niagara, Pictures of, 140-158
Notes on Pictures in National Gallery, 245

Orthochromatic Plates, 115

Panoramic Lens and Camera, 76
Pistolgraph, 76
Pensions to Daguerre and Niepce, 33
Philadelphia, 49
Ponton, Mungo, 22, 103
Poitevin, M., 85, 108
Porta, Baptista G., 3
Potash Bichromate, 22
Pouncy Process, 78
Pictures of the St. Lawrence, 158-169
Pinhole Camera, 117
Pizzighelli's Platinum Printing, 118
Pictures of the Potomac, 183-196
Photography in the North, 226-231
Perspective, 237-244
Photography and the Immured Pompeiians, 303

Rambles among Studios, 196-204
Reade, Rev. J. B., 15-22, 90
Rejlander, O. G., 98
Ritter, John Wm., 5
Rumford, Count, 5
Russell, Col., 117

Sable Island, 47
Salomon, Adam, 84

Sawyer, J. R., 121
Scheele, C. W., 4, 5
Senebier, 5
Simpson, George Wharton, 75, 103
Soda Sulphite, 109
Swan's Carbon Process, 80
Stannotype, 107
Sutton, Thomas, 100
Spencer, J. A., 102
Stereoscopic Pictures, 119
Sharpness and Softness *v.* Hardness, 249
Simple Mode of Intensifying Negatives, 307

Talbot, Henry Fox, 14, 101
Talbot *versus* Laroche, 54
Taylor, Professor Alfred Swaine, 104
The Hudson River, 169-183
The Society's Exhibition, 260
The Use of Clouds in Landscapes, 265
—— as Backgrounds in Portraiture, 269

Union of the North and South London Societies, 253

Vogel, Dr. H. W., 109

Washington, 49
Wedgwood Controversy, 80
Wedgwood, Thomas, 7, 8, 9
Whipple Gallery, 52
Wolcott Reflecting Camera, 28
Wollaston's Diaphragmatic Shutter, 115
Wollaston, Dr., 6
Woodbury Process, 82
Wothlytype Printing Process, 81

INTRODUCTION.

PHOTOGRAPHY, though young in years, is sufficiently aged to be in danger of having much of its early history, its infantile gambols, and vigorous growth, obscured or lost sight of in the glitter and reflection of the brilliant success which surrounds its maturity. Scarcely has the period of an average life psssed away since the labours of the successful experimentalists began; yet, how few of the present generation of workers can lay their fingers on the dates of the birth, christening, and phases of the delightful vocation they pursue. Many know little or nothing of the long and weary travail the minds of the discoverers suffered before their ingenuity gave birth to the beautiful art-science by which they live. What form the infant art assumed in the earlier stages of its life; or when, where, and how, it passed from one phase to another until it arrived at its present state of mature and profitable perfection. Born with the art, as I may say, and having graduated in it, I could, if I felt so disposed, give an interesting, if not amusing, description of its rise and progress, and the many difficulties and disappointments that some of the early practitioners experienced at a time when photographic A B C's were not printed; its "principles and practice" anything but familiarly explained; and when the "dark-room" was as dark as the grave, and as poisonous as a charnel-house, and only occasionally illumined by the glare of a "bull's-eye." But it is not my intention to enter the domain of romance, and give highly coloured or extravagant accounts of the growth of so beautiful and fascinating an art-science. Photography is sufficiently facetious in itself, and too versatile in its powers of delineation of scenes and character, to require any verbose effort of mine to make it attractive. A record of bare facts is all I aim at. Whatever is doubtful I shall leave to the imagination of the reader, or the invention of the romance writer. To arrange in chronological order the various discoveries, inventions, and improvements that have made photography what it is; to do honour to those who have toiled and given, or sold, the fruits of their labour for the advancement of the art; to set at rest, as far as dates can succeed in doing so, any questionable point or order of precedence of merit in invention, application, or modification of a process, and to enable the photographic student to make himself acquainted with the epochs of the art, is the extent of my ambition in compiling these records.

With the hope of rendering this work readily referable and most comprehensive, I shall divide it into four periods. The first will deal broadly and briefly with such facts as can be ascertained that in any way bear on the accidental discovery, early researches, and ultimate success of the pioneers of photography

The second will embrace a fuller description of their successes and results. The third will be devoted to a consideration of patents and impediments; and the fourth to the rise and development of photographic literature and art. A strict chronological arrangement of each period will be maintained, and it is hoped that the advantages to be derived from travelling some of the same ground over again in the various divisions of the subject will fully compensate the reader, and be accepted as sufficient excuse for any unavoidable repetition that may appear in the work. With these few remarks I shall at once enter upon the task of placing before the reader in chronological order the origin, rise, progress, and development of the science and art of photography.

FIRST PERIOD.

THE DARK AGES.

More than three hundred years have elapsed since the influence and actinism of light on chloride of silver was observed by the alchemists of the sixteenth century. This discovery was unquestionably the first thing that suggested to the minds of succeeding chemists and men of science the possibility of obtaining pictures of solid bodies on a plane surface previously coated with a silver salt by means of the sun's rays; but the alchemists were too much absorbed in their vain endeavours to convert the base metals into royal ones to seize the hint, and they lost the opportunity of turning the silver compounds with which they were acquainted into the mine of wealth it eventually became in the nineteenth century. Curiously enough, a mechanical invention of the same period was afterwards employed, with a very trifling modification, for the production of the earliest sun-pictures. This was the camera-obscura invented by Roger Bacon in 1297, and improved by a physician in Padua, Giovanni Baptista Porta, about 1500, and afterwards remodelled by Sir Isaac Newton.

Two more centuries passed away before another step was taken towards the revelation of the marvellous fact that Nature possessed within herself the power to delineate her own beauties, and, as has recently been proved, that the sun could depict his own terrible majesty with a rapidity and fidelity the hand of man could never attain. The second step towards this grand achievement of science was the construction of the double achromatic combination of lenses by J. Dolland. With single combinations of lenses, such pictures as we see of ourselves to-day, and such portraits of the sun as the astronomers obtained during the late total eclipse, could never have been produced. J. Dolland, the eminent optician, was born in London 1706, and died 1762; and had he not made that important improvement in the construction of lenses, the eminent photographic opticians of the present day might have lived and died unknown to wealth and fame.

The observations of the celebrated Swedish chemist, Scheele, formed the next interesting link between the simple and general blackening of a lump of chloride of silver, and the gradations of blackening which ultimately produced the photographic picture on a piece of paper possessing a prepared surface of nitrate of silver and chloride of sodium in combination. Scheele discovered in 1777 that the blackening of the silver compound was due to the reducing power of light, and that the black deposit was *reduced silver;* and it is precisely the same effect of the action of light upon chloride of silver passing through the various densities of the negative that produces the beautiful photographic prints with which we are all familiar at the present time. Scheele was also the first to discover and make known the fact that chloride of silver was blackened or reduced to various depths by the varying action of the prismatic colours. He fixed a glass prism in a window, allowed the refracted sunbeams to fall on a piece of paper strewn with *luna cornua*—fused chloride of silver—and saw that the violet ray was more active than any of the other colours. Anyone, with a piece of sensitized paper and a prism, or piece of a broken lustre, can repeat and see for themselves Scheele's interesting discovery; and anyone that can draw a head or a flower may catch a sunbeam in a small magnifying glass, and make a drawing on sensitized paper with a pencil, as long as the sun is distant from the earth. It is the old story of Columbus and the egg—easy to do when you are shown or told how.

Charles William Scheele was born at Stralsund, Sweden, December 19th, 1742, and died at Koeping, on lake Moeler, May 21st, 1786. He was the real father of photography, for he produced the first photographic picture on record without camera and without lens, with the same chemical compound and the same beautiful and wonderful combination of natural colours which we now employ. Little did he dream what was to follow. But photography, like everything else in this world, is a process of evolution.

Senebier followed up Scheele's experiments with the solar spectrum, and ascertained that chloride of silver was darkened by the violet ray in fifteen minutes, while the red rays were sluggish, and required twenty minutes to produce the same result

John Wm. Ritter, born at Samitz, in Selesia, corroborated the experiments of Scheele, and discovered that chloride of silver was blackened beyond the spectrum on the violet side. He died in 1810; but he had observed what is now called the fluorescent rays of the spectrum—invisible rays which unquestionably exert themselves in the interests and practice of photography.

Many other experiments were made by other chemists and philosophers on the influence of light on various substances, but none of them had any direct bearing on the subject under consideration until Count Rumford, in 1798, communicated to the Royal Society his experiments with chloride of gold. Count Rumford wetted a piece of taffeta ribbon with a solution of chloride of gold, held it horizontally over the clear flame of a wax candle, and saw that the heat decomposed the gold solution, and stained the ribbon a beautiful purple. Though no revived gold was visible, the ribbon appeared to be coated with a rich purple enamel, which showed a metallic lustre of great brilliancy when viewed in the sunlight; but its photographic value lay in the circumstance of the hint it afterwards afforded M. Fizeau in applying a solution of chloride of gold, and, by means of heat, depositing a fine film of metallic gold on the surface of the Daguerreotype image, thereby increasing the brilliancy and permanency of that form of photographic picture. A modification of M. Fizeau's chloride of gold "fixing process" is still used to tone, and imparts a rich purple colour to photographic prints on plain and albumenized papers.

In 1800, Dr. Herschel's "Memoirs on the Heating Power of the Solar Spectrum" were published, and out of his observations on the various effects of differently coloured darkening glasses arose the idea that the chemical properties of the prismatic colours, and coloured glass, might be as different as those which related to heat and light. His suspicions were ultimately verified, and hence the use of yellow or ruby glass in the windows of the "dark-room," as either of those coloured glasses admit the luminous ray and restrain the violet or active photographic ray, and allow all the operations that would otherwise have to be performed in the dark, to be seen and done in comfort, and without injury to the sensitive film.

The researches of Dr. Wollaston, in 1802, had very little reference to photography beyond his examination of the chemical action of the rays of the spectrum, and his observation that the yellow stain of gum guaiacum was converted to a green colour in the violet rays, and that the red rays rapidly destroyed the green tint the violet rays had generated.

1802 is, however, a memorable year in the dark ages of photography, and the disappointment of those enthusiastic and indefatigable pursuers of the sunbeam must have been grievous indeed, when, after years of labour, they found the means of catching shadows as they fell, and discovered that they could not keep them

Thomas Wedgwood, son of the celebrated potter, was not only the first that obtained photographic impressions of objects, but the first to make the attempt to obtain sun pictures in the true sense of the word. Scheele had obtained the first photographic picture of the solar spectrum, but it was by accident, and while pursuing other chemical experiments; whereas Wedgwood went to work avowedly to make the sunbeam his slave, to enlist the sun into the service of art, and to compel the sun to illustrate art, and to depict nature more faithfully than art had ever imitated anything illumined by the sun before. How far he succeeded everyone should know, and no student of photography should ever tire of reading the first published account of his fascinating pastime or delightful vocation, if it were but to remind him of the treasures that surround him, and the value of hyposulphite of soda. What would Thomas Wedgwood not have given for a handful of that now common commodity? There is a mournfulness in the sentence relative to the evanescence of those sun pictures in the Memoir by Wedgwood and Davy that is peculiarly impressive and desponding contrasted with our present notions of instability. We know that sun pictures will, at the least, last for years, while they knew that at the most they would endure but for a few hours. The following extracts from the Memoir published in June, 1802, will, it is hoped, be found sufficiently interesting and in place here to justify their insertion.

"White paper, or white leather moistened with solution of nitrate of silver, undergoes no change when kept in a dark place, but on being exposed to the daylight it speedily changes colour, and after passing through different shades of grey and brown becomes at length nearly black. . . . In the direct beams of the sun, two or three minutes are sufficient to produce the full effect, in the shade several hours are required, and light transmitted through different coloured glasses acts upon it with different degrees of intensity. Thus it is found that red rays, or the common sunbeams passed through red glass, have very little action upon it; yellow and green are more efficacious, but blue and violet light produce the most decided and powerful effects. . . . When the shadow of any figure is thrown upon the prepared surface, the part concealed by it remains white, and the other parts speedily become dark. For copying paintings on glass, the solution should be applied on leather, and in this case it is more readily acted on than when paper is used. After the colour has been once fixed on the leather or paper, it cannot be removed by the application of water, or water and soap, and it is in a high degree permanent. The copy of a painting or the profile, immediately after being taken, must be kept in an obscure place; it may indeed be examined in the shade, but in this case the exposure should be only for a few minutes; by the light of candles or lamps as commonly employed it is not sensibly affected.

No attempts that have been made to prevent the uncoloured parts of the copy or profile from being acted upon by the light have as yet been successful. They have been covered by a thin coating of fine varnish, but this has not destroyed their susceptibility of becoming coloured, and even after repeated washings, sufficient of the active part of the saline matter will adhere to the white parts of leather or paper to cause them to become dark when exposed to the rays of the sun. . . .

The images formed by means of a camera-obscura have been found to be too faint to produce, in any moderate time, an effect upon the nitrate of silver. To copy these images was the first object of Mr. Wedgwood, in his researches on the subject, and for this purpose he first used the nitrate of silver, which was mentioned to him by a friend, as a substance very sensible to the influence of light; but all his numerous experiments as to their primary end proved unsuccessful."

From the foregoing extracts from the first lecture on

photography that ever was delivered or published, it will be seen that those two eminent philosophers and exprimentalists despaired of obtaining pictures in the camera-obscura, and of rendering the pictures obtained by superposition, or cast shadows, in any degree permanent, and that they were utterly ignorant and destitute of any fixing agents. No wonder, then, that all further attempts to pursue these experiments should, for a time, be abandoned in England. Although Thomas Wedgwood's discoveries were not published until 1802, he obtained his first results in 1791, and does not appear to have made any appreciable advance during the remainder of his life. He was born in 1771, and died in 1805. Sir Humphrey Davey was born at Penzance 1778, and died at Geneva in 1828, so that neither of them lived to see the realization of their hopes.

From the time that Wedgwood and Davy relinquished their investigation, the subject appears to have lain dormant until 1814, when Joseph Nicéphore Niepce, of Chalon-sur-Saône, commenced a series of experiments with various resins, with the object of securing or retaining in a permanent state the pictures produced in the camera-obscura, and in 1824, L. J. M. Daguerre turned his attention to the same subject. These two investigators appear to have carried on their experiments in different ways, and in total ignorance of the existence and pursuits of the other, until the year 1826, when they accidentally became acquainted with each other and the nature of their investigations. Their introduction and reciprocal admiration did not, however, induce them to exchange their ideas, or reveal the extent of their success in the researches on which they were occupied, and which both were pursuing so secretly and guardedly. They each preserved a marked reticence on the subject for a considerable time, and it was not until a deed of partnership was executed between them that they confided their hopes and fears, their failures with this substance, and their prospects of success with that; and even after the execution of the deed of partnership they seem to have jealously withheld as much of their knowledge as they decently could under the circumstances.

Towards the close of 1827 M. Niepce visited England, and we receive the first intimation of his success in the production of light-drawn pictures from a note addressed to Mr. Bauer, of Kew. It is rather curious and flattering to find that the earliest intimation of the Frenchman's success is given in England The note which M. Niepce wrote to Mr. Bauer is in French, but the following is a translation of the interesting announcement:—
"Kew, 19th November, 1827. Sir,— When I left France to reside here, I was engaged in researches on the way to retain the image of objects by the action of light. I have obtained some results which make me eager to proceed . . . Nicephore Niepce."
This is the first recorded announcement of his partial success.

In the following December he communicated with the Royal Society of London, and showed several pictures on metal plates. Most of these pictures were specimens of his successful experiments with various resins, and the subjects were rendered visible to the extent which the light had assisted in hardening portions of the resin-covered plates Some were etchings, and had been subjected to the action of acid after the design had been impressed by the action of light. Several of these specimens, I believe, are still extant, and may be seen on application to the proper official at the British Museum M Niepce named these results of his researches Heliography, and Mr Robert Hunt gives their number, and a description of each subject, in his work entitled, "Researches on Light" M Niepce met with some disappointment in England on account of the Royal Society refusing to receive his communication as a secret, and he returned to France rather hurriedly. In a letter dated "Chalons-sur-Saône, 1st March, 1828," he says, "We arrived here 26th February", and, in a letter written by Daguerre, February 3rd, 1828, we find that savant consoling his brother experimentalist for his lack of encouragement in England

In December, 1829, the two French investigators joined issue by executing a deed of co-partnery, in which they agreed to prosecute their researches in future in mutual confidence and for their joint advantage ; but their interchange of thought and experience does not appear to have been of much value or advantage to the other; for an examination of the correspondence between MM. Niepce and Daguerre tends to show that the one somewhat annoyed the other by sticking to his resins, and the other one by recommending the use of iodine. M. Niepce somewhat ungraciously expresses regret at having wasted so much time in experimenting with iodine at M. Daguerre's suggestion, but ultimate results fully justified Daguerre's recommendation, and proved that he was then on the right track, while M Niepce's experiments with resins, asphaltum, and other substances terminated in nothing but tedious manipulations, lengthy exposures, and unsatisfactory results. To M. Niepce, most unquestionably, is due the honour of having produced the first permanent sun pictures, for we have seen that those obtained by Wedgwood and Davy were as fleeting as a shadow, while those exhibited by M. Niepce in 1827 are still in their original condition, and, imperfect as they are, they are likely to retain their permanency for ever. Their fault lay in neither possessing beauty nor commercial applicability.

As M. Niépce died at Chalons-sur-Saone in 1833, and does not appear to have improved his process much, if any, after entering into partnership with M. Daguerre, and as I may not have occasion to allude to him or his researches again, I think this will be the most fitting place to give a brief description of his process, and his share in the labours of bringing up the wonderful baby of science, afterwards named Photography, to a safe and ineffaceable period of its existence.

The Heliographic process of M. Niépce consists of a solution of asphaltum, bitumen of Judea, being spread on metal or glass plates, submitted to the action of light either by superposition or in the camera, and the unaffected parts dissolved away afterwards by means of a suitable solvent. But, in case any student of photography should like to produce one of the first form of permanent sun pictures, I shall give here the details of M. Niépce's own *modus operandi* for preparing the solution of bitumen and coating the plate:—

" I about half fill a wine-glass with this pulverised bitumen; I pour upon it, drop by drop, the essential oil of lavender until the bitumen is completely saturated. I afterwards add as much more of the essential oil as causes the whole to stand about three lines above the mixture, which is then covered and submitted to a gentle heat until the essential oil is fully impregnated with the colouring matter of the bitumen. If this varnish is not of the required consistency, it is to be allowed to evaporate slowly, without heat, in a shallow dish, care being taken to protect it from moisture, by which it is injured and at last decomposed. In winter, or in rainy weather, the precaution is doubly necessary. A tablet of plated silver, or well cleaned and warm glass, is to be highly polished, on which a thin coating of the varnish is to be applied cold, with a light roll of very soft skin; this will impart to it a fine vermilion colour, and cover it with a very thin and equal coating. The plate is then placed upon heated iron, which is wrapped round with several folds of paper, from which, by this method, all moisture had been previously expelled. When the varnish has ceased to simmer, the plate is withdrawn from the heat, and left to cool and dry in a gentle temperature, and protected from a damp atmosphere. In this part of the operation a light disc of metal, with a handle in the centre, should be held before the mouth, in order to condense the moisture of the breath."

In the foregoing description it will be observed how much importance M. Niépce attached to the necessity of protecting the solution and prepared plate from moisture, and that no precautions are given concerning the effect of white light. It must be remembered, however, that the material employed was very insensitive, requiring many hours of exposure either in the camera or under a print or drawing placed in contact with the prepared surface, and consequently such precaution might not have been deemed necessary. Probably M. Niépce worked in a subdued light, but there can be no doubt about the necessity of conducting both the foregoing operations in yellow light. Had M. Niépce performed his operations in a non-actinic light, the plates would certainly have been more sensitive, and the unacted-on parts would have been more soluble; thus rendering both the time of exposure and development more rapid.

After the plate was prepared and dried, it was exposed in the camera, or by superposition, under a print, or other suitable subject, that would lie flat. For the latter, an exposure of two or three hours in bright sunshine was necessary, and the former required six or eight hours in a strong light. Even those prolonged exposures did not produce a visible image, and the resultant picture was not revealed to view until after a tedious process of dissolving, for it could scarcely be called development. M. Niepce himself says, "The next operation then is to disengage the *shrouded* imagery, and this is accomplished by a solvent." The solvent consisted of one measure of the essential oil of lavender and ten of oil of white petroleum or benzole. On removing the tablet from the camera or other object, it was plunged into a bath of the above solvent, and left there until the parts not hardened by light were dissolved. When the picture was fully revealed, it was placed at an angle to drain, and finished by washing it in water.

Except for the purpose of after-etching, M. Niepce's process was of little commercial value then, but it has since been of some service in the practice of photo-lithography. That, I think, is the fullest extent of the commercial or artistic advantages derived from the utmost success of M. Niepce's discoveries; but what he considered his failures, the fact that he employed copper plates coated with silver for his heliographic tablets, and endeavoured to darken the clean or clear parts of the silvered plates with the fumes of iodine for the sake of contrast only, may be safely accepted as the foundation of Daguerre's ultimate success in discovering the extremely beautiful and workable process known as the Daguerreotype.

M. Niepce appears to have done very little more towards perfecting the heliographic process after joining Daguerre ; but the latter effected some improvements, and substituted for the bitumen of Judea the residuum obtained by evaporating the essential oil of lavender, without, however, attaining any important advance in that direction. After the death of M. Nicéphore Niepce, a new agreement was entered into by his son, M. Isidore Niepce, and M. Daguerre, and we must leave those two experimentalists pursuing their discoveries in France while we return to England to pick up the chronological links that unite the history of this wonderful discovery with the time that it was abandoned by Wedgwood and Davy, and the period of its startling and brilliant realisation.

In 1834, Mr. Henry Fox Talbot, of Lacock Abbey, Wilts, " began to put in practice," as he informs us in his memoir read before the Royal Society, a method which *he* " had *devised* some time previously, for employing to purposes of utility the very curious property which has been long known to chemists to be possessed by the nitrate of silver—namely, to discolouration when exposed to the violet rays of light." The statement just quoted places us at once on the debateable ground of our subject, and compels us to pause and consider to what extent photography is indebted to Mr. Talbot for its further development at this period and five years subsequently. In the first place, it is not to be supposed for a moment that a man of Mr. Talbot's position and education could possibly be ignorant of what had been done by Mr. Thomas Wedgwood and Sir Humphrey Davy. Their experiments were published in the Journal of the Royal

Institution of Great Britain in June, 1802, and Mr. Talbot or some of his friends could not have failed to have seen or heard of those published details ; and, in the second place, a comparison between the last records of Wedgwood and Davy's experiments, and the first published details of Mr. Talbot's process, shows not only that the two processes are identically the same, but that Mr. Talbot published his process before he had made a single step in advance of Wedgwood and Davy's discoveries; and that his fixing solution was not a fixer at all, but simply a retardant that delayed the gradual disappearance of the picture only a short time longer. Mr. Talbot has generally been credited with the honour of producing the first permanent sun-pictures on paper; but there are grave reasons for doubting the justice of that honour being entirely, if at all, due to him, and the following facts and extracts will probably tend to set that question at rest, and transfer the laurel to another brow.

To the late Rev. J. B. Reade is incontestably due the honour of having first applied tannin as an accelerator, and hyposulphite of soda as a fixing agent, to the production and retention of light-produced pictures; and having first obtained an ineffaceable photograph upon paper. Mr. Talbot's gallate of silver process was not patented or published till 1841; whereas the Rev. J. B. Reade produced paper negatives by means of gallic acid and nitrate of silver in 1837. It will be remembered that Mr. Wedgwood had discovered and stated that the chloride of silver was more sensitive when applied to white leather, and Mr. Reade, by inductive reasoning, came to the conclusion that tanned paper and silver would be more sensitive to light than ordinary paper coated with nitrate of silver could possibly be. As the reverend philosopher's ideas on that subject are probably the first that ever impregnated the mind of man, and as his experiments and observations are the very earliest in the pursuit of a gallic acid accelerator and developer, I will give them in his own words:—"No one can dispute my claim to be the first to suggest the use of gallic acid as a sensitizer for prepared paper, and hyposulphite of soda as a fixer. These are the keystones of the arch at which Davy and Young had laboured—or, as I may say in the language of another science, we may vary the tones as we please, but here is the fundamental base. My use of gallate of silver was the result of an inference from Wedgwood's experiments with leather, ' which is more readily acted upon than paper' (*Journal of the Royal Institution*, vol. i., p. 171). Mrs. Reade was so good as to give me a pair of light-coloured leather gloves, that I might repeat Wedgwood's experiment, and, as my friend Mr. Ackerman reminds me, her little objection to let me have a second pair led me to say, 'Then I will tan paper.' Accordingly I used an infusion of galls in the first instance in the early part of the year 1837, when I was engaged in taking photographs of microscopic objects. By a new arrangement of lenses in the solar microscope, I produced a convergence of the rays of light, while the rays of heat, owing to their different refractions, were parallel or divergent. This fortunate dispersion of the calorific rays enabled me to use objects mounted in balsam, as well as cemented achromatic object glasses; and, indeed, such was the coolness of the illumination, that even *infusoria* in single drops of water were perfectly happy and playful (*vide* abstracts of the ' Philosophical Transactions,' December 22nd, 1836). The continued expense of an artist—though, at first, I employed my friend, Lens Aldons—to copy the pictures on the screen was out of the question. I therefore fell back, but without any sanguine expectations as to the result, upon the photographic process adopted by Wedgwood, with which I happened to be well acquainted. I was a *weary while*, however, before any satisfactory impression was made, either on chloride or nitrate paper. I succeeded better with the leather; but my fortunate inability to replenish the little stock of this latter article induced me to apply the tannin solution to paper, and thus I was at once placed, by a very decided step, in advance of earlier experimenters, and I had the pleasure of succeeding where Talbot acknowledges that he failed.

"Naturally enough, the solution which I used at first was too strong, but, if you have ever been in what I may call *the agony of a find*, you can conceive my sensations on witnessing the unwilling paper become in a few seconds almost as black as my hat. There was just a passing glimpse of outline, 'and in a moment all was dark.' It was evident, however, that I was in possession of all, and more than all, I wanted, and that the dilution of so powerful an accelerator would probably give successful results. The large amount of dilution greatly surprised me; and, indeed, before I obtained a satisfactory picture, the quantity of gallic acid in the infusion must have been quite homœopathic; but this is in exact accordance with modern practice and known laws. In reference to this point, Sir John Herschel, writing from Slough, in April, 1840, says to Mr. Redman, then of Peckham (where I had resided), 'I am surprised at the weak solution employed, and how, with such, you have been able to get a depth of shadow sufficient for so very sharp a re-transfer is to me marvellous.' I may speak of Mr. Redmond as a photographic pupil of mine, and at my request, he communicated the process to Sir John, which, 'on account of the extreme clearness and sharpness of the results,' to use Sir John's words, much interested him.

"Dr. Diamond also, whose labours are universally appreciated, first saw my early attempts at Peckham in 1837, and heard of my use of gallate of silver, and was thus led to adopt what Admiral Smyth then called 'a quick mode of taking bad pictures'; but, as I told the Admiral in reply, he was born a *baby*. Whether our philosophical baby is 'out of its teens' may be a question; at all events, it is a very fine child, and handles the pencil of nature with consummate skill.

"But of all the persons who heard of my new accelerator, it is most important to state that my old and valued friend, the late Andrew Ross, told Mr. Talbot how first of all, by means of the solar microscope, I threw the image of the object on prepared paper, and then, while the paper was yet wet, washed it over with the infusion of galls, when a sufficiently dense negative was quickly obtained. In the celebrated trial, "Talbot *versus* Laroche," Mr. Talbot, in his cross-examination, and in an almost breathless court, acknowledged that he had received this information from Ross, and from that moment it became the unavoidable impression that he was scarcely justified in taking out a patent for applying my accelerator to any known photogenic paper.

"The three known papers were those impregnated with the nitrate, chloride, and the iodide of silver—the two former used by Wedgwood and Young, and the latter by Davy. It is true that Talbot says of the iodide of silver that it is quite insensitive to light, and so it is as he makes it; but when he reduces it to the condition described by Davy—viz., affected by the presence of a little free nitrate of silver—then he must acknowledge, with Davy, that 'it is far more sensitive to the action of light than either the nitrate or the muriate, and is evidently a distinct compound.' In this state, also, the infusion of galls or gallic acid is, as we all know, most decided and instantaneous, and so I found it to be in my early experiments. Of course I tried the effects of my accelerator on many salts of silver, but especially upon the iodide, in consequence of my knowledge of Davy's papers on iodine in the 'Philosophical Transactions.' These I had previously studied, in conjunction with my chemical friend, Mr. Hodgson, then of Apothecaries' Hall. I did not, however, use iodised paper, which is well described by Talbot in the *Philosophical Magazine* for March, 1838, as a *substitute* for other sensitive papers, but only as one among many experiments alluded to in my letter to Mr. Brayley.

"My pictures were exhibited at the Royal Society, and also at Lord Northampton's, at his lordship's request, in April, 1839, when Mr. Talbot also exhibited his. In my letter to Mr. Brayley, I did not describe iodised pictures, and, therefore, it was held that exhibition in the absence of description left the process legally unknown. Mr. Talbot consequently felt justified in taking out a patent for uniting my *known* accelerator with Davy's *known* sensitive silver compound, adopting my method (already communicated to him) with reference to Wedgwood's papers, and adding specific improvements in manipulation. Whatever varied opinion may consequently be formed as to the defence of the patent in court, there can be but one as to the skill of the patentee.

"It is obvious that, in the process so conducted by me with the solar microscope, I was virtually *within* my camera, standing between the object and the prepared paper. Hence the exciting and developing processes were conducted under *one operation* (subsequently patented by Talbot), and the fact of a latent image being brought out was not forced upon my attention. I did, however, perceive this phenomenon upon one occasion, after I had been suddenly called away, when taking an impression of the *Trientalis Europœa*—and surprised enough I was, and stood in astonishment to look at it. But with all this, I was only, as the judge said, "*very hot.*" I did not realise the *master fact* that the latent image which had been developed was the basis of photographic manipulation. The merit of this discovery is Talbot's, and his only, and I honour him greatly for his skill and earlier discernment. I was, indeed, myself fully aware that the image darkened under the influence of my sensitiser, while I placed my hand before the lens of the instrument to stop out the light; and my solar mezzotint, as I then termed it, was, in fact, brought out and perfected under my own eye by the agency of gallic acid in the infusion, rather than by the influence of direct solar action. But the notion of developing a latent image in these microscopic photographs never crossed my mind, even after I had witnessed such development in the *Trientalis Europœa*. My original notion was that the infusion of galls, added to the wet chloride or nitrate paper while the picture was thrown upon it, produced only a new and highly sensitive compound; whereas, by its peculiar and continuous action after the first impact of light on the now sensitive paper, I was also, as Talbot has shown, employing its property of development as well as excitement. My ignorance of its properties was no bar to its action. However, I threw the *ball*, and Talbot caught it, and no man can be more willing than myself to acknowledge our obligations to this distinguished photographer. He compelled the world to listen to him, and he had something worth hearing to communicate; and it is a sufficient return to me that he publicly acknowledged his obligation to me, with reference to what Sir David Brewster calls 'an essential part of his patent' (*vide North British Review*, No. 14 article—'Photography')

"Talbot did not patent my valuable fixer. Here I had the advantage of having published my use of hyposulphite of soda, which Mr. Hodgson made for me in 1837, when London did not contain an ounce of it for sale. The early operators had no fixer; that was *their fix;* and, so far as any record exists, they got no further in this direction than 'imagining some experiments on the subject!' I tried ammonia, but it acted too energetically on the picture itself to be available for the purpose. It led me, however, to the ammonia nitrate process of printing positives, a description of which process (though patented by Talbot in 1843) I sent to a photographic brother in 1839, and a quotation from my letter of that date has already appeared in one of my communications to *Notes and Queries*. On examining Brande's Chemistry, under the hope of still finding the desired solvent which should have a greater affinity for the simple silver compound on the uncoloured part of the picture than for the portion blackened by light, I happened to see it stated, on Sir John Herschel's authority, that hyposulphite of soda dissolves chloride of silver. I need not now say that I used this fixer with success. The world, however, would not have been long without it, for, when Sir John himself became a photographer in the following year, he first of all used hyposulphite of ammonia, and then permanently fell back upon the properties of his other compound. Two of my solar microscope negatives, taken in 1837, and exhibited with several others by Mr. Brayley in 1839 as illustrations of my letter and of his lecture at the London Institution, are now in the possession of the London Photographic Society. They are, no doubt, the earliest examples of the agency of two chemical compounds which will be co-existent with photography itself, viz., gallate of silver and hyposulphite of soda, and my use of them, as above described, will sanction my claim to be the first to take paper pictures rapidly, and to fix them permanently.

"Such is a short account of my contribution to this interesting branch of science, and, in the pleasure of the discovery, I have a sufficient reward."

These lengthy extracts from the Rev. Mr. Reade's published letter render further comment all but superfluous, but I cannot resist taking advantage of the opportunity here afforded of pointing out to all lovers of photography and natural justice that the progress of the discovery has advanced to a far greater extent by Mr. Reade's reasoning and experiments than it was by Mr. Talbot's ingenuity. The latter, as Mr. Reade observes, only "caught the ball" and threw it into the Patent Office, with some improvements in the manipulations. Mr. Reade generously ascribes all honour and glory to Mr Talbot for his shrewdness in seizing what he had overlooked, viz., the development of the latent image; but there is a quiet current of rebuke running all through Mr Reade's letter about the justice of patenting a known sensitizer and a known accelerator, which he alone had combined and applied to the successful production of a negative on paper. Mr. Talbot's patent process was nothing more, yet he endeavoured to secure a monopoly of what was in substance the discovery and invention of another. Mr. Talbot was either very precipitate, or ill-advised, to rush to the Patent Office with his modification, and even at this distant date it is much to be regretted that he did so, for his rash act has, unhappily for photography, proved a pernicious precedent. Mr. Reade gave his discoveries to the world freely, and the "pleasure of the discovery" was "a sufficient reward." All honour to such discoverers. They, and they only, are the true lovers of science and art, who take up the torch where another laid it down, or lost it, and carry it forward another stage towards perfection, without sullying its brightness or dimming the flame with sordid motives.

The Rev. J. B. Reade lived to see the process *he* discovered and watched over in its embryo state, developed with wondrous rapidity into one of the most extensively applied arts of this marvellous age, and died, regretted and esteemed by all who knew him, December 12th, 1870. Photographers, your occupations are his monument, but let his name be a tablet on your hearts, and his unselfishness your emulation !

The year 1838 gave birth to another photographic discovery, little thought of and of small promise at the time, but out of which have flowed all the various modifications of solar and mechanical carbon printing. This was the discovery of Mr. Mungo Ponton, who first observed and announced the effects of the sun's rays upon bichromate of potash. But that gentleman was unwise in his generation, and did not patent his discovery, so a whole host of patent locusts fell upon the field of research in after years, and quickly seized the manna he had left, to spread on their own bread. Mr. Mungo Ponton spread a solution of bichromate of potash upon paper, submitted it under a suitable object to the sun's rays, and told all the world, without charge, that the light hardened the bichromate to the extent of its action, and that the unacted-upon portions could be dissolved away, leaving the object *white* upon a yellow or orange ground. Other experimenters played variations on Mr. Ponton's bichromate scale, and amongst the performers were M. E. Becquerel, of France, and our own distinguished countryman, Mr. Robert Hunt.

During the years that elapsed between the death of M. Niepce and the period to which I have brought these records, little was heard or known of the researches of M. Daguerre, but he was not idle, nor had he abandoned his iodine ideas. He steadily pursued his subject, and worked with a continuity that gained him the unenviable reputation of a lunatic. His persistency created doubts of his sanity, but he toiled on *solus*, confident that he was not in pursuit of an impossibility, and sanguine of success. That success came, hastened by lucky chance, and early in January, 1839, M. Daguerre announced the interesting and important fact that the problem was solved. Pictures in the camera-obscura could be, not only seen, but caught and retained. M. Daguerre had laboured, sought, and found, and the bare announcement of his wonderful discovery electrified the world of science.

The electric telegraph could not then flash the fascinating intelligence from Paris to London, but the news travelled fast, nevertheless, and the unexpected report of M. Daguerre's triumph hurried Mr. Talbot forward with a similar statement of success. Mr. Talbot declared his triumph on the 31st of January, 1839, and published in the following month the details of a process which was little, if any, in advance of that already known.

Daguerre delayed the publication of his process until a pension of six thousand francs per annum had been secured to himself, and four thousand francs per annum to M. Isidore Niépce for life, with a reversion of one half to their widows. In the midst of political and social struggles France was proud of the glory of such a marvellous discovery, and liberally rewarded her fortunate sons of science with honourable distinction and substantial emolument. She was proud and generous to a chivalrous extent, for she pensioned her sons that she might have the " glory of endowing the world of science and of art with one of the most surprising discoveries" that had been made on her soil; and, because she considered that "the invention did not admit of being secured by patent," but avarice and cupidity frustrated her noble and generous intentions in this country, and England alone was harassed with injunctions and prosecutions, while all the rest of the world participated in the pleasure and profits of the noble gift of France.

In July, 1839, M. Daguerre divulged his secret at the request and expense of the French Government, and the process which bore his name was found to be totally different, both in manipulation and effect, from any sun pictures that had been obtained in England. The Daguerreotype was a latent image produced by light on an iodised silver plate, and developed, or made visible, by the fumes of mercury; but the resultant picture was one of the most shimmering and vapoury imaginable, wanting in solidity, colour, and firmness. In fact, photography as introduced by M. Daguerre was in every sense a wonderfully shadowy and all but invisible thing, and not many removes from the dark ages of its creation. The process was extremely delicate and difficult, slow and tedious to manipulate, and too insensitive to be applied to portraiture with any prospect of success, from fifteen to twenty minutes' exposure in bright sunshine being necessary to obtain a picture. The mode of proceeding was as follows:—A copper plate with a coating of silver was carefully cleaned and polished on the silvered side, that was placed, silver side downwards, over a vessel containing iodine in crystals, until the silvered surface assumed a golden-yellow colour. The plate was then transferred to the camera-obscura, and submitted to the action of light. After the plate had received the requisite amount of exposure, it was placed over a box containing mercury, the fumes of which, on the application of a gentle heat, developed the latent image. The picture was then washed in salt and water, or a solution of hyposulphite of soda, to remove the iodide of silver, washed in clean water afterwards, and dried, and the Daguerreotype was finished according to Daguerre's first published process.

The development of the latent image by mercury subliming was the most marvellous and unlooked for part of the process, and it was for that all-important thing that Daguerre was entirely indebted to chance. Having put one of his apparently useless iodized and exposed silver plates into a cupboard containing a pot of mercury, Daguerre was greatly surprised, on visiting the cupboard some time afterwards, to find the blank looking plate converted into a visible picture. Other plates were iodized and exposed and placed in the cupboard, and the same mysterious process of development was repeated, and it was not until this thing and the other thing had been removed and replaced over and over again, that Daguerre became aware that quicksilver, an article that had been used for making mirrors and reflecting images for years, was the developer of the invisible image. It was indeed a most marvellous and unexpected result. Daguerre had devoted years of labour and made numberless experiments to obtain a transcript of nature drawn by her own hand, but all his studied efforts and weary hours of labour had only resulted in repeated failures and disappointments, and it appeared that Nature herself had grown weary of his bungling, and resolved to show him the way.

The realization of his hopes was more accidental than inferential. The compounds with which he worked, neither produced a visible nor a latent image capable of being developed with any of the chemicals with which he was experimenting. At last accident rendered him more service than reasoning, and occult properties produced the effect his mental and inductive faculties failed to accomplish; and here we observe the great difference between the two successful discoverers, Reade and Daguerre. At this stage of the discovery I ignore Talbot's claim in *toto*. Reade arrived at his results by reasoning, experiment, observation, and judiciously weakening and controlling the re-agent he commenced his researches with. He had the infinite pleasure and disappointment of seeing his first picture flash into existence, and dissappear again almost instantly, but in that instant he saw the cause of his success and failure, and his inductive reasoning reduced his failure to success; whereas Daguerre *found* his result, was puzzled, and utterly at a loss to account for it, and it was only by a process of blindman's buff in his chemical cupboard that he laid his hands on the precious pot of mercury that produced the visible image.

That was a discovery, it is true; but a bungling one, at best. Daguerre only worked intelligently with one-half of the elements of success; the other was thrust in his way, and the most essential part of his achievement was a triumphant accident. Daguerre did half the work—or, rather, one-third—light did the second part, and chance performed the rest, so that Daguerre's share of the honour was only one-third. Reade did two-thirds of the process, the first and third, intelligently; therefore to him alone is due the honour of discovering practical photography. His was a successful application of known properties, equal to an invention; Daguerre's was an accidental result arising from unknown causes and effects, and consequently a discovery of the lowest order. To England, then, and not to France, is the world indebted for the discovery of photography, and in the order of its earliest, greatest, and most successful discoverers and advancers, I place the Rev. J. B. Reade first and highest.

SECOND PERIOD.

DAGUERREOTYPE.

L. J. M. DAGUERRE.

Used Iodine, 1839.

JOHN FREDERICK GODDARD.

Applied Bromine, 1840.

NEW YORK.

Copy of Instantaneous Daguerreotype, 1854.

SECOND PERIOD.

PUBLICITY AND PROGRESS.

1839 has generally been accepted as the year of the birth of Practical Photography, but that may now be considered an error. It was, however, the Year of Publicity, and the progress that followed with such marvellous rapidity may be freely received as an adversely eloquent comment on the principles of secresy and restriction, in any art or science, like photography, which requires the varied suggestions of numerous minds and many years of experiment in different directions before it can be brought to a state of workable certainty and artistic and commercial applicability. Had Reade concealed his success and the nature of his accelerator, Talbot might have been bungling on with modifications of the experiments of Wedgwood and Davy to this day; and had Daguerre not sold the secret of his iodine vapour as a sensitiser, and his accidentally discovered property of mercury as a developer, he might never have got beyond the vapoury images he produced. As it was, Daguerre did little or nothing to improve his process and make it yield the extremely vigorous and beautiful results it did in after years. As in Mr. Reade's case with the Calotype process, Daguerre threw the ball and others caught it. Daguerre's advertised improvements of his process were lamentable failures and roundabout ways to obtain sensitive amalgams—exceedingly ingenious, but excessively bungling and impractical. To make the plates more sensitive to light, and, as Daguerre said, obtain pictures of objects in motion and animated scenes, he suggested that the silver plate should first be cleaned and polished in the usual way, then to deposit successively layers of mercury, and gold, and platinum. But the process was so tedious, unworkable, and unsatisfactory, no one ever attempted to employ it either commercially or scientifically. In publishing his first process, with its working details, Daguerre appears to have surrendered all that he knew, and to have been incapable of carrying his discovery to a higher degree of advancement. Without Mr. Goddard's bromine accelerator and M. Fizeau's chloride of gold fixer and invigorator, the Daguerreotype would never have been either a commercial success or a permanent production.

1840 was almost as important a period in the annals of photography as the year of its enunciation, and to the two valuable improvements and one interesting importation, the Daguerreotype process was indebted for its success all over the world; and photography, even as it is practised now, is probably indebted for its present state of advancement to Mr. John Frederick Goddard, who applied bromine, as an accelerator, to the Daguerreotype process this year. In the early part of the Daguerreotype period it was so insensitive there was very little prospect of being able to take portraits with it through a lens. To meet this difficulty Mr. Wolcott, an American optician, constructed a reflecting camera and brought it to London. It was an ingenious contrivance, but did not fully answer the expectations of the inventor. It certainly did not require such a long exposure with this camera as when the rays from the image or sitter passed through a lens; but, as the sensitised plate was placed *between* the sitter and the reflector, the picture was necessarily small, and neither very sharp nor satisfactory. This was a mechanical contrivance to shorten the time of exposure, which partially succeeded, but it was chemistry, and not mechanics, that effected the desirable result. Both Mr. Goddard and M. Antoine F. J. Claudet, of London, employed chlorine as a means of increasing the sensitiveness of the iodised silver plate, but it was not sufficiently accelerative to meet the requirements of the Daguerreotype process. Subsequently Mr. Goddard discovered that the vapour of bromine, added to that of iodine, imparted an extraordinary degree of sensitiveness to the prepared plate, and reduced the time of sitting from minutes to seconds. The addition of the fumes of bromine to those of iodine formed a compound of bromo-iodide of silver on the surface of the Daguerreotype plate, and not only increased the sensitiveness, but added to the strength and beauty of the resulting picture, and M. Fizeau's method of precipitating a film of gold over the whole surface of the plate still further increased the brilliancy of the picture and ensured its permanency. I have many Daguerreotypes in my possession now that were made over forty years ago, and they are as brilliant and perfect as they were on the day they were taken. I fear no one can say the same for any of Fox Talbot's early prints, or even more recent examples of silver printing.

Another important event of this year was the importation of the first photographic lens, camera, &c., into England. These articles were brought from Paris by Sir Hussey Vivian, present M.P. for Glamorganshire (1889). It was the first lot of such articles that the Custom House officers had seen, and they were at a loss to know how to classify it. Finally they passed it under the general head of Optical Instruments. Sir Hussey told me this, himself, several years before he was made a baronet. What changes fifty years have wrought even in the duties of Custom House officers, for the imports and exports of photographic apparatus and materials must now amount to many thousands per annum!

Having described the conditions and state of progress photography had attained at the time of my first contact with it, I think I may now enter into greater details, and relate my own personal experiences from this period right up to the end of its jubilee celebration.

I was just fourteen years old when photography was made practicable by the publication of the two processes, one by Daguerre, and the other by Fox Talbot, and when I heard or read of the wonderful discovery I was fired with a desire to obtain a sight of these "sun pictures," but the fire was kept smouldering for some time before my desire was gratified. Nothing travelled very fast in those days. Railroads had not long been started, and were not very extensively developed. Telegraphy, by electricity, was almost unknown, and I was a fixture, having just been apprenticed to an engraving firm hundreds of miles from London. But at last I caught sight of one of those marvellous drawings made by the sun in the window of the Post Office of my native town. It was a small Daguerreotype which had been sent there along with a notice that a licence to practise the "art" could be obtained of the patentee. I forget now what amount the patentee demanded for a licence, but I know that at the time referred to it was so far beyond my means and hopes that I never entertained the idea of becoming a licencee. I believe some one in the neighbourhood bought a licence, but either could not or did not make use of it commercially.

Some time after that, a Miss Wigley, from London, came to the town to practise Daguerreotyping, but she did not remain long, and could not, I think, have made a profitable visit. If so, it could scarcely be wondered at, for the sun pictures of that period were such thin, shimmering reflections, and distortions of the human face divine, that very few people were impressed either by the process or the newest wonder of the world. At that early period of photography, the plates were so insensitive, the sittings so long, and the conditions so terrible, it was not easy to induce anyone either to undergo the ordeal of sitting, or to pay the sum of twenty-one shillings for a very small and unsatisfactory portrait. In the infancy of the Daguerreotype process, the sitters were all placed out of doors, in direct sunshine, which naturally made them screw up or shut their eyes, and every feature glistened, and was painfully revealed. Many amusing stories have been told about the trials, mishaps, and disappointments attending those long and painful sittings, but the best that ever came to my knowledge was the following. In the earliest of the forties, a young lady went a considerable distance, in Yorkshire, to sit to an itinerant Daguerreotypist for her portrait, and, being limited for time, could only give one sitting. She was placed before the camera, the slide drawn, lens uncapped, and requested to sit there until the Daguerreotypist returned. He went away, probably to put his "mercury box" in order, or to have a smoke, for it was irksome—both to sitter and operator—to sit or stand doing nothing during those necessarily long exposures. When the operator returned, after an absence of fifteen or twenty minutes, the lady was sitting where he left her, and appeared glad to be relieved from her constrained position. She departed, and he proceeded with the development of the picture. The plate was examined from time to time, in the usual way, but there was no appearance of the lady. The ground, the wall, and the chair whereon she sat, were all visible, but the image of the lady was not; and the operator was completely puzzled, if not alarmed. He left the lady sitting, and found her sitting when he returned, so he was quite unable to account for her mysterious non-appearance in the picture. The mystery was, however, explained in a few days, when the lady called for her portrait, for she admitted that she got up and walked about as soon as he left her, and only sat down again when she heard him returning. The necessity of remaining before the camera was not recognised by that sitter. I afterwards reversed that result myself by focussing the chair, drawing the slide, uncapping the lens, sitting down, and rising leisurely to cap the lens again, and obtained a good portrait without showing a ghost of the chair or anything else. The foregoing is evidence of the insensitiveness of the plates at that early period of the practice of photography; but that state of inertion did not continue long, for as soon as the accelerating properties of bromine became generally known, the time of sitting was greatly reduced, and good Daguerreotype views were obtained by simply uncapping the lens as quickly as possible. I have taken excellent views in that manner myself in England, and, when in America, I obtained instantaneous views of Niagara Falls and other places quite as rapidly and as perfect as any instantaneous views made on gelatine dry plates, one of which I have copied and enlarged to 12 by 10 inches, and may possibly reproduce the small copy in these pages.

In 1845 I came into direct contact with photography for the first time. It was in that year that an Irishman named McGhee came into the neighbourhood to practise the Daguerreotype process. He was not a licencee, but no one appeared to interfere with him, nor serve him with an injunction, for he carried on his little portrait business for a considerable time without molestation. The patentee was either very indifferent to his vested interests, or did not consider these intruders worth going to law with, for there were many raids across the borders by camera men in those early days. Several circumstances combined to facilitate the inroads of Scotch operators into the northern counties of England. Firstly, the patent laws of England did not extend to Scotland at that time, so there was a far greater number of Daguerreotypists in Edinburgh and other Scotch towns in the early days of photography than in any part of England, and many of them made frequent incursions into the forbidden land without troubling themselves about obtaining a licence, but somehow they never remained long at a time; they were either afraid of consequences, or did not meet with patronage sufficient to induce them to continue their sojourns beyond a few of the summer weeks. For many years most of the early Daguerreotypists were birds of passage, frequently on the wing. Among the earliest settlers in London, were Mr. Beard (patentee), Mr. Claudet, and Mr. J. E. Mayall —the latter is still alive, 1889—and in Edinburgh, Messrs. Ross and Thompson, Mr. Howie, Mr. Poppawitz, and Mr. Tunny —the latter was a Calotypist—with most of whom it was my good fortune to become personally acquainted in after years.

Secondly, a great deal of ill-feeling and annoyance were caused by the incomprehensible and somewhat underhanded way in which the English patent was obtained, and these feelings induced many to poach on photographic preserves, and even to defy injunctions; and, while lawsuits were pending, it was not uncommon for non-licencees to practise the new art with the impunity and feelings common to smugglers. Mr. Beard, the English patentee, brought many actions at law against infringers of his patent rights, the most memorable of which was that where Mr. Egerton, 1, Temple Street, Whitefriars, the first dealer in photographic materials, and agent for Voightlander's lenses in London, was the defendant. During that trial it came out in evidence that the patentee had earned as much as forty thousand pounds in one year by taking portraits and fees from licencees. Though the judgment of the Court was adverse to Mr. Egerton, it did not improve the patentee's moral right to his claim, for the trial only made it all the more public that the French Government had allowed M. Daguerre six thousand francs (£240), and M. Isidore Niepce four thousand francs (£160) per annum, on condition that their discoveries should be published, and *made free to all the world*. This trial did not in any way improve Mr. Beard's financial position, for eventually he became a bankrupt, and his establishments in King William Street, London Bridge, and the Polytechnic Institute, in Regent Street, were extin-

D

guished. Mr. Beard, who was the first to practise Daguerreotyping commercially in this country, was originally a coal merchant. I think Mr. Claudet practised the process in London without becoming a licencee, either through previous knowledge, or some private arrangement made with Daguerre before the patent was granted to Mr. Beard. It was while photography was clouded with this atmosphere of dissatisfaction and litigation, that I made my first practical acquaintance with it in the following manner :—

Being anxious to obtain possession of one of those marvellous sun pictures, and hoping to get an idea of the manner in which they were produced, I paid a visit, one sunny morning, to Mr. McGhee, the Daguerreotypist, dressed in my best, with clean shirt, and stiff stand-up collar, as worn in those days. I was a very young man then, and rather particular about the set of my shirt collar, so you may readily judge of my horror when, after making the financial arrangements to the satisfaction of Mr. McGhee, he requested me to put on a blue cotton *quasi* clean " dickey," with a limp collar, that had evidently done similar duty many times before. You may be sure I protested, and inquired the reason why I should cover up my white shirt front with such an objectionable article. I was told if I did not put it on my shirt front would be *solarized*, and come out *blue* or dirty, whereas if I put on the blue "dickey" my shirt front would appear white and clean. What "solarized" meant, I did not know, nor was it further explained, but, as I very naturally wished to appear with a clean shirt front, I submitted to the indignity, and put on the limp and questionably clean " dicky." While the Daguerreotypist was engaged with some mysterious manipulations in a cupboard or closet, I brushed my hair, and contemplated my singular appearance in the mirror somewhat ruefully. O, ye sitters and operators of to-day ! congratulate yourselves on the changes and advantages that have been wrought in the practice of photography since then. When Mr. McGhee appeared again with something like two wooden books in his hand, he requested me to follow him into the garden, which was only a back yard. At the foot of the garden, and against a brick wall with a piece of grey cloth nailed over it, I was requested to sit down on an old chair; then he placed before me an instrument which looked like a very ugly theodolite on a tripod stand—that was my first sight of a camera—and, after putting his head under a black cloth, told me to look at a mark on the other side of the garden, without winking or moving till he said "done." How long I sat I don't know, but it seemed an awfully long time, and I have no doubt it was, for I know that I used to ask people to sit five and ten minutes, afterwards. The sittings over, I was requested to re-enter the house, and then I thought I would see something of the process; but no. Again Mr. McGhee went into the mysterious chamber, and shut the door quickly. In a little time he returned and told me that the sittings were satisfactory —he had taken two—and that he would finish and deliver them next day. Then I left without obtaining the ghost of an idea of the *modus operandi* of producing portraits by the sun, beyond the fact that a camera had been placed before me. Next day the portraits were delivered according to promise, but I confess I was somewhat disappointed at getting so little for my money. It was a very small picture that could not be seen in every light, and not particularly like myself, but a scowling-looking individual, with a limp collar, and rather dirty looking face. Whatever would *mashers* have said or done, if they had gone to be photographed in those days of photographic darkness? I was, however, somewhat consoled by the thought that I, at last, possessed one of those wonderful sun pictures, though I was ignorant of the means of production.

Soon after having my portrait taken, Mr. McGhee disappeared, and there was no one left in the neighbourhood who knew anything of the mysterious manipulations of Daguerreotyping. I had, nevertheless, resolved to possess an apparatus and obtain the necessary information, but there was no one to tell me what to buy, where to buy it, nor what to do with it. At last an old friend of mine who had been on a visit to Edinburgh, had purchased an apparatus and some materials with the view of taking Daguerreotypes himself, but finding that he could not, was willing to sell it to me, though he could not tell me how to use it, beyond showing me an image of the house opposite upon the ground glass of the camera. I believe my friend let me have the apparatus for what it cost him, which was about £15, and it consisted of a quarter-plate portrait lens by Slater, mahogany camera, tripod stand, buff sticks, coating and mercury boxes of the roughest description, a few chemicals and silvered plates, and a rather singular but portable dark room. Of the uses of the chemicals I knew very little, and of their nature nothing which led to very serious consequences, which I shall relate in the proper place. Having obtained possession of this marvellous apparatus, my next ardent aspiration was to make a successful use of it. I distinctly remember, even at this distant date, with what nervous curiosity I examined all the articles when I unpacked them in my father's house, and with what wonder, not unmixed with apprehension, my father looked upon that display of unknown, and to him apparently nameless and useless toys. "More like a lot of conjuror's traps than anything else," he exclaimed, after I had set them all out. And a few days after he told one of my young friends that he thought I had gone out of my mind to take up with that "Daggertype" business; the name itself was a stumbling block in those days, for people called the process "dagtype, docktype, and daggertype" more frequently than by its proper name, Daguerreotype. What a contrast now-a-days, when almost every father is an amateur photographer, and encourages both his sons and daughters to become the same.

My father was a very good parent, in his way, and encouraged me, to the fullest extent of his means, in the study of music and painting, and even sent me to the Government School of Design, where I studied drawing under W. B. Scott; but the new-fangled method of taking portraits did not harmonise with his conservative and practical notions. One cause of his disapprobation and dissatisfaction was, doubtless, my many failures; in fact, I may say, inability to show him any result. I had acquired an apparatus of the roughest and most primitive construction, but no knowledge of its use or the behaviour of the chemicals employed, beyond the bare numerical order in which they were to be used, and there was no one within a hundred miles of where I lived, that I knew of, who could give me lessons or the slightest hint respecting the process. I had worn out the patience of all my relations and friends in fruitless sittings. I had set fire to my singular dark room, and nearly set fire to the house, by attempting to refill the spirit lamp while alight, and I was ill and suffering from salivation through inhaling the fumes of mercury in my blind, anxious, and enthusiastic endeavours to obtain a sun picture. It is not long since an eminent photographer told me that I was an enthusiast, but if he had seen me in those days he would, in all probability, have told me that I was mad. Though ill, I was not mad; I was only determined not to be beaten. I was resolved to keep pegging away until I obtained a satisfactory result. My friends laughed at me when I asked them to sit for a trial, and they either refused, or sat with a very bad grace, as if it really were a trial to them; but fancy, fair and kindly readers, what it must have been to me! Finding that my living models fought shy of me and my trials, I then thought of getting a lay figure, and borrowed a large doll —quite as big as a baby—of one of my lady friends. I stuck it up in a garden and pegged away at it for nearly six months. At the end of that time I was able to produce a portrait of the doll with tolerable certainty and success. Then I ventured to ask my friends to sit again, but my process was too slow for life studies, and my live sitters generally moved so much, their portraits were not recognisable. There were no head-rests in those days, at least I did not possess one, or it might have been pleasanter for my sitters and easier for myself. What surprised me very much—and I thought it a singular thing at the time—was my success in copying an engraving of Thorburn's Miniature of the Queen. I made several good and beautiful copies of that engraving, and sent one to an artist friend, then in Devonshire, who wrote to say that it was beautiful, and that if he could get a Daguerreotype portrait with the eyes as clear as that, he would sit at once; but all the "Dagtypes" he had hitherto seen had only black holes where the eyes should be. Unfortunately, that was my own experience. I could copy from the flat well enough, but when I went to the round I went wrong. Ultimately I discovered the cause of all that, and found a remedy, but oh! the weary labour and mental worry I underwent before I mastered the difficulties of the most troublesome and uncertain, yet most beautiful and permanent of all the photographic processes that ever was discovered or invented; and now it is a lost art. No one practises it, and I don't think that there are half-a-dozen men living—myself included—that could at this day go through all the manipulations necessary to produce a good Daguerreotype portrait or picture; yet, when the process was at the height of its popularity, a great number of people pursued it as a profession in all parts of the civilized world, and in the United States of America alone it was estimated in 1854 that there were not less than thirty thousand people making their living as Daguerreans. Few, if any, of the photographers of to-day—whether amateur or professional—know anyting of the forms or uses of plates, buffs, lathes, sensitizing or developing boxes, gilding stands, or other Daguerreotype appliances; and I am quite certain that there is not a dealer in all England that can furnish at this date a complete set of Daguerreotype apparatus.

It was in 1849 that I gilded my first picture—a portrait of one of my friends playing a guitar. I possess that picture now, and, after a lapse of forty years, it is as good and bright as it was on the day that it was taken. It was not a first-class production, but I hoped to do better soon, and on the strength of that hope determined to commence business as a professional Daguerreotypist. While I was considering whether I should pitch my tent permanently in my native town, or take to a nomadic kind of life, similar to what other Daguerreotypists were pursuing, I was helped to a decision by the sudden appearance of a respectable and experienced Daguerreotypist who came and built a " glass house "—the first of its kind—in my native town. This somewhat disarranged my plans, but on the whole it was rather opportune and advantageous than otherwise, for it afforded me an unexpected opportunity of gaining a great deal of practical experience on easy terms. The new comer was Mr. George Brown, who had been an " operator " for Mr. Beard, in London, and as he exhibited much finer specimens of the Daguerreotype process than any I had hitherto seen, I engaged myself to assist him for six months at a small salary. I showed him what I had done, and he showed and told me all that he knew in connection with photography, and thus commenced a business relation that ripened into a friendship that endured as long as he lived.

At the end of the six months' engagement I left Mr. Brown, to commence business on my own account, but as neither of us considered that there was room for two Daguerreotypists in a town with a population of *one hundred and twenty thousand*, I was driven to adopt the nomadic mode of life peculiar to the itinerant photographer of the period. That was in 1850. Up to that time I had done nothing in Calotype work. Mr. Brown was strictly a Daguerreotypist, but Mr. Parry, at that time a glass dealer and amateur photographer, was working at the Calotype process, but not very successfully, for nearly all his efforts were spoiled by decomposition, which he could not then account for or overcome, but he eventually became one of the best Calotypists in the neighbourhood, and I became the possessor of some of the finest Calotype negatives he ever produced, many of which are still in my possession. Mr. Parry relinquished his glass business, and became a professional photographer soon after the introduction of the collodion process. Another amateur photographer that I met in those early days was a flute player in the orchestra of the theatre. He produced very good Calotype negatives with a single lens, and was very enthusiastic, but extremely reticent on all photographic matters. About this period I made the acquaintance of Mr. J. W. Swan : I had known him for some time previously when he was apprentice and assistant to Mr. Mawson, chemist, in Mosley Street, Newcastle-on-Tyne. Neither Mr. Mawson nor Mr. Swan were known to the photographic world at that time. Mr. Mawson was most popular as a dealer in German yeast, and I think it was not until after Archer published his process that they began to make collodion and deal in photographic materials—at any rate, I did not buy any photographic goods of them until 1852, when I first began to use Mawson's collodion. In October, 1850, I went to Hexham, about twenty miles west of Newcastle-on-Tyne, to make my first appearance as a professional Daguerreotypist. I rented a sitting-room with a good window and clear view, so as to take "parlour portraits." I could only take small pictures—two and a half by two inches—for which I charged half a guinea, and was favoured with a few sittings; but it was a slow place, and I left it in a few weeks.

The next move I made was to Seaham Harbour, and there I did a little better business, but the place was too small and the people too poor for me to continue long. Half guineas were not plentiful, even among the tradespeople, and there were very few gentlefolk in the neighbourhood. Some of the townspeople were very kind to me, and invited me to their homes, and although my sojourn was not very profitable, it was very pleasant. I had many pleasant rambles on the sands, and often looked at Seaham Hall and thought of Byron and his matrimonial disappointment in his marriage with Miss Milbank.

From Seaham Harbour I went to Middlesborough, hoping to do more business among a larger population, but it appeared as if I were only going from bad to worse. At that date the population was about thirty thousand, but chiefly people of the working classes, employed at Balchow and Vaughn's and kindred works. I made portraits of some of the members of Mr. Balchow's family, Mr. Geordison, and some of the resident Quakers, but altogether I did not do much more than pay expenses. I managed, however, to stay there till the year 1851, when I caught the World's Fair fever, so I packed up my apparatus and other things I did not require immediately, and sent them to my father's house, and with a few changes in my carpet-bag, and a little money in my pocket, I started off to see the Great Exhibition in London. I went by way of York and Hull, with the two-fold object of seeing some friends in both places, and to prospect on the business chances they might afford. At York I found Mr. Pumphrey was located, but as he did not appear to be fully occupied with sitters—for I found him trying to take a couple of boys fighting in a back yard—I thought there was not room for another Daguerreotypist in York. In a few days I went to Hull, but even there the ground was preoccupied, so I took the first steamer for London. We sailed on a Saturday night, and after a pleasant voyage arrived at the wharf below London Bridge early on Sunday evening. I put up at the "Yorkshire Grey," in Thames Street, where I met several people from the North, also on a visit to London to see the Great Exhibition. This being my first visit to London, I was anxious to get a sight of the streets and crowds therein, so, after obtaining some refreshment, I strolled out with one of my fellow-passengers to receive my first impressions of the great metropolis. The evening was fine, and, being nearly the longest day, there was light enough to enable me to see the God-forsaken appearance of Thames Street, the dismal aspect of Fish Street Hill, and the gloomy column called "The Monument" that stands there to remind citizens and strangers of the Great Fire of 1666; but I was both amazed and amused with the life and bustle I saw on London Bridge and other places in the immediate neighbourhood, but my eyes and ears soon became fatigued with the sights and sounds of the lively and noisy thoroughfares. After a night's rest, which was frequently broken by cries of "Stop thief!" and the screams of women, I arose and made an early start for the Great Exhibition of 1851. Of all the wonderful things in that most wonderful exhibition, I was most interested in the photographic exhibits and the beautiful specimens of American Daguerreotypes, both portraits and landscapes, especially the views of Niagara Falls, which made me determine to visit America as soon as ever I could make the necessary arrangements.

While examining and admiring those very beautiful Daguerreotypes, I little thought that I was standing, as it were, between the birth of one process and the death of another; but so it was, for the newly-born collodion process very soon annihilated the Daguerreotype, although the latter process had just reached the zenith of its beauty. In the March number of the *Chemist*, Archer's Collodion Process was published, and that was like the announcement of the birth of an infant Hercules, that was destined to slay a beautiful youth whose charms had only arrived at maturity. But there was really a singular and melancholy coincidence in the birth of the Collodion Process and the early death of the Daguerreotype, for Daguerre himself died on July 10th, 1851, so that both Daguerre and his process appeared to receive their death blows in the same year. I don't suppose that Daguerre died from a shock to his system, caused by the publication of a rival process, for it is not likely that he knew anything about the invention of a process that was destined, in a very few years, to abolish his own—living as he was in the retirement of his native village, and enjoying his well-earned pension

As Daguerre was the first of the successful discoverers of photography to be summoned by death, I will here give a brief sketch of his life and pursuits prior to his association with Nicéphore Niepce and photography. Louis Jacques Mandé Daguerre was born at Cormeilles, near Paris, in 1787, of poor and somewhat careless parents, who appear to have bestowed upon him more names than attention. Though they did not endow him with a good education, they had the good sense to observe the bent of his mind and apprentice him to a theatrical scene painter. In that situation he soon made his mark, and his artistic and mechanical abilities, combined with industry, painstaking, and boldness of conception, soon raised him to the front rank of his profession, in which he gained both honour and profit. Like all true artists, he was fond of sketching from nature; and, to save time and secure true proportion, he employed such optical appliances as were then at his command. Some of his biographers say that he, like Fox Talbot, employed the camera lucida; others the camera obscura; as there is a considerable difference between the two it would be interesting to know which it really was. At any rate it was one of these instruments which gave him the notion and created the desire to secure the views as they were presented by the lens or reflector. Much of his time was devoted to the painting and construction of a diorama which was first exhibited in 1822, and created quite a sensation in Paris. As early as 1824 he commenced his photographic experiments, with very little knowledge on the subject; but with the hope and determination of succeeding, by some means or other, in securing the pictures as Nature painted them on the screen or receiver. Doubtless he was sanguine enough then to hope to be able to obtain colours as well as drawings, but he died without seeing that accomplished, and so will many others. What he did succeed in accomplishing was marvellous, and quite entitled him to all the honour and emolument he received, but he only lived about twelve years after his discovery. He was, however, saved the mortification of seeing his beautiful discovery discarded and cast away in the hey-day of its beauty and perfection.

After a few weeks sojourn in London, seeing all the sights and revisiting all the Daguerreotype studios, I turned my back on the great city and my footsteps homewards again. As soon as I reached home I unpacked my apparatus and made arrangements for another campaign with the camera at some of the sea-side resorts, with the hope of making up for lost time and money through visiting London.

I had looked at Scarborough and found the Brothers Holroyd located there; at Whitby, Mr. Stonehouse; and I did not like the appearance of Redcar, so I settled upon Tynemouth, and did fairly well for a short season. About the end of October I went on to Carlisle, but a Scotchman had already preceded me there, and I thought one Daguerreotypist was quite enough for so small a place, and pushed on to Penrith, where I settled for the winter and gradually worked up a little connection, and formed some life-long friendships. I was the first Daguerreotypist who had visited the town of Penrith, and while there I made Daguerreotypes of Sir George and Lady Musgrave and family, and some members of the Lonsdale family. It was through the kindness of Miss Lowther that I was induced to go to Whitehaven, but I did not do much business there, so, after a bad winter, I resolved to go to America in the spring, and made arrangements for the voyage immediately. Thinking that I would find better apparatus and appliances in America, I disposed of my "Tent and Kit," closed up my affairs, bid adieu to my relatives and friends, and departed.

To obtain the benefit and experience of a long sea voyage, I secured a cabin passage in a sailing ship named the *Amazon*, and sailed from Shields towards the end of April, 1853. We crossed the Tyne bar late in the evening with a fair wind, and sailed away for the Pentland Frith so as to gain the Atlantic by sailing all round the North of Scotland. I was rather upset the first night, but recovered my appetite next morning. We entered the Pentland Frith on the Saturday afternoon, and were running through the Channel splendidly, when the carpenter came to report water in the well—I forget how many feet—but he thought it would not be safe to attempt crossing the Atlantic. I was a little alarmed at this, but the captain took it very coolly, and ordered the ship to be pumped every watch. Being the only passenger, I became a kind of chum and companion to the captain, and as we sat over our grog that night in the cabin our conversation naturally turned upon the condition of the ship, when he remarked that he was disappointed, and that he "expected he had got a sound ship under his feet this time." These words did not make much impression upon me then, but I had reason to comprehend their meaning afterwards. I was awoke early on the Sunday morning by the noise caused by the working of the pumps, and on going on deck found that we were becalmed, lying off the coast of Caithnesshire, and the water pouring out of the pump-hole in a continuous stream. After breakfast, and while sitting on the taffrail of the quarterdeck along with the captain, waiting for a breeze, I asked him if he intended to cross the Atlantic in such a leaky vessel. He answered "Yes, and the men are all willing." So I thought if these men were not afraid of the ship foundering, I need not be; but I had reasons afterwards for coming to an opposite conclusion.

Towards evening the breeze sprang up briskly, and away we

went, the ship heading W.N.W., as the captain said he wanted to make the northern passage. Next morning we were in a rather rough sea, and a gale of wind blowing. One of the yards was broken with the force of the wind, and the sail and broken yard dangled about the rigging for a considerable time before the sail could be hauled in and the wreckage cleared up. We had several days of bad weather, and one morning when I got up I found the ship heading East. I naturally concluded that we were returning, but the captain said that he had only turned the ship about to enable the men to stop a leak in her bows. The carpenter afterwards told me that the water came in there like a river during the night. Thus we went on through variable weather until at last we sighted two huge icebergs, and then Newfoundland, when the captain informed me that he intended now to coast up to New York. We got out of sight of land occasionally, and one day, after the captain had taken his observations and worked out the ship's position, he called my attention to the chart, and observed that he intended to sail between an island and the mainland, but as the Channel was subject to strong and variable currents, it was a rather dangerous experiment. Being in such a leaky ship, I thought he wanted to hug the land as much as possible, which I considered a very wise and safe proceeding, but he had ulterior objects in view, which the sequel will reveal.

On the night of the 31st of May, after a long yarn from the captain about how he was once wrecked on an iceberg, I turned in with a feeling of perfect safety, for the sea was calm, the night clear, and the wind fair and free; but about daylight next morning I was awoke with a shock, a sudden tramping on deck, and the mate shouting down the companion stairs, "Captain, the ship's ashore." Both the captain and I rushed on deck just as we jumped out of our berths, but we could not see anything of the land or shore, for we were enveloped in a thick fog. We heard the breakers and felt the thud of the waves as they broke upon the ship, but whether we had struck on a rock or grounded on a sandy beach we could not then ascertain. The captain ordered the sails to be "slewed back," and a hawser to be thrown astern, but all efforts to get the ship off were in vain, for with every wave the ship forged more and more on to the shore.

As the morning advanced, the fog cleared away a little, which enabled us to see dimly through the mist the top of a bank of yellow sand. This sight settled the doubt as to our whereabouts, and the captain immediately gave the order "Prepare to abandon the ship." The long boat was at once got ready, and lowered with considerable difficulty, for the ship was then more among the breakers. After a good deal of delay and danger, we all succeeded in leaving the ship and clearing the breakers. We were exposed in the open boats all that day and night, and about ten o'clock next morning we effected a landing on the lee side of the island, which we ascertained to be Sable Island, a bald crown of one of the banks of Newfoundland. Here we received help, shelter, and provisions, all provided by the Home and Colonial Governments, for the relief of shipwrecked people, for this island was one of the places where ships were both accidentally and wilfully wrecked. We were obliged to stay there sixteen days before we could get a vessel to take us to Halifax, Nova Scotia, the nearest port, and would possibly have had to remain on the island much longer, but for a mutiny among the crew. I could describe some strange and startling incidents in connection with the wreck and mutiny, but I will not allow myself to be tempted further into the vale of divergence, as the chief object I have in view is my reminiscence of photography.

On leaving Sable Island I was taken to Halifax, where I waited the arrival of the cunard steamer *Niagara*, to take me on to Boston; thence I proceeded by rail and steamer to New York, where I arrived about the end of June, 1853.

On landing in New York I only knew one individual, and not knowing how far I should have to go to find him I put up at an hotel on Broadway, but soon found that too expensive for my means, and went to a private boarding house as soon as I could

Visiting all the leading Daguerreotypists on Broadway, I was somewhat astonished at their splendid reception rooms, and the vast number of large and excellent specimens exhibited. Their plain Daguerreotypes were all of fine quality, and free from the "buff lines" so noticeable in English work at that period; but all their attempts at colouring were miserable failures, and when I showed one of my coloured specimens to Mr. Gurney, he said, "Well, if you can colour one of my pictures like that I'll believe you;" which I soon did, and very much to his astonishment. In those days I prepared my own colours, and Mr. Gurney bought a box immediately. The principal Daguerreotypists in New York at that time were Messrs. Brady, Gurney, Kent, Lawrence, Mead Brothers, and Samuel Root, and I called upon them all before I entered into any business arrangements, finally engaging myself to Messrs. Mead Brothers as a colourist and teacher of colouring for six months, and while fulfilling that engagement I gave lessons to several "Daguerreans," and made the acquaintance of men from all parts of the Union, for I soon obtained some notoriety throughout the States in consequence of a man named Humphrey attacking me and my colouring process in a photographic journal which bore his name, as well as in the *New York Tribune*. I replied to his attack in the columns of the *Tribune*, but I saw that he had a friend on the staff, and I did not feel inclined to continue the controversy. Mr. Humphrey knew nothing about my process, but began and continued the discussion on his knowledge of what was known as the "Isinglass Process," which was not mine. After completing my engagements with Messrs. Mead Brothers, I made arrangements to supply the stock dealers with my prepared colours, and travel the States myself to introduce them to all the Daguerreans residing in the towns and cities I should visit.

In the principal cities I found all the Daguerreans quite equal to the best in New York, and all doing good business, and I gave lessons in colouring to most of them. In Newark I met Messrs. Benjamin and Polson ; in Philadelphia, Marcus Root and Dr. Bushnel. I encountered a great many *doctors* and *professors* in the business in America. In Baltimore, Maryland—then a slave State—many of the Daguerreans owned slaves. In Washington D.C., I renewed my acquaintance with Mr. George Adams, one of the best Daguerreans in the City ; and while visiting him a very curious thing occurred. One of the representatives of the South came in to have his portrait taken, and the first thing he did was to lay a revolver and a bowie knife on the table beside him. He had just come from the House of Representatives. His excuse for such a proceeding was that he had bought some slaves at the market at Alexandria, and was going to take them home that night. He was a very tall man, and when he stood up against the background his head was above it. As he wanted to be taken standing, this put Mr. Adams into a dilemma, and he asked what he should do. I thought the only thing that could be done was to move the background up and down during exposure, which we did, and so obviated the appearance of a line crossing the head.

While staying in Washington I attended one of the levees at the White House, and was introduced to President Pearce. There was no fuss or difficulty in gaining admission. I had only to present my card at the door, and the City Marshall at once led me into the room where the President, surrounded by some of his Cabinet, was waiting to receive, and I was introduced. After a cordial shake of his hand, I passed on to another saloon where there was music and promenading in mixed costumes, for most of the men were dressed as they liked, and some of the ladies wore bonnets. It was the weekly *sans ceremonie* reception. Finding many of the people of Washington very agreeable and hospitable, I stayed there a considerable time. When I started on the southern journey I did intend to go on to New Orleans, but I stayed so long in Philadelphia and Washington the summer was too far advanced, and as a rather severe outbreak of yellow fever had occurred, I returned to New York and took a journey northward, visiting Niagara Falls, and going on to Canada. I sailed up the Hudson River, stopping at Albany and Troy. At the latter place I met an Englishman, named Irvine, a Daguerrean who treated me hospitably, and for whom I coloured several Daguerreotypes. He wanted me to stay with him, but that I declined. Thence I proceeded to Rochester, and there found that one of my New York pupils had been before me, representing himself as Werge the colourist, for when I introduced myself to the principal Daguerrean he told me that Werge—a very different man—had been there two or three weeks ago. I discovered who the fellow was, and that he had practised a piece of Yankee smartness for which I had no redress. From Rochester I proceeded to Buffalo, where I met with another instance of Yankee smartness of a different kind. I had sold some colours to a man there who paid me in dollar bills, the usual currency of the country, but when I tendered one of these bills for payment at the hotel, it was refused. I next offered it on board a steamboat, but there it was also declined. When I had an opportunity I returned it to the man who gave it to me, and requested him to send me a good one instead. He was honest enough to do that, and impudent enough to tell me that he knew it was bad when he gave it to me, but as I was a stranger he thought I might pass it off easily.

I next went to Niagara Falls, where it was my good fortune to encounter two very different specimens of American character in the persons of Mr. Easterly and Mr. Babbitt, the former a visitor and the latter a resident Daguerrean, who held a monopoly from General Porter to Daguerreotype the Falls and visitors. He had a pavilion on the American side of the Falls, under which his camera was in position all day long, and when a group of visitors stood on the shore to survey the Falls from that point, he took the group—without their knowledge— and showed it to the visitors before they left. In almost every instance he sold the picture at a good price ; the people were generally delighted to be taken at the Falls. I need hardly say that they were all taken instantaneously, and embraced a good general view, including the American Fall, Goat Island, the Horse Shoe Fall, and the Canadian shore. Many of these views I coloured for Mr. Babbitt, but there was always a beautiful green colour on the brink of the Horse Shoe Fall which I never could match. For many years I possessed one of Mr. Babbitt's Daguerreotype views, as well as others taken by Mr. Easterly and myself, but I had the misfortune to be deprived of them all by fire. Some years after I lent them to an exhibition in Glasgow, which was burnt down, and all the exhibits destroyed. After a delightful sojourn of three weeks at Niagara Falls, I took steamer on the lower Niagara River, sailed down to Lake Ontario, and down the River St. Lawrence, shooting the Lachine Rapids, and on to Montreal.

In the Canadian City I did not find business very lively, so after viewing the fine Cathedral of Notre Dame, the mountain, and other places, I left Montreal and proceeded by rail to Boston. The difference between the two cities was immense. Montreal was dull and sleepy, Boston was all bustle and life, and the people were as unlike as the cities. On my arrival in Boston, I put up at the Quincy Adams Hotel, and spent the first few days in looking about the somewhat quaint and interesting old city, hunting up Franklin Associations, and revolutionary landmarks, Bunker Hill, and other places of interest. Having satisfied my appetite for these things, I began to look about me with an eye to business, and called upon the chief Daguerreans and photographers in Boston. Messrs. Southworth and Hawes possessed the largest Daguerreotype establishment, and did an excellent business In their "Saloon" I saw the largest and finest revolving stereoscope that was ever exhibited. The pictures were all whole-plate Daguerreotypes, and set vertically on the perpendicular drum on which they revolved. The drum was turned by a handle attached to cog wheels, so that a person sitting before it could see the stereoscopic pictures with the utmost ease. It was an expensive instrument, but it was a splendid advertisement, for it drew crowds to their saloon to see it and to sit, and their enterprise met with its reward.

At Mr. Whipple's gallery, in Washington Street, a dual photography was carried on, for he made both Daguerreotypes and what he called "crystallotypes," which were simply plain silver prints obtained from collodion negatives. Mr. Whipple. was the first American photographer who saw the great commercial advantages of the collodion process over the Daguerreotype, and he grafted it on the elder branch of photography almost as soon as it was introduced. Indeed, Mr. Whipple's establishment may be considered the very cradle of American photography as far as collodion negatives and silver prints are concerned, for he was the very first to take hold of it with spirit, and as early as 1853 he was doing a large business in photographs, and teaching the art to others. Although I had taken collodion negatives in England with Mawson's collodion in 1852, I paid Mr. Whipple fifty dollars to be shown how he made his collodion, sivler bath, developer, printing, &c., &c., for which purpose he handed me over to his active and intelligent assistant and newly-made partner, Mr. Black. This gave me the run of the establishment, and I was somewhat surprised to find how vast and varied were his mechanical appliances for reducing labour and expediting work. The successful practice of the Daguerreotype art greatly depended on the cleanness and highly polished surface of the silvered plates, and to secure these necessary conditions, Mr.

Whipple had, with characteristic and Yankee-like ingenuity, obtained the assistance of a steam engine which not only "drove" all the circular cleaning and buffing wheels, but an immense circular fan which kept the studio and sitters delightfully cool. Machinery and ingenuity did a great many things in Mr. Whipple's establishment in the early days of photography. Long before the Ambrotype days, pictures were taken on glass and thrown upon canvas by means of the oxyhydrogen light for the use of artists. At that early period of the history of photography, Messrs. Whipple and Black did an immense "printing and publishing" trade, and their facilities were "something considerable." Their toning, fixing, and washing baths were almost worthy the name of vats.

Messrs. Masury and Silsby were also early producers of photographs in Boston, and in 1854 employed a very clever operator, Mr. Turner, who obtained beautiful and brilliant negatives by iron development. On the whole, I think Boston was ahead of New York for enterprise and the use of mechanical appliances in connection with photography. I sold my colours to most of the Daguerreotypists, and entered into business relations with two of the dealers, Messrs. French and Cramer, to stock them, and then started for New York to make arrangements for my return to England.

When I returned to New York the season was over, and everyone was supposed to be away at Saratoga Springs, Niagara Falls, Rockaway, and other fashionable resorts; but I found the Daguerreotype galleries all open and doing a considerable stroke of business among the cotton planters and slave holders, who had left the sultry south for the cooler atmosphere of the more northern States. The Daguerreotype process was then in the zenith of its perfection and popularity, and largely patronised by gentlemen from the south, especially for large or double whole-plates, about 16 by 12 inches, for which they paid fifty dollars each. It was only the best houses that made a feature of these large pictures, for it was not many of the Daguerreans that possessed a "mammoth tube and box"—*i.e.*, lens and camera —or the necessary machinery to "get up" such large surfaces, but all employed the best mechanical means for cleaning and polishing their plates, and it was this that enabled the Americans to produce more brilliant pictures than we did. Many people used to say it was the climate, but it was nothing of the kind. The superiority of the American Daguerreotype was entirely due to mechanical appliances. Having completed my business arrangements and left my colours on sale with the principal stock dealers, including the Scovill Manufacturing Company, Messrs Anthony, and Levi Chapman.

I sailed from New York in October 1854, and arrived in England in due time without any mishap, and visiting London again as soon as I could, I called at Mr. Mayall's gallery in Regent Street to see Dr. Bushnell, whom I knew in Philadelphia, and who was then operating for Mr. Mayall. While there Mr. Mayall came in from the Guildhall, and announced the result of the famous trial, "Talbot *versus* Laroche," a verbatim report of which is given in the Journal of the Photographic Society for December 21st, 1854. Mr. Mayall was quite jubilant, and well he might be, for the verdict for the defendant removed the trammels which Mr. Fox Talbot attempted to impose upon the practice of the collodion process, which was Frederick Scott Archer's gift to photographers. That was the first time that I had met Mr. Mayall, though I had heard of him and followed him both at Philadelphia and New York, and even at Niagara Falls. At that time Mr. Mayall was relinquishing the Daguerreotype process, though one of the earliest practitioners, for he was in business as a Daguerreotypist in Philadelphia from 1842 to 1846, and I know that he made a Daguerreotype portrait of James Anderson, the tragedian, in Philadelphia, on Sunday, May 18th, 1845. During part of the time that he was in Philadelphia he was in partnership with Marcus Root, and the name of the firm was "Highschool and Root," and about the end of 1846 Mr. Mayall opened a Daguerreotype studio in the Adelaide Gallery, King William Street, Strand, London, under the name of Professor Highschool, and soon after that he opened a Daguerreotype gallery in his own name in the Strand, which establishment he sold to Mr. Jabez Hughes in 1855. The best Daguerreotypists in London in 1854 were Mr. Beard, King William Street, London Bridge; Messrs. Kilburn, T. R. Williams and Claudet, in Regent Street; and W. H. Kent, in Oxford Street. The latter had just returned from America, and brought all the latest improvements with him. Messrs. Henneman and Malone were in Regent Street doing calotype portraits. Henneman had been a servant to Fox Talbot, and worked his process under favourable conditions. Mr. Lock was also in Regent Street, doing coloured photographs. He offered me a situation at once, if I could colour photographs as well as I could colour Daguerreotypes, but I could not, for the processes were totally different. M. Manson, an old Frenchman, was the chief Daguerreotype colourist in London, and worked for all the principal Daguerreotypists. I met the old gentleman first in 1851, and knew him for many years afterwards. He also made colours for sale. Not meeting with anything to suit me in London, I returned to the North, calling at Birmingham on my way, where I met Mr. Whitlock, the chief Daguerreotypist there, and a Mr. Monson, who professed to make Daguerreotypes and all other types. Paying a visit to Mr. Elisha Mander, the well-known photographic case maker, I learnt that Mr. Jabez Hughes, then in business in Glasgow, was in want of an assistant, a colourist especially. Having met Mr. Hughes in Glasgow in 1852, and knowing what kind of man he was, I wrote to him, and was engaged in a few days. 1 went to Glasgow in January, 1855, and then commenced business relations and friendship with Mr. Hughes that lasted unbroken until his death in 1884. My chief occupation was to colour the Daguerreotypes taken by Mr. Hughes, and occasionally take sitters, when Mr. Hughes was busy, in another studio. I had not, however, been long in Glasgow, when Mr. Hughes determined to return to London. At first he wished me to accompany him, but it was ultimately arranged that I should purchase the business, and remain in Glasgow, which I did, and took possession in June, Mr. Hughes going to Mr. Mayall's old place in the Strand, London. Mr. Hughes had been in Glasgow for nearly seven years, and had done a very good business, going first as operator to Mr. Bernard, and succeeding to the business just as I was doing. While Mr. Hughes was in Glasgow he was very popular, not only as a Daguerreotypist, but as a lecturer. He delivered a lecture on photography at the Literary and Philosophical Society, became an active member of the Glasgow Photographic Society, and an enthusiastic member of the St. Mark's Lodge of Freemasons. Only a day or two before he left Glasgow, he occupied the chair at a meeting of photographers, comprising Daguerreotypists and collodion workers, to consider what means could be adopted to check the downward tendency of prices even in those early days. I was present, and remember seeing a lady Daguerreotypist among the company, and she expressed her opinion quite decidedly. Efforts were made to enter into a compact to maintain good prices, but nothing came of it. Like all such bandings together, the band was quickly and easily broken.

I had the good fortune to retain the best of Mr. Hughes's customers, and make new ones of my own, as well as many staunch and valuable friends, both among what I may term laymen and brother Masons, while I resided in Glasgow. Most of my sitters were of the professional classes, and the *elite* of the city, among whom were Sir Archibald Alison, the historian, Col. (now General) Sir Archibald Alison, Dr. Arnott, Professor Ramsey, and many of the princely merchants and manufacturers. Some of my other patrons—for I did all kinds of photographic work—were the late Norman Macbeth, Daniel McNee (afterwards Sir Daniel), and President of the Scottish Academy of Art, and also Her Majesty the Queen, for she bought two of my photographs of Glasgow Cathedral, and a copy of my illustration of Hood's "Song of the Shirt," copies of which I possess now, and doubtless so does Her Majesty. One of the most interesting portraits I remember taking while I was in Glasgow was that of John Robertson, who constructed the first marine steam engine. He was associated with Henry Bell, and fitted the "Comet" with her engine. Mr. Napier senr., the celebrated engineer on the Clyde, brought Robertson to sit to me, and ordered a great many copies. I also took a portrait of Harry Clasper, of rowing and boat-building notoriety, which was engraved and published in the *Illustrated London News*. Several of my portraits were engraved both on wood and steel, and published. At the photographic exhibition in connection with the meeting of the British Association held in Glasgow, in 1855, I saw the largest collodion positive on glass that ever was made to my knowledge. The picture was thirty-six inches long, a view of Gourock, or some such place down the Clyde, taken by Mr. Kibble. The glass was British plate, and cost about £1. I thought it a great evidence of British pluck to attempt such a size. When I saw Mr. Kibble I told him so, and expressed an opinion that I thought it a waste of time, labour, and money not to have made a negative when he was at such work. He took the hint, and at the next photographic exhibition he showed a silver print the same size. Mr. Kibble was an undoubted enthusiast, and kept a donkey to drag his huge camera from place to place. My pictures frequently appeared at the Glasgow exhibition, but at one, which was burnt down, I lost all my Daguerreotype views of Niagara Falls, Whipple's views of the moon, and many other valuable pictures, portraits, and views, which could never be replaced.

THIRD PERIOD.

COLLODION TRIUMPHANT.

In 1857 I abandoned the Daguerreotype process entirely, and took to collodion solely; and, strangely enough, that was the year that Frederick Scott Archer, the inventor, died. Like Daguerre, he did not long survive the publication and popularity of his invention, nor did he live long enough to see his process superseded by another. In years, honours, and emoluments, he fell far short of Daguerre, but his process had a much longer existence, was of far more commercial value, benefitting private individuals and public bodies, and creating an industry that expanded rapidly, and gave employment to thousands all over the world; yet he profited little by his invention, and when he died, a widow and three children were left destitute. Fortunately a few influential friends bestirred themselves in their interest, and when the appeal was made to photographers and the public to the Archer Testimonial, the following is what appeared in the pages of *Punch*, June 13th, 1857:—

"To the Sons of the Sun.

"The inventor of collodion has died, leaving his invention unpatented, to enrich thousands, and his family unportioned to the battle of life. Now, one expects a photographer to be almost as sensitive as the collodion to which Mr. Scott Archer helped him. A deposit of silver is wanted (gold will do), and certain faces, now in the dark chamber, will light up wonderfully, with

THIRD PERIOD.

COLLODION.

FREDERICK SCOTT ARCHER.

From Glass Positive by R. Cade, Ipswich, 1855.

HEVER CASTLE, KENT.

Copy of Glass Positive taken by F. Scott Archer in 1849.

an effect never before equalled by photography. A respectable ancient writes that the statue of Fortitude was the only one admitted to the Temple of the Sun. Instead whereof, do you, photographers, set up Gratitude in your little glass temples of the sun, and sacrifice, according to your means, in memory of the benefactor who gave you the deity for a household god. Now, answers must not be negatives."

The result of that appeal, and the labours of the gentlemen who so generously interested themselves on behalf of the widow and orphans, was highly creditable to photographers, the Photographic Society, Her Majesty's Ministers, and Her Majesty the Queen. What those labours were, few now can have any conception; but I think the very best way to convey an idea of those labours and their successful results will be to reprint a copy of the final report of the committee.

THE REPORT OF THE COMMITTEE OF THE ARCHER TESTIMONIAL.

"The Committee of the Archer Testimonial, considering it necessary to furnish a statement of the course pursued towards the attainment of their object, desire to lay before the subscribers and the public generally a full report of their proceedings.

"Shortly after the death of Mr. F. Scott Archer, a preliminary meeting of a few friends was held, and it was determined that a printed address should be issued to the photographic world.

"Sir William Newton, cordially co-operating in the movement, at once made application to Her Most Gracious Majesty. The Queen, with her usual promptitude and kindness of heart, forwarded a donation of £20 towards the Testimonial. The Photographic Society of London, at the same time, proposed a grant of £50, and this liberality on the part of the Society was followed by an announcement of a list of donations from individual members, which induced your Committee to believe that if an appeal were made to the public, and those practising the photographic art, a sum might be raised sufficiently large, not only to relieve the immediate wants of the widow and children, but to purchase a small annuity, and thus in a slight degree compensate for the heavy loss they had sustained by the premature death of one to whom the photographic art had already become deeply indebted.

"To aid in the accomplishment of this design, Mr. Mayall placed the use of his rooms at the service of a committee then about to be formed. Sir William Newton and Mr. Roger Fenton consented to act as treasurers to the fund, and the Union, and London and Westminster Banks kindly undertook to receive subscriptions.

"Your Committee first met on the 8th day of June, 1857, Mr. Digby Wyatt being called to the chair, when it was resolved to ask the consent of Professors Delamotte and Goodeve to become joint secretaries. These duties were willingly accepted, and subscription lists opened in various localities in furtherance of the Testimonial.

"Your Committee met on the 8th day of July, and again on the 4th day of September, when, on each occasion, receipts were announced and paid into the bankers.

"The Society of Arts having kindly offered, through their Secretary, the use of apartments in the house of the Society for any further meetings, your Committee deemed it expedient to accept the same, and passed a vote of thanks to Mr. Mayall for the accommodation previously afforded by that gentleman.

"Your Committee, believing that the interests of the fund would be better served by a short delay in their proceedings, resolved on deferring their next meeting until the month of November, or until the Photographic Society should resume its meetings, when a full attendance of members might be anticipated; it being apparent that individually and collectively persons in the provinces had withheld their subscriptions until the grant of the Photographic Society of London had been formally sanctioned at a special meeting convened for the purpose, and that their object—the purchase of an annuity for Mrs. Archer and her children—could only be effected by the most active co-operation among all classes.

"Your Committee again met on the 26th of November, when it was resolved to report progress to the general body of subscribers, and that a public meeting be called for the purpose, at which the Lord Chief Baron Pollock should be requested to preside. To this request the Lord Chief Baron most kindly and promptly acceded; and your Committee determined to seek the co-operation of their photographic friends and the public to enable them to carry out in its fullest integrity the immediate object of securing some small acknowledgment for the eminent services rendered to photography by the late Mr. Archer.

"At this meeting it was stated that an impression existed, which to some extent still exists, that Mr Archer was not the originator of the Collodion Process; your Committee, therefore, think it their duty to state emphatically that they are fully satisfied of the great importance of the services rendered by him, as an original inventor, to the art of photography.

"Professor Hunt, having studied during twenty years the beautiful art of photography in all its details, submitted to the Committee the following explanation of Mr. Archer's just right:—

"'As there appears to be some misconception of the real claim of Mr. Archer to be considered as a *discoverer*, it is thought desirable to state briefly and distinctly what we owe to him. There can be no doubt that much of the uncertainty which has been thought by some persons to surround the introduction of collodion, has arisen from the unobtrusive character of Mr. Archer himself, who deferred for a considerable period *the publication of the process of which he was the discoverer*.

"'When Professor Schönbein, of Basle, introduced gun-cotton at the meeting of the British Association at Southampton in 1846, the solubility of this curious substance in ether was alluded to. Within a short time collodion was employed in our hospitals for the purposes of covering with a film impervious to air abraded surfaces on the body; its peculiar electrical condition was also known and exhibited by Mr. Hall, of Dartford, and others.

"'The beautiful character of the collodion film speedily led to the idea of using it as a medium for receiving photographic agents, and experiments were made by spreading the collodion on paper and on glass, to form with it sensitive tablets. These experiments were all failures, owing to the circumstance that the collodion was regarded merely as a sheet upon which the photographic materials were to be spread; the dry collodion film being in all cases employed.

"'To Mr. Archer, who spent freely both time and money in experimental research, it first occurred to dissolve in the collodion itself the iodide of potassium. By this means he removed every difficulty, and became the inventor of the collodion process. The pictures thus obtained were exhibited, and some of the details of the process communicated by Mr. Scott Archer in confidence to friends before he published his process. This led, very unfortunately, to experiments by others in the same direction, and hence there have arisen claims in opposition to those of this lamented photographer. Everyone, however, acquainted with the early history of the collodion process freely admits that Mr. Archer was the *sole inventor of iodized collodion*, and of those manipulatory details which still, with very slight modifications, constitute the collodion process, and he was the first person who published any account of the application of this remarkable accelerating agent, by which the most important movement has been given to the art of photography.'

"Your committee, in May last, heard with deep regret of the sudden death of the widow, Mrs. Archer, which melancholy event caused a postponement of the general meeting resolved upon in November last. Sir Wm. Newton thereupon resolved to make another effort to obtain a pension for the three orphan children, now more destitute than ever, and so earnestly did he urge their claim upon the Minister, Lord Derby, that a reply came the same day from his lordship's private secretary, saying, 'The Queen has been pleased to approve of a pension of fifty pounds per annum being paid from the Civil List to the children of the late Mr. Frederick Scott Archer, in consideration of the scientific discoveries of their father,' his lordship adding his regrets 'that the means at his disposal have not enabled him to do more in this case.' Your committee, to mark their sense of the value of the services rendered to the cause by Sir William Newton, thereupon passed a vote of thanks to him. In conclusion, your committee have to state that a trust deed has been prepared, free of charge, by Henry White, Esq., of 7, Southampton Street, which conveys the fund collected to trustees, to be by them invested in the public securities for the sole benefit of the orphan children. The sum in the Union Bank now amounts to £549 11s. 4d., exclusive of interest, and the various sums—in all about £68—paid over to Mrs. Archer last year. Thus far, the result is a subject for congratulation to the subscribers and your committee, whose labours have hitherto not been in vain. Your committee are, nevertheless, of opinion that an appeal to Parliament might be productive of a larger recognition of the claim of these orphan children— a claim not undeserving the recognition of the Legislature, when the inestimable boon bestowed upon the country is duly considered. Since March 1851, when Mr. Archer described his process in the pages of the *Chemist*, how many thousands must in some way or other have been made acquainted with the immense advantages it offers over all other processes in the arts, and how many instances could be adduced in testimony of its usefulness? For instance, its value to the Government during the last war, in the engineering department, the construction of field works, and in recording observations of historical and scientific interest. Your committee noticed that an attractive feature of the Photographic Society's last exhibition was a series of drawings and plans, executed by the Royal Engineers, in reduction of various ordnance maps, at a saving estimated at £30,000 to the country. The non-commissioned officers of this corps are now trained in this art, and sent to different foreign stations, so that in a few years there will be a network of photographic stations spread over the world, and having their results recorded in the War Department, and, in a short time, all the world will be brought under the subjugation of art.

"Mr. Warren De la Rue exhibited to the Astronomical Society, November, 1857, photographs of the moon and Jupiter, taken by the collodion process in five seconds, of which the Astronomer-Royal said, 'that a step of very great importance had been made, and that, either as regards the self-delineation of clusters of stars, nebulæ, and planets, or the self-registration of observations, it is impossible at present to estimate the value.' When admiring the magnificent photographic prints which are now to be seen in almost every part of the civilised world, an involuntary sense of gratitude towards the discoverer of the collodion process must be experienced, and it cannot but be felt how much the world is indebted to Mr. Archer for having placed at its command the means by which such beautiful objects are presented. How many thousands amongst those who owe their means of subsistence to this process must have experienced such a feeling of gratitude? It is upon such considerations that the public have been, and still are, invited to assist in securing for the orphan children of the late Mr. Archer some fitting appreciation of the service which he rendered to science, art, his country—nay, to the whole world.

"M. DIGBY WYATT, *Chairman*,
"JABEZ HOGG, *Secretary to Committee.*
"*Society of Arts, July,* 1858."

After reading that report, and especially Mr. Hunt's remarks, it will appear evident to all that even that act of charity, gratitude, and justice could not be carried through without someone raising objections and questioning the claims of Frederick Scott Archer as the original inventor of the Collodion process. Nearly all the biographers and historians of photography have coupled other names with Archer's, either as assistants or co-inventors, but I have evidence in my possession that will prove that neither Fry nor Diamond afforded Archer any assistance whatever, and that Archer preceded all the other claimants in his application of collodion. In support of the first part of this statement, I shall give extracts from Mrs. Archer's letter, now in my possession, which, I think, will set that matter at rest for ever. Mrs. Archer, writing from Bishop Stortford on December 7th, 1857, says. " When Mr. A. prepared pupils for India he always taught the paper process as well as the Collodion, for fear the chemicals should cause disappointment in a hot climate, as I believe that the negative paper he prepared differed from that in general use. I enclosed a specimen made in our glass house.

"In Mr. Hunt's book, as well as Mr. Horne's, Mr. Fry's name is joined with Mr. Archer's as the originators of the Collodion process.

" Should Mr. Hunt seem to require any corroboration of what I have stated respecting Mr. Fry, I can send you many of Mr. Fry's notes of invitation, when Mr. A. merely gave him lessons in the application of collodion, and Mr. Brown gave me the correspondence which passed between him and Mr. Fry on the subject at the time Mr. Horne's book was published. I did not send up those papers, for, unless required, it is useless to dwell on old grievances, but I should like such a man as Mr. Hunt to understand *how* the association of the two names originated."

As to priority of application, the following letter ought to settle that point —

"*Alma Cottage, Bishop Stortford.*
"*9th December*, 1857.

"Sir,—My hunting has at length proved successful. In the enclosed book you will find notes respecting the paper pulp, albumen, tanno-gelatine, and collodion. You will therein see Mr. Archer's notes of iod-collodion in 1849. You may wonder that I could not find this note-book before, but the numbers of papers that there are, and the extreme disorder, defy description. My head was in such a deplorable state before I left that I could arrange nothing. Those around me were most anxious to destroy *all the papers*, and I had great trouble to keep all with Mr. Archer's handwriting upon them, however dirty and rubbishing they might appear, so they were huddled together, a complete chaos. I look back with the greatest thankfulness that my brain did not completely lose its balance, for I had not a single relative who entered into Mr. Archer's pursuits, so that they could not possibly assist me.

"Mr. Archer being of so reserved a character, I had to *find out* where everything was, and my search has been amongst different things. I need not tell you that I hope this dirty enclosure will be taken care of.

"The paper pulp occupied much time; in fact, notes were only made of articles which had been much tried, which might probably be brought into use.—I am, sir, yours faithfully,

"*J. Hogg, Esq.* F. G. Archer."

If the foregoing is not evidence sufficient, I have by me a very good *glass positive* of Hever Castle, Kent, which was taken in the spring of 1849, and two collodion negatives made by Mr. Archer in the autumn of 1848; and these dates are all vouched for by Mr. Jabez Hogg, who was Mr Archer's medical attendant and friend, and knew him long before he began his experiments with collodion—whereas I cannot find a trace even of the *suggestion* of the application of collodion in the practice of photography either by Gustave Le Gray or J. R. Bingham prior to 1849; while Mr. Archer's note-book proves that he was not only iodizing collodion at that date, but making experiments with paper pulp and *gelatine;* so that Mr. Archer was not only the inventor of the collodion process, but was on the track of its destroyer even at that early date. He also published his method of bleaching positives and intensifying negatives with bichloride of mercury.

Frederick Scott Archer was born at Bishop Stortford in 1813, but there is little known of his early life, and what little there is I will allow Mrs. Archer to tell in her own way.

"DEAR SIR,—I do not know whether the enclosed is what you require; if not, be kind enough to let me know, and I must try to supply you with something better. I thought you merely required particulars relating to photography. Otherwise Mr. Archer's career was a singular one : Losing his parents in childhood, he lived in a world of his own; I think you know he was apprenticed to a bullion dealer in the city, where the most beautiful antique gems and coins of all nations being constantly before him, gave him the desire to model the figures, and led him to the study of numismatics. He worked so hard at nights at these pursuits that his master gave up the last two years of his time to save his life. He only requested him to be on the premises, on account of his extreme confidence in him.

"Many other peculiarities I could mention, but I dare say you know them already.

"I will send a small case to you, containing some early specimens and gutta-percha negatives, with a copy of Mr. A.'s portrait, which I found on leaving Great Russell Street, and have had several printed from it. It is not a good photograph, but I think you will consider it a likeness. I am, yours faithfully,

"*J. Hogg, Esq.* F. G. ARCHER."

Frederick Scott Archer pursued the double occupation of

sculptor and photographer at 105, Great Russell Street. It was there he so persistently persevered in his photographic experiments, and there he died in May, 1857, and was interred in Kensal Green Cemetery. A reference to the report of the Committee will show what was done for his bereaved family—a widow and three children. Mrs. Archer followed her husband in March, 1858, and two of the children died early; but one, Alice (unmarried), is still alive and in receipt of the Crown pension of fifty pounds per annum.

While the collodion episode in the history of photography is before my readers, and especially as the process is rapidly becoming extinct, I think this will be a suitable place to insert Archer's instructions for making a *soluble* gun-cotton, iodizing collodion, developing, and fixing the photographic image.

Gun-Cotton (or Pyroxaline, as it was afterwards named).

Take of dry nitre in powder ... ... 40 parts
Sulphuric acid ... ... 60 ,,
Cotton ... ... 2 ,,

The sulphuric acid and the nitre were mixed together, and immediately the latter was all dissolved, the gun-cotton was added and well stirred with a glass rod for about two minutes; then the cotton was plunged into a large bowl of water and well washed with repeated changes of water until the acid and nitre were washed away. The cotton was then pressed and dried, and converted into collodion by dissolving 30 grains of gun-cotton in 18 fluid ounces of ether and 2 ounces of alcohol—putting the cotton into the ether first, and then adding the alcohol; the collodion allowed to settle and decanted prior to iodizing. The latter operation was performed by adding a sufficient quantity of iodide of silver to each ounce of the plain collodion. Mr. Archer tells how to make the iodide of silver, but the quantity is regulated by the quantity of alcohol in the collodion. When the iodized collodion was ready for use, a glass plate was cleaned and coated with it, and then sensitized by immersion in a bath of nitrate of silver solution—30 grains of nitrate of silver to each ounce of distilled water. From three to five minutes' immersion in the silver bath was generally sufficient to sensitize the plate. This, of course, had to be done in what is commonly called a *dark-room*. After exposure in the camera, the picture was developed by pouring over the surface of the plate a solution of pyrogallic acid of the following proportions:—

Pyrogallic acid	5 grains
Distilled water	10 ounces
Glacial acetic acid	40 minims

After the development of the picture it was washed and fixed in a solution of hyposulphite of soda, 4 ounces to 1 pint of water. The plate was then washed and dried. This is an epitome of the whole of Archer's process for making either negatives or positives on glass, the difference being effected by varying the time of exposure and development. Of course the process was somewhat modified and simplified by experience and commercial enterprise. Later on bromides were added to the collodion, an iron developer employed, and cyanide of potassium as a fixing agent; but the principle remained the same from first to last.

When pyrogallic acid was first employed in photography, it was quoted at 21s. per oz., and, if I remember rightly, I paid 3s. for the first *drachm* that I purchased. On referring to an old price list I find Daguerreotype plates, 2½ by 2 inches, quoted at 12s. per dozen; nitrate of silver, 5s. 6d. per oz.; chloride of gold, 5s. 6d. for 15 grains; hyposulphite of soda at 5s. per lb.; and a half-plate rapid portrait lens by Voightlander, of Vienna, at £60. Those were the days when photography might well be considered expensive, and none but the wealthy could indulge in its pleasures and fascinations.

While I lived in Glasgow, competition was tolerably keen,

even then, and amongst the best "glass positive men" were Messrs Bibo, Bowman, J. Urie, and Young and Son, as the latter styled himself; and in photographic portraiture, plain and coloured, by the collodion process, were Messrs. Macnab and J. Stuart. From the time that I relinquished the Daguerreotype process, in 1857, I devoted my attention to the production of high-class collodion negatives. I never took kindly to *glass positives*, though I had done some as early as 1852. They were never equal in beauty and delicacy to a good Daguerreotype, and their low tone was to me very objectionable. I considered the Ferrotype the best form of collodion positive, and did several of them, but my chief work was plain and coloured prints from collodion negatives, also small portraits on visiting cards.

Early in January, 1860, my home and business were destroyed by fire, and I lost all my old and new specimens of Daguerreotypes and photographs, all my Daguerreotype and other apparatus, and nearly everything I possessed. As I was only partially insured, I suffered considerable loss. After settling my affairs I decided on going to America again and trying my luck in New York. Family ties influenced this decision considerably, or I should not have left Glasgow, where I was both prosperous and respected. To obtain an idea of the latest and best aspects of photography, I visited London and Paris.

The carte-de-visite form of photography had not exhibited much vitality at that period in London, but in Paris it was beginning to be popular. While in London I accompanied Mr. Jabez Hughes to the meeting of the Photographic Society, Feb. 7th, 1860, the Right Honorable the Lord Chief Baron Pollock in the chair, when the report of the Collodion Committee was delivered. The committee, consisting of F. Bedford, P. Delamotte, Dr. Diamond, Roger Fenton, Jabez Hughes, T. A. Malone, J. H. Morgan, H. P. Robinson, Alfred Rosling, W. Russell Sedgefield, J. Spencer, and T. R. Williams, strongly recommended Mr. Hardwich's formula. That was my first visit to the Society, and I certainly did not think then that I should ever see it again, or become and be a member for twenty-two years.

I sailed from Liverpool in the ss. *City of Baltimore* in March, and reached New York safely in April, 1860. I took time to look about me, and visited all the "galleries" on Broadway, and other places, before deciding where I should locate myself. Many changes had taken place during the six years I had been absent. Nearly all the old Daguerreotypists were still in existence, but all of them, with the exception of Mr. Brady, had abandoned the Daguerreotype process, and Mr. Brady only retained it for small work. Most of the chief galleries had been moved higher up Broadway, and a mania of magnificence had taken possession of most of the photographers. Mr. Anson was the first to make a move in that direction by opening a "superb gallery" on the ground floor in Broadway right opposite the Metropolitan Hotel, filling his windows with life-sized photographs coloured in oil at the back, which he called Diaphanotypes. He did a large business in that class of work, especially among visitors from the Southern States; but that was soon to end, for already there were rumours of war, but few then gave it any serious consideration.

Messrs. Gurney and Sons' gallery was also a very fine one, but not on the ground floor. Their "saloon" was upstairs. This house was one of the oldest in New York in connection with photography. In the very early days, Mr. Gurney, senr., was one of the most eminent "professors" of the Daguerreotype process, and was one of the committee appointed to wait upon the Rev. Wm. Hill, a preacher in the Catskills, to negotiate with the reverend gentlemen (?) for his vaunted secret of photography in natural colours. As the art progressed, or the necessity for change arose, Mr. Gurney was ready to introduce every novelty, and, in later years, in conjunction with Mr. Fredericks, then in partnership with Mr. Gurney, he introduced the "Hallotype," not Hillotype, and the "Ivorytype." Both these processes had their day. The former was photography spoiled by the application of Canada balsam and very little art; the latter was the application of a great deal of art to spoil a photograph. The largest of all the large galleries on Broadway was that of Messrs. Fredericks and Co. The whole of the ground and first floor were thrown into one "crystal front," and made a very attractive appearance. The windows were filled with life-sized portraits painted in oil, crayons, and other styles, and the walls of the interior were covered with life-sized portraits of eminent men and beautiful women. The floor was richly carpeted, and the furnishing superb. A gallery ran round the walls to enable the visitors to view the upper pictures, and obtain a general view of the "saloon," the *tout ensemble* of which was magnificent. From the ground floor an elegant staircase led to the galleries, toilet and waiting rooms, and thence to the operating rooms or studios. Some of the Parisian galleries were fine, but nothing to be compared with Fredericks', and the finest establishment in London did not bear the slightest comparison.

Mr. Brady was another of the early workers of the Daguerreotype process, and probably the last of his *confrères* to abandon it. He commenced business in the early forties in Fulton Street, a long way down Broadway, but as the sea of commerce pressed on and rolled over the strand of fashion, he was obliged to move higher and higher up Broadway, until he reached the corner of Tenth Street, nearly opposite Grace Church. Mr. Brady appeared to set the Franklin maxim, "Three removes as bad as a fire," at defiance, for he had made three or four moves to my knowledge—each one higher and higher to more elegant and expensive premises, each remove entailing the cost of more and more expensive furnishing, until his latest effort in upholstery culminated in a superb suite of black walnut and green silk velvet; in short, Longfellow's "Excelsior" appeared to be the motto of Mr. Brady.

Messrs Mead Brothers, Samuel Root, James Cady, and George Adams ought to receive "honourable mention" in connection with the art in New York, for they were excellent operators in the Daguerreotype days, and all were equally good manipulators of the collodion process and silver printing.

After casting and sounding about, like a mariner seeking a haven on a strange coast, I finally decided on buying a half interest in the gallery of Mead Brothers, 805, Broadway; Harry Mead retaining his, or his wife's share of the business, but leaving me to manage the "uptown" branch. This turned out to be an unfortunate speculation, which involved me in a lawsuit with one of Mead's creditors, and compelled me to get rid of a very unsatisfactory partner in the best way and at any cost that I could. Mead's creditor, by some process of law that I could never understand, stripped the gallery of all that belonged to my partner, and even put in a claim for half of the fixtures. Over this I lost my temper, and had to pay, not the piper, but the lawyer. I also found that Mrs. Henry Mead had a bill of sale on her husband's interest in the business, which I ended by buying her out. Husband and wife are very seldom one in America. Soon after getting the gallery into my own hands, refurnishing and rearranging, the Prince of Wales's visit to New York was arranged, and as the windows of my gallery commanded a good view of Broadway, I let most of them very advantageously, retaining the use of one only for myself and family. There were so many delays, however, at the City Hall and other places on the day of the procession, that it was almost dark when the Prince reached 805, Broadway, and all my guests were both weary of waiting so long, and disappointed at seeing so little of England's future King.

When I recommenced business on Broadway on my own account there was only one firm taking cartes-de-visite, and I introduced that form of portrait to my customers, but they did not take very kindly to it, though a house not far from me was doing a very good business in that style at three dollars a dozen, and Messrs. Rockwood and Co. appeared to be monopolising all the carte-de-visite business that was being done in New York; but eventually I got in the thin edge of the wedge by exhibiting *four* for one dollar. This ruse brought in sitters, and I began to do very well until Abraham Lincoln issued his proclamation calling for one hundred thousand men to stamp out the Southern rebellion. I remember that morning most distinctly. It was a miserably wet morning in April, 1861, and all kinds of business received a shock. People looked bewildered, and thought of nothing but saving their money and reducing their expenses. It had a blighting effect on my business, and I, not knowing, like others, where it might land me, determined to get rid of my responsibilities at any cost, so I sold my business for a great deal less than it was worth, and at a very serious loss. The outbreak of that gigantic civil war and a severe family bereavement combined, induced me to return to England as soon as possible. Before leaving America, in all probability for ever, I went to Washington to bid some friends farewell, and while there I went into Virginia with a friend on Sunday morning, July 21st, and in the afternoon saw the smoke and heard the cannonading of the first battle of Bull Run, and witnessed, next morning, the rout and rush into Washington of the demoralised fragments of the Federal army. I wrote and sent a description of the stampede to a friend in Glasgow, which he handed over to the *Glasgow Herald* for publication, and I have reason to believe that my description of that memorable rout was the first that was published in Great Britain.

As soon as I could settle my affairs I left New York with my family, and arrived in London on the 15th of September, 1861. It was a beautiful sunny day when I landed, and, after all the trouble and excitement I had so recently seen and experienced, London, despite its business and bustle, appeared like a heaven of peace.

Mr. Jabez Hughes was about the last to wish me "Godspeed" when I left England, so he was the first I went to see when I returned. I found, to my disappointment, that he was in Paris, but Mrs. Hughes gave me a hearty welcome. After a few days' sojourn in London I went to Glasgow with the view of recommencing in that city, where I had many friends; but while there, and on the very day that I was about to sign for the lease of a house, Mr. Hughes wrote to offer me the management of his business in Oxford Street. It did not take me long to decide, and by return post that same night I wrote accepting the offer. I concluded all other arrangements as quickly as possible, returned to London, and entered upon my managerial duties on the 1st November, 1861. I had long wished and looked out for an opportunity to settle in London and enlarge my circle of photographic acquaintance and experience, so I put on my new harness with alacrity and pleasure.

Among the earliest of my new acquaintances was George Wharton Simpson, Editor of the PHOTOGRAPHIC NEWS. He called at Oxford Street one evening while I was the guest of Mr. Hughes, by whom we were introduced, and we spent a long, chatty, and pleasant evening together, talking over my American experience and matters photographic; but, to my surprise, much of our conversation appeared in the next issue of his journal (*vide* PHOTOGRAPHIC NEWS, October 11th, 1861, pp. 480-1). But that was a power, I afterwards ascertained, which he possessed to an eminent degree, and which he utilized most successfully at his "Wednesday evenings at home," when he entertained his photographic friends at Canonbury Road, N. Very delightful and enjoyable those evenings were, and he never failed to cull paragraphs for the PHOTOGRAPHIC NEWS from the busy brains of his numerous visitors. He was a genial host, and his wife was a charming hostess; and his daughter Eva, now the wife of William Black the novelist, often increased the charm of those evenings by the exhibition of her musical abilities. It is often a wonder to me that other editors of photographic journals don't pursue a similar plan, for those social re-unions were not only pleasant, but profitable to old friend Simpson. Through Mr. Simpson's "at homes," and my connection with Mr. Hughes, I made the acquaintance of nearly all the eminent photographers of the time, amongst whom may be mentioned W. G. Lacy, of Ryde, I.W. The latter was a very sad and brief acquaintanceship, for he died in Mr. Hughes's sitting-room on the 21st November, 1861, in the presence of G. Wharton Simpson, Jabez Hughes, and myself, and, strangely enough, it was entirely through this death that Mr. Hughes went to Ryde, and became photographer to the Queen. Mr. Lacy made his will in Mr. Hughes's sitting-room, and Mr. Simpson sole executor, who sold Mr. Lacy's business in the Arcade, Ryde, I.W., to Mr. Hughes, and in the March following he took possession, leaving me solely in charge of his business in Oxford Street, London.

About this time Mr. Skaife introduced his ingenious pistolgraph, but it was rather in advance of the times, for the dryplates then in the market were not quite quick enough for "snap shots," though I have seen some fairly good pictures taken with the apparatus.

At this period a fierce controversy was raging about lunar photography, but it was all unnecessary, as the moon had photographed herself under the guidance of Mr. Whipple, of Boston, U.S., as early as 1853, and all that was required to obtain a lunar picture was sufficient exposure.

On December 3rd, 1861, Thomas Ross read a paper and exhibited a panoramic lens and camera at a meeting of the Photographic Society, and on the 15th October, 1889, I saw the same apparatus, in perfect condition, exhibited as a curiosity at the Photographic Society's Exhibition. No wonder the apparatus was in such good condition, for I should think it had never been used but once. The plates were 10 inches long, and curved like the crescent of a new moon. Cleaning board, dark slide, and printing-frame, were all curved. Fancy the expense and trouble attending the use of such an apparatus; I should think it had few buyers. Certainly I never sold one, and I never met with any person who had bought one.

Amateurs have ever been the most restless and discontented disciples of the "Fathers of Photography," always craving for something new, and seeking to lessen their labours and increase their facilities, and to these causes we are chiefly indebted for the marvellous development and radical changes of photography. No sooner was the Daguerreotype process perfected than it was superseded by *wet* collodion, and that was barely a workable process when it became the anxiety of every amateur to have a *dry* collodion process, and multitudes of men were at work endeavouring to make, modify, or invent a means that would enable them to use the camera as a sort of sketch-book, and make their finished picture at home at their leisure. Hence the number of Dry Plate processes published about this period, and the controversies carried on by the many enthusiastic champions of the various methods. Beer was pitted against tea and coffee, honey against albumen, gin against gum, but none of them were equal to wet collodion.

The International Exhibition of 1862 did little or nothing in the interests of photography. It is true there was a scattered and skied exhibition at the top of a high tower, but as there was no "lift," I suspect very few people went to see the exhibits. I certainly was not there more than once myself. Among the exhibitors of apparatus were the names of Messrs. McLean, Melhuish and Co., Murray and Heath, P. Meagher, T. Ottewill and Co., but there was nothing very remarkable among their exhibits. There was some very good workmanship, but the articles exhibited were not beyond the quality of the everyday manufacture of the best camera and apparatus makers.

The chief contributors to the exhibition of photographs were Messrs. Mayall, T. R. Williams, and Herbert Watkins in portraiture; and in landscapes, &c., Messrs. Francis Bedford, Rejlander, Rouch, Stephen Thompson, James Mudd, William Mayland, H. P. Robinson, and Breeze. By some carelessness or stupidity on the part of the attendants or constructors of the Exhibition, nearly all Mr. Breeze's beautiful exhibits—stereoscopes and stereoscopic transparencies—were destroyed by the fall of a skylight. Perhaps the best thing that the International Exhibition did for photography was the issue of the Jurors' Report, as it was prefaced with a brief History of Photography up to date, not perfectly correct regarding the Rev. J. B. Reade's labours, but otherwise good, the authorship of which I attribute to the late Dr. Diamond; but the awards—ah! well, awards never were quite satisfactory. Commendees thought they should have been medalists, and the latter thought something else. Thomas Ross, J. H. Dallmeyer, and Negretti and Zambra were the English recipients of medals, and Voigtlander and Son and C. Dietzler received medals for their lenses.

Early in 1862 the Harrison Globe Lens was attracting attention, and, as much was claimed for it both in width of angle and rapidity, I imported from New York a 5 by 4 and a whole plate as samples. The 5 by 4 was an excellent lens, and embraced a much wider angle than any other lens known, and Mr. Hughes employed it to photograph the bridal bed and suite of apartments of the Prince and Princess of Wales at Osborn, Isle of Wight, and I feel certain that no other lens would have done the work so well. I have copies of the photograph by me now. They are circular pictures of five inches in diameter, and every article and decoration visible in the chambers are as sharp and crisp as possible. I showed the lens to Mr. Dallmeyer, and he thought he could make a better one; his Wide-Angle Rectilinear was the result.

Mr. John Pouncy, of Dorchester, introduced his "patent

process for permanent printing" this year, but it never made much headway. It was an oleagenous process, mixed with bichromate of potash, or bitumen of Judea, and always smelt of bad fat. I possessed examples at the time, but took no care of them, and no one else did in all probability; but it appeared to me to be the best means of transferring photographic impressions to wood blocks for the engraver's purpose. Thomas Sutton, B.A., published a book on Pouncy's process and carbon printing, but the process had inherent defects which were not overcome, so nothing could make it a success. Sutton's "History of Carbon Printing" was sufficiently interesting to attract both readers and buyers at the time.

I have previously stated that Daguerre introduced and left his process in an imperfect and uncommercial condition, and that it was John Frederick Goddard, then lecturer at the Adelaide Gallery, London, and inventor of the polariscope, who discovered the accelerating properties of bromine, and by which, with iodine, he obtained a bromo-iodide of silver on the surface of the silvered plate employed in the Daguerreotype process, thereby reducing the time of exposure from twenty minutes to twenty seconds, and making the process available for portraiture with an ordinary double combination lens. Somehow or other, this worthy gentleman had fallen into adverse circumstances, and was obliged to eat the bread of charity in his old age. The facts of this sad case coming to the knowledge of Mr. Hughes and others, an appeal, written by Mr. Hughes, was published in the PHOTOGRAPHIC NEWS, December 11th, 1863. As Mr. Hughes and myself had benefited by Mr. Goddard's improvement in the practice of the Daguerreotype, we took an active interest in the matter, and, by canvassing friends and customers, succeeded in obtaining a considerable proportion of the sum total subscribed for the relief of Mr. Goddard. Enough was obtained to make him independent and comfortable for the remainder of his life. Mr. T. R. Williams was appointed almoner by the committee, but his office was not for long, as Mr. Goddard died Dec. 28th, 1866.

On the 5th of April, 1864, I attended a meeting of the Photographic Society at King's College, and heard Mr. J W. Swan read a paper on his new patent carbon process. It was a crowded meeting, and an intense interest pervaded the minds of both members and visitors The examples exhibited were very beautiful, but at that early stage they began to show a weakness, which clung to the collodion support as long as it was employed Some of the specimens which I obtained at the time left the mounting boards, and the films were torn asunder by opposing forces, and the pictures completely destroyed. I have one in my possession now in that unsatisfactory condition Mr. Swan's process was undoubtedly an advance in the right direction, but it was still imperfect, and required further improvement. Many of the members failed to see where the patent rights came in, and Mr. Swan himself appeared to have qualms of conscience on the subject, for he rather apologetically announced in his paper, that he had obtained a patent, though his first intention was to allow it to be practised without any restriction. I think myself it would have been wiser to have adhered to his original intention ; however, it was left to others to do more to advance the carbon process than he did.

During this year (1865) an effort was made to establish a claim of priority in favour of Thomas Wedgwood for the honour of having made photographs on silver plates, and negatives on paper, and examples of such alleged early works were submitted to the inspection of members of the Photographic Society, but it was most satisfactorily determined that the photographs on the silver plates were weak Daguerreotypes of a posterior date, and that the photographic prints, on paper, of a breakfast-table were from a calotype negative taken by Fox Talbot. Messrs. Henneman and Dr. Diamond proved this most conclusively. Other prints then exhibited, and alleged to be photographs, were nothing but prints from metal plates, produced by some process of engraving, probably Aquatint. I saw some of the examples at the time, and, as recently as Nov. 1st, 1889, I have seen some of them again, and I think the "Breakfast Table" and a view of "Wedgwood's Pottery" are silver prints, though very much faded, from calotype negatives. The other prints, such as the "Piper" and "A Vase," are from engraved plates. No one can desire to lessen Thomas Wedgwood's claims to pre-eminence among the early experimentalists with chloride of silver, but there cannot now be any denial to the claims of the Rev. J. B. Reade in 1837, and Fox Talbot in 1840, of being the earliest producers of photographic negatives on paper, from which numerous prints could be obtained.

The Wothlytype printing process was introduced to the notice of photographers and the public this year : first, by a blatant article in the *Times,* which was both inaccurate and misleading, for it stated that both nitrate of silver and hyposulphite of soda were dispensed with in the process ; secondly, by the issue of advertisements and prospectuses for the formation of a Limited Liability Company. I went to the Patent Office and examined the specification, and found that both nitrate of silver and hyposulphite of soda were essential to the practice of the process, and that there was no greater guarantee of permanency in the use of the Wothlytype than in ordinary silver printing.

On March 14th, 1865, George Wharton Simpson, editor and proprietor of the *Photographic News,* read a paper at a meeting of the Photographic Society on a new printing process with collodio-chloride of silver on paper. Many beautiful examples were exhibited, but the method never became popular, chiefly on account of the troubles of toning with sulpho-cyanide of ammonium. The same or a similar process, substituting gelatine for collodion, is known and practised now under the name of Aristotype, but not very extensively, because of the same defects and difficulties attending the Simpsontype. Another new method of positive printing was introduced this year by Mr. John M. Burgess, of Norwich, which he called "Eburneum." It was not in reality a new mode of printing, but an ingenious application of the collodion transfer, or stripping process. The back of the collodion positive print was coated with a mixture of gelatine and oxide of zine, and when dry stripped from the glass. The finished picture resembled a print on very fine ivory, and possessed both delicate half-tones and brilliant shadows. I possess some of them now, and they are as beautiful as they were at first, after a lapse of nearly quarter of a century. It was a very troublesome and tedious process, and I don't think many people practised it. Certainly I don't know any one that does so at the present time.

This was the year of the Dublin International Exhibition. I went to see it and report thereon, and my opinions and criticisms of the photographic and other departments will be found and may be perused in "Contributions to Photographic Literature." On the whole, it was a very excellent exhibition, and I thoroughly enjoyed the trip.

A new carbon process by M. Carey Lea was published this year. The ingredients were similar to those employed by Swan and others, but differently handled. No pigment was mixed with the gelatine before exposure, but it was rubbed on after exposure and washing, and with care any colour or number of colours might be applied, and so produce a polychromatic picture, but I don't know any one that ever did so. I think it could easily be applied to making photographic transfers to blocks for the use of wood engravers.

December 5th, 1865, Mr. Walter Woodbury demonstrated and exhibited examples of the beautiful mechanical process that bears his name to the members of the Photographic Society. The process was not entirely photographic. The province of photography ceased on the production of the gelatine relief.

All that followed was strictly mechanical. It is somewhat singular that a majority of the inventions and modifications of processes that were introduced this year related to carbon and permanency.

Thursday, January 11th, 1866, I read, at the South London Photographic Society, a paper on "Errors in Pictorial Backgrounds." As the paper, as well as the discussion thereon, is published *in extenso* in the journals of the period, it is not necessary for me to repeat it here, but I may as well state briefly my reasons for reading the paper. At that time pictorial backgrounds and crowded accessories were greatly in use, and it was seldom, if ever, that the horizontal line of the painted background, and the horizontal line indicated by the position of the camera, coincided. Consequently the photographic pictures obtained under such conditions invariably exhibited this incongruity, and it was with the hope of removing these defects, or violations of art rules and optical laws, that I ventured to call attention to the subject and suggest a remedy. A little later, I wrote an article, "Notes on Pictures in the National Gallery," which was published in the *Photographic News* of March 29th, in support of the arguments already adduced in my paper on "Errors in Pictorial Backgrounds," and I recommend every portrait photographer to study those pictures.

February 13th I was elected a member of the Photographic Society of London.

Quite a sensation was created in the Spring of this year by the introduction of what were termed "Magic Photographs." Some one was impudent enough to patent the process, although it was nothing but a resurrection of what was published in 1840 by Sir John Herschel, which consisted of bleaching an ordinary silver print to invisibilty with bichloride of mercury, and restoring it by an application of hyposulphite of soda. I introduced another form of magic photograph, in various monochromatic colours, similar to Sir John Herschel's cyanotype, and I have several of these pictures in my possession now, both blue, purple, and red, dated 1866, as bright and beautiful as they were the day they were made. But the demand for these magic photographs was suddenly stopped by some one introducing indecent pictures. In all probability these objectionable pictures came from abroad, and the most scrupulous of the home producers suffered in consequence, as none of the purchasers could possibly know what would appear when the developer or redeveloper was applied.

On June 14th Mr. F. W. Hart read a paper, and demonstrated before the South London Photographic Society, on his method of rendering silver prints permanent. "A consummation devoutly to be wished," but unfortunately some prints in my possession that were treated to a bath of his eliminator show unmistakable signs of fading. In my opinion, there is nothing so efficacious as warm water washing, and some prints that I toned, fixed, and washed myself over thirty years ago, are perfect.

The "cabinet" form of portrait was introduced this year by Mr. F. R. Window, and it eventually became the fashionable size, and almost wiped out the carte-de-visite. The latter, however, had held its position for about nine years, and the time for change had arrived. Beyond the introduction of the cabinet portrait, nothing very novel or ingenious had been introduced, but a very good review of photography up to date appeared in the October issue of the *British Quarterly Review* This was a very ably written article from the pen of my old friend, Mr. George Wharton Simpson

No radical improvement or advance in photography was made in 1867, but M. Adam-Salomon created a little sensation by exhibiting some very fine samples of his work in the Paris Exhibition. They were remarkable chiefly for their pose, lighting, retouching, and tone. A few of them were afterwards seen in London, and that of Dr. Diamond was probably the most satiafactory. M. Salomon was a sculptor in Paris, and his art training and feeling in that branch of the Fine Arts naturally assisted him in photography

The Duc de Luynes' prize of 8,000 francs for the best mechanical printing process was this year awarded to M. Poitevin. In making the award, the Commission gave a very excellent resumé of all that had previously been done in that direction, and endeavoured to show why they thought M. Poitevin entitled to the prize; but for all that I think it will be difficult to prove that any of M. Poitevin's mechanical processes ever came into use.

On June 13th, in the absence of Mr. Jabez Hughes, I read his paper, "About Leptographic Printing," before the South London Photographic Society. This Leptographic paper was claimed to be the invention of two photographers in Madrid, but it was evidently only a modification of Mr. Simpson's collodio-chloride of silver process.

About this period I got into a controversy—on very different subjects, it is true—but it made me determine to abandon for the future the practice of writing critical notices under the cover of a *nom de plume*. I had, under the *nom de plume* of "Union Jack," written in favour of a union of *all* the photographic societies then in London. This brought Mr. A. H. Wall down on me, but that did not affect me very much, nor was I personally distressed about the other, but I thought it best to abandon a dangerous practice Under the *nom de plume* of "Lux Graphicus" I had contributed a great many articles to the *Photographic News*, and, in a review of the Society's exhibition, published Nov 22nd, 1867, I expressed an honest opinion on Mr. Robinson's picture entitled "Sleep." It was not so favourable and flattering, perhaps, as he would have liked, but it was an honest criticism, and written without any intention of giving pain or offence.

The close of this year was marked by a very sad catastrophe intimately associated with photography, by the death of Mr. Mawson at Newcastle-on-Tyne; he was killed by an explosion of nitro-glycerine. Mr. Mawson, in conjunction with Mr. J. W. Swan, was one of the earliest and most successful manufacturers of collodion, and, as early as 1852, I made negatives with that medium, though I did not employ collodion solely until 1857, when I abandoned for ever the beautiful and fascinating Daguerreotype.

On Friday, December 27th, Antoine Jean Francois Claudet, F.R.S., &c., &c, died suddenly in the 71st year of his age. He was one of the earliest workers and improvers of the Daguerreotype process in this country, and one of the last to relinquish its practice in London. Mr. Claudet bought a share of the English patent of Mr. Berry, the agent, while he was a partner in the firm of Claudet and Houghton in 1840, and commenced business as a professional Daguerreotypist soon afterwards. Before the introduction of bromine as an accelerator by Mr. Goddard, Mr. Claudet had discovered that chloride of iodine increased the sensitiveness of the Daguerreotype plate, and he read a paper on that subject before the Royal Society in 1841. He was a member of the council of the Photographic Society for many years, and a copious contributor to its proceedings, as well as to photographic literature. In his intercourse with his *confrères* he was always courteous, and when I called upon him in 1851 he received me most kindly. I met him again in Glasgow, and many times in London, and always considered him the best specimen of a Frenchman I had ever met. Towards his clients he was firm, respectful, and sometimes generous, as the following characteristic anecdote will show. He had taken a portrait of a child, which, for some reason or other, was not liked, and demurred at. He said, "Ah! well, the matter is easily settled. I'll keep the picture, and return your money"; and so he thought the case was ended; but by-and-bye the picture was asked for, and he refused to give it up. Proceedings were taken to compel him to surrender it, which he defended. In stating the case, the counsel remarked that the child was dead. Mr. Claudet immediately stopped the counsel and the case by exclaiming, "Ah! they did not tell me that before. Now, I make the parents a present of the portrait." I am happy to say that I possess a good portrait of Mr. Claudet, taken in November, 1867, with his *Topaz lens*, ⅜-inch aperture. Strangely enough, Mr. Claudet's studio in Regent Street was seriously damaged by fire within a month of his death, and all his valuable Daguerreotypes, negatives, pictures, and papers destroyed.

On April 9th, 1868, I exhibited, at the South London Photographic Society, examples of nearly all the types of photography then known, amongst them a Daguerreotype by Daguerre, many of which are now in the Science Department of the South Kensington Museum, and were presented by me to form the nucleus of a national exhibition of the rise and progress of photography, for which I received the "thanks of the Lords of the Council on Education," dated April 22nd, 1886

There was nothing very remarkable done in 1868 to forward the interests or development of photography, yet that year narrowly escaped being made memorable, for Mr. W. H. Harrison, now editor of the *Photographic News*, actually prepared, exposed, and developed a gelatino-bromide dry plate, but did not pursue the matter further. 1869 also passed without adding much to the advancement of photography, and I fear the same may be said of 1870, with the exception of the publication, by Thos. Sutton, of Gaudin's gelatino-iodide process.

On February 21st, 1870, Robert J. Bingham died in Brussels. When the Daguerreotype process was first introduced to this country, Mr Bingham was chemical assistant to Prof. Faraday at the Royal Institution. He took an immediate interest in the wonderful discovery, and made an improvement in the application of bromine vapour, which entitled him to the gratitude of all Daguerreotypists. When Mr Goddard applied bromine to the process, he employed "bromine water," but, in very hot weather, the aqueous vapour condensed upon the surface of the plate, and interrupted the sensitising process. Mr. Bingham obviated this evil by charging hydrate of lime with bromine vapour, which not only removed the trouble of condensation, but increased the sensitiveness of the prepared plate. This was a great boon to all Daguerreotypists, and many a time I thanked him mentally long before I had the pleasure of meeting him in London. Mr. Bingham also wrote a valuable manual on the Daguerreotype and other photographic processes, which was published by Geo. Knight and Sons, Foster Lane, Cheapside. Some years before his death, Mr. Bingham settled in Paris, and became a professional photographer, but chiefly as a publisher of photographic copies of paintings and drawings.

Abel Niepce de St. Victor, best known without the Abel, died suddenly on April 6th, 1870. Born at St. Cyr, July 26th, 1805. After passing through his studies at the Military School of Saumur, he became an officer in a cavalry regiment. Being studious and fond of chemistry, he was fortunate enough to effect some saving to the Government in the dyeing of fabrics employed in making certain military uniforms, for which he received compensation and promotion. His photographic fame rests upon two achievements : firstly, his application of iodized albumen to glass for negative purposes in 1848, a process considerably in advance of Talbot's paper negatives, but it was quickly superseded by collodion; secondly, his researches on "heliochromy," or photography in natural colours. Niepce de St. Victor, like others before and since, was only partially successful in obtaining some colour reproductions, but totally unsuccessful in rendering those colours permanent. In proof of both these statements I will quote from the Juror's Report, on the subject, of the International Exhibition, 1862 :—"The obtaining of fixed natural colours by means of photography still remains, as was before remarked, to be accomplished; but the jurors have pleasure in recording that some very striking results of experiments in this direction were forwarded for their inspection by a veteran in photographic research and discovery, M. Niepce de St. Victor. These, about a dozen in number, $3\frac{1}{2}$ by $2\frac{1}{2}$ inches, consisted of reproductions of prints of figures with parti-coloured draperies. Each tint in the pictures exhibited, they were assured, was a faithful reproduction of the original. Amongst the colours were blues, yellows, reds, greens, &c., all very vivid. Some of the tints gradually faded and disappeared in the light whilst under examination, and a few remained permanent for some hours. The possibility of producing natural colour thus established is a fact most interesting and important, and too much praise cannot be awarded to the skilful research which has been to this extent crowned with success. The jury record their obligations to their chairman, Baron Gross, at whose personal solicitation they were enabled to obtain a sight of these remarkable pictures." Such was the condition of photography in natural colours towards the close of 1862, and so it is now after a lapse of twenty-eight years. In 1870 several examples of Niepce de St. Victor's heliochromy were sent to the Photographic Society of London, and I had them in my hands and examined them carefully in gaslight; they could not be looked at in daylight at all. I certainly saw *faint* traces of colour, but whether I saw them in their original vigour, or after they had faded, I cannot say. All I can say is that the tints were very feeble, and that they had not been obtained *through the lens.* They were, at their best, only contact impressions of coloured prints obtained after many hours of exposure. The examples had been sent to the Photographic Society with the hope of selling them for the benefit of the widow, but the Society was too wise to invest in such evanescent property. However, a subscription was raised both in England and France for the benefit of the widow and orphans of Niepce de St. Victor.

December, 1870, was marked by the death of one of the eminent pioneers of photography. On the 12th, the Rev. J. B. Reade passed away at Bishopsbourne Rectory, Canterbury, in the sixty-ninth year of his age. I have already, I think, established Mr. Reade's claim to the honour of being the first to produce a photograpnic negative on paper developed with gallic acid, and I regret that I am unable to trace the existence of those two negatives alluded to in Mr. Reade's published letter. Mr. Reade told me himself that he gave those two historic negatives to Dr. Diamond, when Secretary to the Photographic Society, to be lodged with that body for safety, proof, and reference; but they are not now in the possession of the Photographic Society, and what became of them no one knows. Several years ago I caused enquiries to be made, and Dr. Diamond was written to by Mr. H. Baden Pritchard, then Secretary, but Dr. Diamond's reply was to the effect that he had no recollection of them, and that Mr. Reade was given to hallucinations. Considering the positions that Mr. Reade held, both in the world and various learned and scientific societies, I don't think that he could ever have been afflicted with such a mental weakness. He was a clergyman in the Church of England, an amateur astronomer and microscopist, one of the fathers of photography, and a member of Council of the Photographic Society, and President of the Microscopical Society at the time of his death. I had many a conversation with him years ago, and I never detected either weakness or wandering in his mind; therefore I could not doubt the truth of his statement relative to the custodianship of the first paper negative that was taken through the lens of a solar microscope. Mr. Reade was a kind and affable man; and, though a great sufferer on his last bed of sickness, he wrote loving, grateful, and Christian like letters to many of his friends, some of which I have seen, and I have photographed his signature to one of them to attach to his portrait, which I happily possess.

In 1871 the coming revolution in photography was faintly heralded by Dr. R. L. Maddox, publishing in the *British Journal of Photography*, "An Experiment with Gelatino-Bromide." Successful as the experiment was it did not lead to any extensive adoption of the process at the time, but it did most unqestionably exhibit the capabilities of gelatino-bromide.

As that communication to the *British Journal of Photography* contained and first made public the working details of a process that was destined to supersede collodion, I will here insert a copy of Dr. Maddox's letter *in extenso*.

"An Experiment with Gelatino-Bromide.

"The collodio-bromide processes have for some time held a considerable place in the pages of the *British Journal of Photography*, and obtained such a prominent chance of being eventually the process of the day in the dry way, that a few remarks upon the application of another medium may perhaps not be uninteresting to the readers of the journal, though little more can be stated than the result of somewhat careless experiments tried at first on an exceedingly dull afternoon. It is not for a moment supposed to be new, for the chances of novelty in photography are small, seeing the legion of ardent workers, and the ground already trodden by its devotees, so that for outsiders little remains except to take the result of labours so industriously and largely circulated through these pages, and be thankful.

"Gelatine, which forms the medium of so many printing processes, and which doubtless is yet to form the base of many more, was tried in the place of collodion in this manner:— Thirty grains of Nelson's gelatine were washed in cold water, then left to swell for several hours, when all the water was poured off, and the gelatine set in a wide-mouthed bottle, with the addition of four drachms of pure water, and two small drops of *aqua regia*, and then placed in a basin of hot water for solution. Eight grains of bromide of cadmium dissolved in half a drachm of pure water were now added, and the solution stirred gently. Fifteen grains of nitrate of silver were next dissolved in half a drachm of water in a test tube, and the whole taken into the dark room, when the latter was added to the former slowly, stirring the mixture the whole time. This gave a fine milky emulsion, and was left for a little while to settle. A few plates of glass well cleaned were next levelled on a metal plate put over a small lamp; they were, when fully warmed, coated by the emulsion spread to the edges by a glass rod, then returned to their places, and left to dry. When dry, the plates had a thin opalescent appearance, and the deposit of bromide seemed to be very evenly spread in the substance of the substratum.

"These plates were printed from, in succession, from different negatives, one of which had been taken years since on albumen with oxgall and diluted phosphoric acid, sensitised in an acid nitrate. and developed with pyrogallic acid, furnishing a beautiful warm brown tint.

"The exposure varied from the first plate thirty seconds to a minute and a-half, as the light was very poor. No vestige of an outline appeared on removal from the printing-frame. The plates were dipped in water to the surface, and over them was poured a plain solution of pyrogallic acid, four grains to the ounce of water. Soon a faint but clean image was seen, which gradually intensified up to a certain point, then browned all over; hence, the development in the others was stopped at an early stage, the plate washed, and the development continued with fresh pyro, with one drop of a ten-grain solution of nitrate of silver, then re-washed and cleared by a solution of hyposulphite of soda.

"The resulting tints were very delicate in detail, of a colour varying between a bistre and olive tint, and after washing dried with a brilliant surface. The colour of the print varied greatly according to the exposure. From the colour and delicacy it struck me that with care to strain the gelatine, or use only the clearest portion, such a process might be utilised for transparencies for the lantern, and the sensitive plates be readily prepared.

Some plates were fumed with ammonia; these fogged under the pyro solution The proportions set down were only taken at random, and are certainly not as sensitive as might be procured under trials. The remaining emulsion was left shut up in a box in the dark-room, and tried on the third day after preparation; but the sensibility had, it seems, greatly diminished, though the emulsion, when rendered fluid by gently warming, appeared creamy, and the bromide thoroughly suspended. Some of this was now applied to some pieces of paper by means of a glass rod, and hung up to surface dry, then dried fully on the warmed level plate, and treated as sensitised paper.

One kind of paper, that evidently was largely adulterated by some earthy base, dried without any brilliancy, but gave, under exposure of a negative for thirty seconds, very nicely toned prints when developed with a weak solution of pyro. Some old albumenised paper of Marion's was tried, the emulsion being poured both on the albumen side, and, in other pieces, on the plain side; but the salting evidently greatly interfered, the resulting prints being dirty-looking and greyed all over.

These papers, fumed with ammonia, turned grey under development. They printed very slowly, even in strong sunlight, and were none of them left long enough to develop into a full print. After washing they were cleared by weak hypo solution. It is very possible the iron developer may be employed for the glass prints, provided the acidification does not render the gelatine soft under a development.

The slowness may depend in part on the proportions of bromide and nitrate not being correctly balanced, especially as the ordinary, not the anhydrous, bromide was used, and on the quantities being too small for the proportion of gelatine.

Whether the plates would be more sensitive if used when only surface dry is a question of experiment; also, whether other bromides than the one tried may not prove more advantageous in the presence of the neutral salt resulting from the decomposition, or the omission or decrease of the quantity of *aqua regia*. Very probably also the development by gallic acid and acetate of lead developer may furnish better results than the plain pyro.

"As there will be no chance of my being able to continue these experiments, they are placed in their crude state before the readers of the Journal, and may eventually receive correction and improvement under abler hands. So far as can be judged, the process seems quite worth more carefully conducted experiments, and, if found advantageous, adds another handle to the photographer's wheel. R. L. MADDOX, M.D."

After perusing the above, it will be evident to any one that Dr. Maddox very nearly arrived at perfection in his early experiments. The slowness that he complains of was caused entirely by not washing the emulsion to discharge the excess of bromide, and the want of density was due to the absence of a restrainer and ammonia in the developer. He only made positive prints from negatives; but the same emulsion, had it been washed, would have made negatives in the camera in much less time. Thus, it will be seen, that Dr. Maddox, like the Rev. J. B. Reade, threw the ball, and others caught it; for the gelatine process, as given by Dr. Maddox, is only modified, not altered, by the numerous dry-plate and gelatino-bromide paper manufacturers of to-day.

Meanwhile collodion held the field, and many practical men thought it would never be superseded.

In this year Sir John Herschel died at a ripe old age, seventy-nine. Photographers should revere his memory, for it was he who made photography practical by publishing his observation that hyposulphite of soda possessed the power of dissolving chloride and other salts of silver.

FOURTH PERIOD.

GELATINE.

DR. R. L. MADDOX.
From Photograph by J. Thomson.
GELATINO-BROMIDE EMULSION 1871

R. KENNETT.
From Photograph by J. Werge, 1887.
GELATINO-BROMIDE PELLICLE 1873 DRY PLATES 18/4

FOURTH PERIOD.

GELATINE SUCCESSFUL.

In 1873, Mr. J. Burgess, of Peckham, London, advertised his gelatino-bromide emulsion, but as it would not keep in consequence of decomposition setting in speedily, it was not commercial, and therefore unsuccessful. It evidently required the addition of some preservative, or antiseptic, to keep it in a workable condition, and Mr. J. Traill Taylor, editor of the *British Journal of Photography*, made some experiments in that direction by adding various essential oils; but Mr. Gray—afterwards the well-known dry-plate maker—was most successful in preserving the gelatine emulsion from decomposition by the addition of a little oil of peppermint, but it was not the emulsion form of gelatino-bromide of silver that was destined to secure its universal adoption and success.

At a meeting of the South London Photographic Society, held in the large room of the Society of Arts, John Street, Adelphi, Mr. Burgess endeavoured to account for his emulsion decomposing, but he did not suggest a remedy, so the process ceased to attract further attention. Mr. Kennett was present, and it was probably Mr. Burgess's failure with emulsion that induced him to make his experiments with a sensitive pellicle. Be that as it may, Mr. Kennett did succeed in making a workable gelatino-bromide pellicle, and obtained a patent for it on the 20th of November, 1873. I procured some, and tried it at once. It gave excellent results, but preparing the plates was a messy and sticky operation, which I feared would be prejudicial to its usefulness and success. This I reported to Mr. Kennett immediately, and found that his own experience corroborated mine, for he had already received numerous complaints of this objection, while others failed through misapprehension of his instruction; and very comical were some of these misinterpretations. One attempted to coat the plates with the *end* of the stirring-rod, while another set them to drain in a rack, and those that did succeed in coating the plates properly, invariably spoiled them by over-exposure or in development. He was overwhelmed with correspondence and visitors, and to lessen his troubles I strongly advised him to prepare the plates himself, and sell them in that form ready for use. He took my advice, and in March, 1874, issued his first batch of gelatino-bromide dry-plates; but even that did not remove his vexation of spirit, nor lessen his troublesome correspondence. Most of his clients were sceptical, and exposed the plates too long, or worked under wet-plate conditions in their dark-rooms, and fog and failure were the natural consequences. Most, if not all, of his clients at that time were amateurs, and it was not until years after, that professional photographers adopted the dry and abandoned the wet process. In fact, it is doubtful if the profession ever tried Mr. Kennett's dry plates at all, for it was not until J. W. Swan and Wratten and Wainwright issued their dry plates, that I could induce any professional photographer to give these new plates a trial, and I have a very vivid recollection of the scepticism and conservatism exhibited by the most eminent photographers on the first introduction of gelatino-bromide dry plates.

For example, when I called upon Messrs. Elliott and Fry to introduce to their notice these rapid plates, I saw Mr. Fry, and told him how rapid they were. He was incredulous, and smilingly informed me that I was an enthusiast. It was a dull November morning, 1878, and I challenged him, not to fight, but to give me an opportunity of producing as good a picture in quarter the time they were giving in the studio, no matter what that time was. This rather astonished him, and he invited me up to the studio to prove my statement. I ascertained that they were giving *ninety* seconds—a minute and a-half!—on a wet collodion plate, 10 by 8. I knew their size, and had it with me, as well as the developer. Mr. Fry stood and told the operator, Mr. Benares, to take the time from me. Looking at the quality of the light, I gave *twenty* seconds, but Mr. Benares was disposed to be incredulous also, and, after counting twenty, went on with " one for the plate, and one more for Mr. Werge," but I told him to stop, or I would have nothing more to do with the business. The plate had twenty-two or three seconds' exposure, and when I developed in their dark room, it was just those two or three seconds over-exposed. Nevertheless, Mr. Fry brought me a print from that negative in a few days, and acknowledged that it was one of the finest negatives he had ever seen. They were convinced, and adopted the new dry plates immediately. But it was not so with all, for many of the most prominent photographers would not at first have anything to do with gelatine plates, and remained quite satisfied with collodion; but the time came when they were glad to change their opinion, and give up the wet for the dry plates, but it was a long time, for Mr. Kennett introduced his dry plates in 1874, and it was not until 1879 and 1880 that professional photographers had adopted and taken kindly to gelatine plates generally.

With amateurs it was very different, and many of their exhibits in the various exhibitions were from gelatine negatives obtained upon plates prepared by themselves, or commercial makers. In the London Photographic Society's exhibition of 1874, and following, several prints from gelatine negatives were exhibited, and in 1879 they were pretty general. Among the many exhibited that year was Mr. Gale's swallow-picture, which created at the time a great deal of interest and controversy, and Mr. Gale was invited over and over again to acknowledge whether the appearance of the bird was the result of skill, accident, or "trickery;" but I don't think that he ever gratified anyone's curiosity on the subject. I can, however, state very confidently that he was innocent of any "trickery" in introducing the bird by double printing, for the late Mr. Dudley Radcliffe told me at the time that he (Mr. Radcliffe) not only prepared the plate, but developed the negative, and was surprised to see the bird there. This may have been the reason why Mr. Gale was so reticent on the subject, but I am anticipating, and must go back to preserve my plan of chronological progression.

In 1875 a considerable impetus was given to carbon printing, both for small work and enlarging by the introduction of the Lambertype process. Similar work had been done before, but, as Mr. Leon Lambert used to say, he made it "facile"; and he certainly did so, and induced many photographers to adopt his beautiful, but troublesome, chromotype process. There were two Lamberts in the tent—one a very clever manipulator, the other a clever advertiser—and between the two they managed to sell a great many licences, and carry away a considerable sum of money. I was intimate with them both while they remained in England, and they were both pleasant and honourable men.

On January 18th, 1875, O. G. Rejlander died, much to the regret of all who took an interest in the art phase of photography. Rejlander has himself told us how, when, and where he first fell in love with photography. In 1851 he was not impressed with the Daguerreotypes at the great exhibition, nor with "reddish landscape photographs" that he saw in Regent Street, but when in Rome, in 1852, he was struck with the beauty of some photographs of statuary, which he bought and studied, and made up his mind to study photography as soon as he returned to England. How he did that will be best told by himself :—" In 1853, having inquired in London for the best teacher, I was directed to Henneman. We agreed for so much for three or five lessons ; but, as I was in a hurry to get back to the country, I took all the lessons in one afternoon! Three hours in the calotype and waxed-paper process, and half-an-hour sufficed for the collodion process!! He spoke, I wrote; but I was too clever. It would have saved me a year or more of trouble and expense had I attended carefully to the rudiments of the art for a month." His first attempt at "double printing" was exhibited in London in 1855, and was named in the catalogue, *group printed from three negatives*. Again, I must allow Mr. Rejlander to describe his reasons for persevering in the art of "double printing":—"I had taken a group of two. They were expressive and composed well. The light was good, and the chemistry of it successful. A very good artist was staying in the neighbourhood, engaged on some commission. He called; saw the picture; was very much delighted with it, and so was I. Before he left my house he looked at the picture again, and said it was " marvellous," but added, " Now, if I had drawn that, I should have introduced another figure between them, or some light object, to keep them together. You see, there is where you photographers are at fault. Good morning!" I snapped my fingers after he left—but not at him—and exclaimed aloud, 'I can do it!' Two days afterwards I called at my artist-friend's hotel as proud as—anybody. He looked at my picture and at me, and took snuff twice. He said, 'This is another picture.' 'No,' said I, 'it is the same, except with the addition you suggested.' 'Never,' he exclaimed; 'and how is it possible? You should patent that!'" Rejlander was too much of an artist to take anything to the Patent Office.

When I first saw his celebrated composition picture, "The Two Ways of Life," in the Art Treasures Exhibition at

Manchester in 1857, I wondered how he could have got so many men and women to become models, and be able to sit or stand in such varied and strained positions for the length of time then required by the wet collodion process; but my wonder ceased when I became acquainted with him in after years, and ascertained that he had the command of a celebrated troupe, who gave *tableaux vivants* representations of statues and groups from paintings under the direction and name of "Madame Wharton's *pose plastique* troupe." What became of the original "Two Ways of Life" I do not know, but the late Henry Greenwood possessed it at the time of Rejlander's death, for I remember endeavouring to induce Mr. Greenwood to allow it to be offered as a bait to the highest contributor to the Rejlander fund; but Mr. Greenwood's characteristic reply was, "Take my purse, but leave me my 'Two Ways of Life.'" Mr. Rejlander kindly gave me a reduced copy of his "Two Ways of Life," and many other examples of his works, both in the nude and semi-nude. Fortunately Rejlander did not confine himself to such productions, but made hundreds of draped studies, both comic and serious, such as "Ginx's Baby," "Did She?" "Beyond the Bible," and "Homeless." Where are they all now? I fear most of them have faded away, for Rejlander was a somewhat careless operator, and he died before the more permanent process of platinum printing was introduced. When Rejlander died, his widow tried to make a living by printing from his negatives, but I fear they soon got scattered. Rejlander was a genial soul and a pleasant companion, and he had many kind friends among members of the Solar Club, as well as other clubs with which he was associated.

There is one more death in this year to be recorded, that of Thomas Sutton, B.A., the founder and for many years editor of *Photographic Notes*, and the inventor of a panoramic camera of a very clumsy character that bore his name, and that was all. Mr. Sutton was a very clever man with rather warped notions, and in the management of his *Photographic Notes* he descended to the undignified position of a caricaturist, and published illustrations of an uncomplimentary description, some of which were offensive in the extreme, and created a great deal of irritation in some minds at the time.

In 1877 Carey Lea gave his ferrous-oxalate developer to the world, but it was not welcomed by many English photographers for negative development, though it possessed many advantages over alkaline pyro. It was, however, generally employed by foreign photographers, and is now largely in use by English photographers, especially for the development of bromide paper, either for contact printing or enlargements. In the early part of this year, Messrs. Wratten and Wainwright commenced to make gelatino-bromide dry plates, and during the hot summer months Mr. Wratten found it necessary to precipitate the gelatine emulsion with alcohol. This removed the necessity of dialysing, and helped to lessen the evils of decomposition and "frilling."

The most noticeable death in the photographic world of this year was that of Henry Fox Talbot. He was born on February the 11th, 1800, and died September 17th, 1877, thus attaining a ripe old age. I am not disposed to deny his claims to the honour of doing a great deal to forward the advancement of photography, but what strikes me very much is the mercenary spirit in which he did it, especially when I consider the position he occupied, and the pecuniary means at his command. In the first place, he rushed to the Patent Office with his gallo-nitrate developer, and then every little improvement or modification that he afterwards made was carefully protected by patent rights. With a churlishness of spirit and narrow-mindedness it is almost impossible to conceive or forgive, he tried his utmost to stop the formation of the London Photographic Society, and it was only after pressing solicitations from Sir Charles Eastlake, President of the Royal Academy, and first President of the London Photographic Society, that he withdrew his objections. The [late Peter le Neve Foster, Secretary of the Society of Arts, told me this years after, and when it was proposed to make Fox Talbot an honorary member of the Photographic Society, Mr. Foster was opposed to the proposition. Then the action that he brought against Silvester Laroche was unjustifiable, for there really was no resemblance between the collodion and calotype means of making a negative, except in the common use of the camera, and the means of making prints was the same as that employed by Thomas Wedgwood, while the fixing process with hyposulphite of soda was first resorted to by the Rev. J. B. Reade, on the published information of Sir John Herschel.

On March 29th, 1878, Mr. Charles Bennett published his method of increasing the sensitiveness of gelatino-bromide plates. It may be briefly described as a prolonged cooking of the gelatine emulsion at a temperature of 90°, and, according to Mr. Bennett's experience, the longer it was cooked the more sensitive it became, with a corresponding reduction of density when the prepared plates were exposed and developed.

April 20th of this year Mr. J. A. Spencer died, after a lingering illness, of cancer in the throat. Mr. Spencer was, at one period in the history of photography, the largest manufacturer of albumenised paper in this country, and carried on his business at Shepherd's Bush. In 1866 he told me that he broke about 2,000 eggs daily, merely to obtain the whites or albumen. The yolks being of no use to him, he sold them, when he could, to glove makers, leather dressers, and confectioners, but they could not consume all he offered for sale, and he buried the rest in his garden until his neighbours complained of the nuisance, so that it became ultimately a very difficult thing for him to dispose of his waste yolks in any manner. After the introduction of Swan's improved carbon process, he turned his attention to the manufacture of carbon tissue, and in a short time he became one of the partners in the Autotype Company, and the name of the firm at that period was Spencer, Sawyer, and Bird; but he ceased to be a partner some time before his death.

At the South London Technical Meeting, held in the great hall of the Society of Arts, I exhibited my non-actinic developing tray, and developed a gelatine dry plate in the full blaze of gas-light. A short extract from a leader in the *Photographic News* of November 14th, 1879, will be sufficient to satisfy all who are interested in the matter. "Amongst the many ingenious appliances exhibited at the recent South London meeting, none excited greater interest than the developing tray of Mr. Werge, in which he developed in the full gas-light of the room a gelatine plate which had been exposed in the morning, and exhibited to the meeting the result in a clean transparency, without fog, or any trace of the abnormal action of light. . . We can here simply record the fact, interesting to many, that the demonstration before the South London meeting was a perfect success."

1880 had a rather melancholy beginning, for on January the 15th, Mr. George Whaiton Simpson died suddenly, which was a great shock to every one that knew him. I had seen him only a few days before in his usual good health, and he looked far more like outliving me than I him; besides, he was a year my junior. The extract above quoted was the last time he honoured me by mentioning my name in his writings, though he had done so many times before, both pleasantly and in defending me against some ill-natured and unwarrantable attacks in the journal which he so ably conducted for twenty years.

Mungo Ponton died August 3rd, 1880. Though his discovery did little or nothing towards the development of photography proper, it is impossible to allow him to pass out of this world without honourable mention, for his discovery led to the creation and development of numerous and important photo-mechanical industries, which give employment to numbers of men and women. When Mungo Ponton announced his discovery in the *Edinburgh New Philosophical Journal* in 1839, he probably never dreamt that it would be of any commercial value, or he might have secured rights and royalties on all the patent processes that grew out of it; for Poitevin's patent, 1855, Beauregard's, 1857, Pouncey's, 1858 and 1863, J. W. Swan's, 1864, Woodbury's, 1866, all the Autotype and Lambertype and kindred patents, as well as all the forms of Collotype printing, are based on Ponton's discovery. But so it is: the originator of anything seldom seeks any advantage beyond the honour attached to the making of a great invention or discovery. It is generally the petty improvers that rush to the Patent Office to secure rights and emoluments, regardless of the claims of the founders of their patented processes.

On March 2nd, 1880, I delivered a lecture on "The Origin, Progress, and Practice of Photography" before the Lewisham and Blackheath Scientific Association, in which I reviewed the development of photography from its earliest inception up to date, exhibited examples, and gave demonstrations before a very attentive and apparently gratified audience.

On the 27th May, 1880, Professor Alfred Swaine Taylor died at his residence, 15, St. James's Terrace, Regent's Park, in his seventy-fourth year. He was born on the 11th December, 1806, at Northfleet in Kent, and in 1823 he entered as a student the united hospitals of Guy's and St. Thomas's, and became the pupil of Sir Astley Cooper and Mr. Joseph Henry Green. His success as a student and eminence as a professor, lecturer, and author are too well known to require any comment from me on those subjects, but it is not so generally known how much photography was indebted to him at the earliest period of its birth. In 1838 Dr. Taylor published his celebrated work, "The Elements of Medical Jurisprudence," and in 1840 he published a pamphlet "On the Art of Photogenic Drawing," in which he advocated the superiority of ammonia nitrate of silver over chloride of silver as a sensitiser, and hyposulphite of lime over hyposulphite of soda as a fixer, and the latter he advocated up to the year of his death, as the following letter will show:—

"*St. James's Terrace, February* 10*th,* 1880.
"Mr. Werge.

"Dear Sir,—I have great pleasure in sending you for the purpose of your lecture some of my now ancient photographs. They show the early struggles which we had to make. The mounted drawings were all made with the *ammonia nitrate* of silver; I send samples of the paper used. In general the paper selected contained chloride enough to form ammonia chloride I send samples of unused paper, procured in 1839—some salted afterwards.

"All these drawings (which are dated) have been preserved by the hyposulphite of *lime* (not soda). The hypo of lime does not form a definite compound with silver, like soda; hence it is easily washed away, and this is why the drawings are tolerably preserved after forty years. All are on plain paper. Ammonia nitrate does not answer well on albumenized paper. The art of toning by gold was not known in those ancient days, but the faded drawings on *plain paper*, as you will see, admit of restoration, in dark purple, by placing them in a very dilute solution of chloride of gold, and putting them in the dark for twenty-four hours. The gold replaces the reduced silver and sulphide of silver. I send you the only copy I have of my photogenic drawing. Five hundred were printed, and all were sold or given away. Please take care of it. The loose photographs in red tape are scenes in Egypt and Greece, taken about 1850 from wax paper negatives (camera views) made by Mr. D Colnaghi, now English Consul at Florence. If you can call here I shall be glad to say more to you on the matter.—Yours truly,

"Alfred S. Taylor."

The above was the last of many letters on photographic matters that I had received from Dr Taylor, and the last time I had the pleasure of seeing him was when I returned the photographs and pamphlet alluded to therein, only a short time before his death. Dr. Taylor never lost his interest in photography, and was always both willing and pleased to enter into conversation on the subject He had worked at photography through all its changes, despite his many professional engagements, from its dawn in 1839, right up to the introduction of gelatino-bromide dry plates, and in 1879 he came and sat to me for his portrait on one of what he called "these wonderful dry plates," and watched the process of development with as much interest as any enthusiastic tyro would have done, and I am proud to say that I had the pleasure of taking the portrait and exhibiting the process of development of the latest aspect of photography to one of its most enthusiastic and talented pioneers.

Dr. Taylor was a man of remarkable energy and versatility. He was a prolific writer and an admirable artist. On his walls were numerous beautiful drawings, and his windows were filled with charmingly illusive transparencies, all the work of his own hands; and once, when expressing my wonder that he could find time to do so many things, he remarked that "a man could always find time to do anything he wished if his heart was with his work " Doubtless it is so, and his life and what he did in it were proofs of the truth and wisdom of his observation.

Hydroquinone as a developer was introduced this year by Eder and Toth, but it did not make much progress at first. It is more in use now, but I do not consider it equal to oxalate of iron.

A considerable fillip was, this year, given to printing on gelatino-bromide paper by the issue of " The Argentic Gelatino-Bromide Worker's Guide," published by W. T. Morgan and Co. The work was written by John Burgess, who made and sold a bromide emulsion some years before, and it contained some excellent working instructions. In the book is a modification and simplification of J M. Burgess's Eburneum Process, though that process was the invention of Mr. J. Burgess, of Norwich; but a recent application of the gelatino-bromide emulsion to celluloid slabs by Mr. Fitch has made the Ivorytype process as simple and certain as the exposure and development of gelatino-bromide paper.

On January 30th, 1881, died Mr. J R. Johnson, of pantoscopic celebrity. Mr. Johnson was the inventor of many useful things, both photographic and otherwise. He was the chief promoter of the Autotype Company, in which the late Mr. Winsor was so deeply interested; and his double transfer process, published in 1869, contributed greatly to the successful development and practice of the Carbon process. The invention of the Pantoscopic Camera, and what he did to forward the formation of the Autotype Company and simplify carbon printing, may be considered the sum total of his claim to photographic recognition.

The chief photographic novelty of 1881 was Mr Woodbury's Stannotype process, a modification and simplification of what is best known as the Woodburytype. Instead of forcing the gelatine relief into a block of type-metal by immense pressure to make the matrix, he "faced" a reversed relief with tin foil, thus obtaining a printing matrix in less time and at less expense. I have seen some very beautiful examples of this process, but somehow or other it is not much employed.

The man who unquestionably made the first photographic portrait died on the 4th of January, 1882, and I think it is impossible for me to notice that event without giving a brief description of the circumstance, even though I incur the risk of telling to some of my readers a tale twice told. When Daguerre's success was first announced in the Academy of Science in 1839, M. Arago stated that Daguerre had not yet succeeded in taking portraits, but that he hoped to do so soon. The details of the process were not published until July, and in the autumn of that year Dr. Draper succeeded in obtaining a portrait of his assistant, and that was the first likeness of a human being ever known to have been secured by photography. It would be interesting to know if that Daguerreotype is in existence now. Dr. Draper was Professor of Chemistry in the University of New York, and as soon as the news of the discovery reached New York he fitted an ordinary spectacle lens into a cigar case, and commenced his experiments first by taking views out of a window, and afterwards by taking portraits. To shorten the time of exposure for the latter, he whitened the faces of his sitters. In April, 1840, Dr. Draper and Professor Moise opened a portrait gallery on the top of the University Buildings, New York, and did a splendid business among the very best people of the City at the minimum price of five dollars a portrait, and they would be very small even at that price.

One more of the early workers in photography died this year on the 4th of March. Louis Alphonse Poitevin was not a father of photography in a creative sense, but, like Walter Woodbury, an appropriater of photography in furthering the development of photo-mechanical printing. His first effort in that direction was to obtain copper plates, or moulds, from Daguerreotype pictures by the aid of electrical deposits, and he discovered a method of photo-chemical engraving, for which he was awarded a silver medal by the Société d'Encouragement des Arts, but the process was of no practical value. His chief and most valuable experiments were with gelatine and bichromates, and his labours in that direction were rewarded by the receipt of a considerable portion of the Duc de Luynes' prize for permanent photographic printing processes, which consisted of photo-lithography and Collotype printing. Born in 1819, he was sixty-three years old when he died.

A useful addition to the pyrogallic acid developer was this year given by Mr. Herbert B. Berkeley. Hitherto, nearly all pyro-developed gelatine plates were stained a deep yellow colour by the action of ammonia. but the use of sulphite of soda, as suggested by Mr. Berkeley, considerably lessened this evil.

In 1883, Captain Abney rendered a signal service to the members of the Photographic Society, and photographers in general, by publishing in the Journal of the Society a translation of Captain Pizzighelli and Baron A. Hubl's booklet on platinotype. After giving a *resume* of the early experiments with platinum by Herschel, Hunt, and others, the theory and practice of platinotype printing are clearly explained, and it was undoubtedly due to the publication of this translation that platinotype printing was very much popularised. In proof of the accuracy of this opinion, every following photographic exhibition showed an increasing number of exhibits in platinotype.

No great novelty was brought into the world of photography in 1884, but there were signs of a steady advance, and an increasing number of workers with dry plates. I should not, however, neglect allusion to the publication of Dr. H. W. Vogel's experiments with eosine, cyanocine, and other kindred bodies by which he increased the sensitiveness of both wet collodion and gelatine plates to the action of the yellow rays considerably (*vide* Journal of Society, May 30th) The Berlin Society for the Advancement of Photography acquired and published these experiments for the general good, and yet Tailfer and Clayton obtained patent right monopolies for making eosine gelatine plates in France, Austria, and England. This proceeding seems very much akin to the sharp practice displayed by Mr. Beard in securing a patent right monopoly in the Daguerreotype process which was *given to the world* by the French Government in 1839. Germany very properly refused to grant a patent under these circumstances

On April 14th, 1885, Mr. Walter Bird read a paper at the

meeting of the Photographic Society of Great Britain, "On the Photographic Reproductions of Pictures in the National Gallery," by A. Braun et Cie. I was present, and it appeared to me that the "effects" in some of the pictures exhibited were not produced by any chemical mode of translation of colour, but by some method of after-treatment of the negative which was more likely to be by skilled labour than by any chemical process. This belief induced me to read a paper at the next meeting—May 12th—"On the After-Treatment of Negatives," in which I showed what could be done both by chemical means and art-labour to assist photography in translating the monographic effects of colour more in accordance with the scale of luminosity adopted and adhered to by the most eminent engravers both in line and mezzotint.

At the next meeting—June 9th—Mr. J. R. Sawyer reopened the discussion on the above subject by reading a paper and exhibiting examples of his own experiments, and Mr. Sawyer admitted that he was " bound to confess that while every effort should be made to discover chemical combinations which will give the utmost value that can be practicably obtained in the reproduction (?) of colours, yet that, in all probability, art—and art not inferior to that of a competent engraver—will be necessary to assist photography in rendering the very subtle combinations of colour that present themselves in a fine painting;" and Colonel H. Stuart Wortley proved that the copy of Turner's "Old Téméraire" was not only "retouched," but wrongly translated, as the various shades of yellow in the original picture were represented in the copy as if they had been all of the same tint. Mr. Sawyer made use of the phrase "reproduction of colours," but that was an error. He should have said—and undoubtedly meant—translation of colours, for photography is, unfortunately, incapable of reproducing colours. Among Mr. Sawyer's examples was a curious and contradictory evidence that isochromatic plates translated yellow tints better than ordinary bromide plates, yet wrongly, for three different shades of yellow were translated as if they had been all one tint. I had noticed this myself when copying paintings and coloured prints, but in photographing the natural colours of fruits and flowers the result was different, and I attributed the mal-translation of pigment yellows to the amount of white with which they had been mixed by the painter. Be that as it may, I always obtained the best translation from natural colours, and a group of flowers which contained a beautiful sulphur coloured dahlia illustrates and confirms this statement in a most remarkable and satisfactory manner. It is, therefore, the more to be regretted that there is any restriction placed upon the individual experiment and development of this interesting aspect of photography.

This was the year of The International Inventions Exhibition, and the photographic feature of which was the historical collection exhibited by some of the members of the Photographic Society of Great Britain, and I think that collection was sufficiently interesting to justify my giving, in these pages, the entire list as published in the *Photographic Journal* :—

"We subjoin a full and complete statement of the whole of the exhibits, with the names of the contributors :—

"Capt Abney, R.E., F.R.S.—Papyrotype process, executed at the School of Military Engineering, Chatham.

"W. Andrews—Wet collodion negatives, intensified by the Schlippes salt method.

"T. and R. Annan—Calotype process (negative and print), taken by D. O. Hill.

"F. Beasley, jun.—Collodio-albumen negatives.

"W. Bedford—One of Archer's first cameras for collodion process, stereoscopic arrangement by Archer to fit a larger camera.

"Valentine Blanchard—Instantaneous views, wet collodion, 1856-65. Illustrations of a method of enlargement, as proposed by V. Blanchard, 1873. Modification of the Brewster stereoscope by Oliver Wendell Holmes

"Bullock (Bros.)—Photo-lithography, 1866 (Bullock's patent).

"T. Bolas, F.C.S.—Detective camera, 1876. Negative photograph on bitumen, made insoluble by the action of light. Carbon negatives stripped by Wenderoth's process.

"E. Clifton—Portrait of Daguerre. Crystalotype by J. R. Whipple, 1854. Specimens from "Pretsch" photo-galvanographic plates, 1856.

"T. S. Davis, F.C.S.—A combined preparation and wash bottle for gelatine emulsion. Adjustable gauge for cutting photographic glasses.

"De la Rue and Co.—Surface printing from blocks executed by Paul Pretsch, 1860.

"W. England—Old Daguerreotype developing box. Old ditto sensitizing box. Old camera, 1860, with rapid inside shutter. Instantaneous views in Paris, wet collodion, 1856-65.

"Edinburgh Photographic Society—Archer's water lens.

"James Glaisher, F.R.S.—Nature printing, taken over thirty years ago.

G. Fowler Jones—Prints from negatives by Le Gray's ceroline process.

"R. Kennett—Scaife's pistolgraph. Globe lens.

"Dr. Maddox—Some of the earliest gelatino-bromide negatives, by the originator of the process, 1871.

"Mudd and Son—Collodio-albumen negatives.

"R. C. Murray—Early Talbotype photographs, 1844-45.

"H. Neville—Camera with Sutton's patent panoramic lens.

"Mrs. H. Baden Pritchard—Impressions from pewter plates of heliographic drawing, by Nicephore Niepce, 1827. Original letter, by Nicephore Niepce, sent to the Royal Society, 1827. View of Kew, taken by Nicephore Niepce, 1827.

"H. P. Robinson—Heliographic picture, by Nicephore Niepce, 1826. Photo-etched plate (from a print), by Niepce in 1827. Heliograph (from a print), by Niepce, 1827. One of the earliest printing frames, made for Fox Talbot's photogenic drawing, 1839. The first nitrate of silver bath used by Scott Archer in his discovery of the collodion process, 1850.

"Ross and Co.—One of Archer's earliest fluid lenses. The first photographic compound portrait lens, made by Andrew Ross, 1841. Photographic camera, believed to be the first made in England.

"Sands and Hunter—Old lens, with adjustable diaphragm, by Archer, 1851. Old stereoscopic camera, with mechanical arrangement for transferring plates to and from the dark slide.

"T. L Scowen—Parallel bar stereoscopic camera Latimer Clarke.

"John Spiller, F.C.S., F I.C.—The first preserved plates (three to twenty-one days), 1854 Illustrations of the French Pigeon Post.

"J. W. Swan, F.C S.—Electro intaglios from carbon reliefs (Thorwalsden's "Night and Morning"). Photo-mezzotints were taken from these in gelatinous inks, 1860, by J. W. Swan, by the process now known as Woodburytype. Plaster cast from a carbon print of Kenilworth, showing the relief, taken in 1864, by J. W. Swan. Carbon prints twenty years old (photographed and printed in various colours by J. W. Swan). Old print (in red) by T. and R Annan, by Swan's process. Carbon print, twenty years old (printed in 1864) by double transfer.

"B. B. Turner—Talbotype. Negatives and prints from same. Single lens made by Andrew Ross, 1851.

"J. Werge—Examples of printing with various metals on plain paper, 1839-42. The Fathers of Photography. Examples and dates of the introduction of early photographs. Daguerreotype, 1839. Collodion positive, 1851. Ambrotype, 1853. Ferrotype, 1855.

"W. Willis, Jun.—Specimen of aniline process. Historical illustrations of the development of the platinotype process.

"W. B Woodbury—Photo-relief printing process. Woodbury mould and Woodburytype print from same, 1866. Stannotype printing press, with mould. Machine for measuring reliefs. Woodbury lantern slides. Early Daguerreotype on copper. Positive photograph on glass. Woodbury balloon camera. Microscopical objects in plaster from gelatine reliefs. Woodbury collographic process. Woodbury photo-chromograph system, coloured from the back, 1869. Woodbury actinometer. Despatch-box camera. Watermark or photo-filigrain process. Transparency on gelatine. The first specimen of Woodbury printing exhibited, including the first mould printed from, and also proofs backed with luminous paint

"Colonel H. Stuart Wortley—Early photo-zincographs, 1861-2. Experimental prints with uranium collodion, 1867 (modifica- of Wothly's process). Set of apparatus complete for making gelatine emulsion, and preparing gelatine plates, 1877-8. No. 1. Apparatus for cutting gelatine plates either by hand-turning or treadle. No. 2. Stove for keeping emulsion warm for any time at a fixed temperature in pure air, and for the final drying of the plates. No 3. Apparatus for squeezing emulsion out into water. No. 4. Apparatus for mixing emulsion. Instantaneous shutter, with horizontal motion by finger or pneumatic tube ; adjustable wings for cutting off sky, and varying length of exposure."

It is a very remarkable circumstance that none of the contributors to that historical collection could include among their interesting exhibits portraits of either Nicephore Niepce or Frederick Scott Archer. Among my "Fathers of Photography" were portraits of Daguerre, Rev. J. B. Reade, Fox Talbot, Dr. Alfred Swaine Taylor, and Sir John Herschel. It was suggested that those historical exhibits should be left at the close of the exhibition to form a nucleus to a permanent photographic exhibition in Kensington Museum. I readily contributed my exhibits towards such a laudable object. They were accepted, and these exhibits may be seen at any time in the West

Gallery of the Science Department of the South Kensington Museum.

At the exhibition of the Photographic Society of Great Britain this year, I exhibited "Wollaston's Diaphragmatic Shutter," in my opinion the best snap shutter that ever was invented, but it had two very serious drawbacks, for it was both *heavy* and *expensive*.

In 1886 more than usual interest was exhibited by photographers in what was misnamed as the isochromatic, or orthochromatic process, and this interest was probably created by the papers read and discussions that followed at the meetings of the Photographic Society in the previous year. Messrs. Dixon and Gray—the latter a young man in the employ of Messrs. Dixon and Son—commenced a series of experiments with certain dyes with the hope of obtaining a truer translation of colour when copying oil paintings or water-colour drawings, a class of work in which they were largely interested, and had obtained a considerable reputation for such reproductions as photography was then capable of rendering, and one of the results of these experiments was exhibited, and obtained a medal, at the exhibition of the Photographic Society in October. Messrs. Dixon and Sons' exhibit was a very surprising one, and created quite a sensation, as nothing equal to it had ever been shown before. The subject was a drawing of a yellow flower and green leaves against a blue ground—the yellow the most luminous, the green next, and the blue the darkest. In ordinary wet or dry-plate photography these effects would have been reversed, but by Dixon and Gray's process the relative luminosities of these three colours were almost perfectly translated. Messrs. Dixon and Gray did not publish their process, but prepared existing gelatine dry plates by their method, and sold them at an enhanced price. They were not, however, permitted to supply anyone long, for B. J. Edwards, who had obtained a monopoly of Tailfer and Clayton's patent rights in England, served them with an injunction, or threatened them with legal proceedings, so they discontinued preparing their orthochromatic plates for sale. By some special arrangement they were allowed to prepare plates for their own use, provided they used Edwards' XL dry plates.

It so happened, however, that this proviso was not a hardship, for Mr. Dixon told me himself that he had found Edwards' plates the most suitable for their process. The hardship lay in not being able to apply their own discovery or preparation to any dry plates for sale for the public use and benefit. This prohibition was the more to be regretted because no other commercial isochromatic or orthochromatic plates had or have appeared to possess the same qualities of translation. The suppression of the Dixon and Gray preparation of plates is the more surprising when I find eosine is mentioned in the Clayton and Tailfer claim, whereas Mr. Dixon assured me that eosine was not employed by them. Mr. Edwards only acquired his monopoly and right to interfere with the commercial application of an independent discovery on Nov. 18th, 1886, and there is little to be gained in England by the publication of the experiments of such men as Vogel, Eder, Ives, and Abney, if one man can prevent all others making use of them.

This year death removed from our midst one, and perhaps the greatest, of the martyrs of photography—Sylvester Laroche. This was the man that fought the battle for freedom from the shackles of monopoly. He won the fight, but lost his money, and the photographers of the day failed to make him a suitable recompense. There was one honourable exception, and Mr. Sylvester told me himself that Mr. J. E. Mayall gave him £100 towards his legal expenses. Laroche's surname was Sylvester, but as there was a whole family of that name photographers, he added Laroche to distinguish himself from his brothers. Sylvester Laroche was an artist, and worked very cleverly in pastel, but somehow or other he never appeared to prosper.

Nothing particular marked the photographic record of 1887, but death was busy in removing men who had made their mark both in the early and later days of photography. First, on March 19th, Robert Hunt, the most copious writer on photography in its earlier period. As early as 1844 he published the first edition of his "Researches on Light," in which he was considerably assisted by Sir John Herschel, and it is astonishing to find what a mine of photographic information that early work contains.

The next was Colonel Russell, better known, photographically, as Major Russell. He was born in 1820, and died on May 16th, 1887. He was best known for his tannin process and alkaline developer, with a bromide solution as a restrainer. For a long time his tannin process was very popular among collodion dry-plate workers, and very beautiful pictures were taken on Russell's Tannin Plates, but it is many years since they were ruthlessly brushed aside, like all other collodion dry-plates, by the now universally employed gelatino-bromide plates or films.

A revival of interest in pinhole photography was awakened this year, and several modes of constructing a pinhole camera were published; but I remember seeing a wonderful picture by a *keyhole* camera long before I became a photographer. I had called to see an old lady who lived opposite a mill and farm. It was a bright, sunny afternoon, and, when I was leaving, I was astonished to see a beautiful picture of the mill and farm on the wall of the hall. "Ah!" said the old lady; "that's my camera-obscura. When the sun shines on the mill at this time of day, I am sure to have a picture of the mill brought through the keyhole." It was something like this that suggested the camera-obscura to Roger Bacon and Baptista Porta. So it is not necessary to have such a small hole to obtain a picture, but it is necessary to have the smallest hole possible to obtain the *sharpest* picture.

Pizzighelli's visible platinotype printing paper was introduced this year, and I welcomed it as a boon, for the double reasons of its simplicity and permanency. I had been longing for years for such a process, for I, like Roger Fenton, had come to the conclusion that there was no future for photography, in consequence of the instability of silver prints. They would be much more durable than they are if they were only washed in several changes of warm water, but few people will be at the trouble to do that, some because they don't know the efficacy of warm water, and others because it lowers the tone. An eminent photographer once asked me how to render silver prints permanent; but when I told him there was nothing equal to warm water washing, he exclaimed, "Oh! but that spoils the tone." When a photographer sacrifices durability to tone, he is scarcely acting honestly towards his customers. Admitted that there is nothing so beautiful in photography as a good silver print when it has its first bloom on it, neither is there anything so grievously disappointing as a silver print in its last stage of decay. It is quite time that the *durability* of a photograph should be the first consideration of every photographer, as well as the amateur. Years ago I proposed and published a plan of raising a fund to induce chemists and scientists to consider the subject, but not a single photographer responded by subscribing his guinea.

A very simple and interesting means of making photographs at night was introduced this year by Dr. Piffard, an amateur photographer of New York, and the extreme simplicity and efficacy of his method was surprising. For good portraiture it is not equal to the electric light, but for family groups, at home occupations or amusements, it is superior, and I have taken such groups with Piffard's magnesium flash light, which no other means of lighting would have enabled me to produce. I have taken groups of people playing at cards, billiards, and other games in their own homes with the simplest of apparatus, the ordinary lens and camera, plus an old tea tray—but to obtain the best results, the quickest lens and the quickest dry plates should be employed, and I have always found the best position for the light to be on the top of the camera.

1888 is chiefly remarkable for the attempted revival of the stereoscope, and Mr. W. F. Donkin read an interesting and instructive paper on the subject, in which he endeavoured to account for its disappearance, explain its principles, and give an historical account of its early construction, and modern or subsequent improvements. As to its immense popularity thirty to thirty-five years ago, that was due to its novelty, and the marvellous effect of solidity the pictures assumed when viewed in the stereoscope; but it soon ceased to be popular when the views became stale, and people grew tired of looking at them; to keep up the interest they had to be continually buying fresh ones, and of this they soon got tired also; and when hosts saw that their guests were bored with sights so often seen, they put them out of sight altogether, and I fear that nothing will, for the same reasons, bring about a revival of the revolving or any other form of stereoscopes, for views. It is becoming much the same now with lantern slides— possessors and their friends grow weary of the subjects seen so frequently, and hiring instead of buying slides is becoming the practice of those who own an optical lantern.

With stereoscopic portraits it was not so, for there was always a personal and family interest attached to them, and I made a great many stereoscopic portraits by the Daguerreotype process; but even they were somewhat ruthlessly and precipitately displaced when the carte-de-visite mania took possession of the public mind. However, I see no reason why stereoscopic portraiture should not be revived if good pictures were produced on ivoryine, and it appears to me that substance is most suitable for the purpose, as the pictures can be examined either by reflected or transmitted light. Every one interested in stereoscopic photography should "read, mark, learn, and inwardly digest," the late Mr. Donkin's able and instructive paper on "Stereoscopes and Binocular Vision," published in the journal of the Photographic Society, January 27th, 1888. This was unhappily the last paper that Mr. Donkin read at the Photographic Society, for he was unfortunately lost in the Caucasus the following autumn. W. F. Donkin, M.A., F.C.S., F.I.C., was for several years Honorary Secretary of the Photographic Society and of the Alpine Club, and, at the November meeting of the Photographic Society, the President, James Glaisher, F.R.S., made the following remarks on the melancholy event:—"There is, I am sure, but one feeling in regard to the fact that the gentleman who usually sits on my right is not here to-night. Our Secretary, W. F. Donkin, is, I fear, irretrievably lost in the Caucasus. The feeling of every member of this Society is one of respect and esteem towards him. During the time he held the post of Secretary, his uniform courtesy won him the respect of all. I fear we shall see him no more." This fear was afterwards confirmed by the search party, which was headed by Mr. C. T. Dent, President of the Alpine Club. The late Mr. Donkin was both an expert Alpine climber and photographer, and many of his photographs of Alpine scenery have been published and admired.

Every year compels me to record the death of some old and experienced photographer, or some artist associated with photography from its earliest introduction. Among the latter was Norman Macbeth, R.S.A., an eminent portrait painter, who was quick to see and ready to avail himself of the invaluable services of a new art, or means of improving art, both in drawing and detail, and make the newly-discovered power a help in his own labours, and an economiser of the time of his sitters. The first time I had the pleasure of meeting him was in Glasgow in 1855, when he brought one of his sitters to me to be Daguerreotyped, and he preferred a Daguerreotype as long as he could get one, on account of its extreme delicacy and details in the shadows; but he could not obtain any more Daguerreotypes after 1857, for at that time I abandoned the Daguerreotype for ever, and was the last to practise the process in Glasgow, and probably throughout Great Britain.

From the time that Mr. Macbeth commenced taking photographs himself, he took a keen interest in photography to the last, and only about a month before he died, he read an able, instructive, and interesting paper on the "Construction and Requirements of Portrait Art" before the members of the London and Provincial Photographic Association; and that paper should be in the possession, and frequent perusal, of every student of photographic portraiture. Although an artist in feeling and by profession, Mr. Macbeth was no niggard in his praises of artistic photography, and I have frequently heard him expatiate lovingly on the artistic productions of Rejlander, Robinson, and Hubbard; but, like all artists, he abominated retouching, and denounced it in the strongest terms, and regretted its prevalence and practice as destructive of truth, and "truth in photography," he used to say, "was its greatest recommendation."

The annals of 1889—the jubilee year of published and commercial photography—commence with the record of death. On the 21st of January, Mr. John Robert Sawyer died at Naples in the 61st year of his age. Mr. Sawyer had been for many years a member of the Autotype Company, and his foresight and indefatigability were largely instrumental in making that Company a commercial success. It was anything but a success from the time that it was commenced by the late Mr. Winsor and Mr. J. R. Johnson, but from the moment that Mr. J. R. Sawyer became "director of works," the company rapidly became a flourishing concern, and possesses now a world-wide reputation.

Mr. Sawyer was one of the early workers in photography, and for several years conducted a photographic business in the city of Norwich. It was there that circumstances induced him to give his attention to some form of permanent photography with the view of employing it to illustrate a work on the carving and sculpture in Norwich Cathedral, particularly the fine work in the roof of the nave. Mr. Sawyer naturally turned his attention, in the first place, to the autotype process, but it was then in its infancy, and the price prohibitory. The collotype process then became his hope and refuge, but that also was in its infancy, and not practised in England. Mr. Sawyer therefore started for Berlin early in 1869, and there met a certain Herr Ghémoser, a clever expert in the collotype process, from whom he obtained valuable information and working instructions. On his return home, Mr. Sawyer laboured at the collotype process until he overcame most of its difficulties, and on January 1st, 1871, he entered into partnership with Mr. Walter Bird, and removed to London with the intention of making the collotype process a feature in the business. Messrs. Sawyer and Bird commenced their London experiences in Regent Street, but on January 1st, 1872, they entered into an agreement with the Autotype Fine Art Company to work the collotype process as a branch of their business. Meanwhile, another partner, Mr. John Spencer, had joined the firm, and at the end of that year Messrs. Spencer, Sawyer, Bird and Co. purchased the Autotype patents, plant, and stock at Ealing Dene, and all its interest in the wholesale trade; and, in 1874, they bought up the whole of the Fine Art business, including the stock in Rathbone Place, and became the Autotype Company.

The great photographic feature of this year was the Convention held on August 19th in St. James's Hall, Regent Street, London, in celebration of the jubilee of practical photography, which was inaugurated by the delivery of an address by the president, Mr. Andrew Pringle. The address was a fairly good résumé of all that had been done for the advancement of photography during the past fifty years.

The exhibition of photographs was somewhat of a failure; little was shown that possessed any historical interest, and that little was contributed by myself. There was a considerable display of apparatus of almost every description, but there was nothing that had not been seen, or could have been seen, in the shops of the exhibitors.

The papers that were read were of considerable interest, and imparted no small amount of information, especially Mr. Thos. R. Dallmeyer's on "False Rendering of Photographic Images by the Misapplication of Lenses"; Mr. C. H. Bothamley's on "Orthochromatic Photography with Gelatine Plates"; Mr. Thomas Bolas's on "The Photo-mechanical Printing Methods as employed in the Jubilee Year of Photography"; but by far the most popular, wonderful, and instructive, was Professor E. Muybridge's lecture, with illustrations, on "The Movements of Animals." The sight of the formidable batteries of lenses was startling enough, but when the actions of the horse, and other animals, were shown in the "Zoopraxiscope," the effect on the sense of sight was both astounding and convincing, and I began to marvel how artists could have lived and laboured in the wrong direction for so many years, especially when the lecturer showed that a prehistoric artist had scratched on a bone a rude but truthful representation of an animal in motion. Both the sight and intelligence of that prehistoric artist must have been keener than the senses of animal painters of the nineteenth century.

Taking it all in all, the Jubilee Convention was an immense success, and brought photographers and amateurs to London from the most distant parts of the country. Looking round the Hall on the opening night, and scanning the features of those present, I was coming to the conclusion that I was the oldest photographer present, when I espied Mr. Baynham Jones, a man of eighty-three winters, and certainly the oldest amateur photographer living; so I willingly ceded the honour of seniority to him, and as soon as he espied me he clambered over the rails to come and sit at my side and talk over the past, and quite unknown to many present, aspects and difficulties of photography. Mr. Baynham Jones was an enthusiastic photographer from the very first, for in 1839, as soon as Daguerre's process was published, he made himself a camera out of a cigar-box and the lens of his opera glass, and, being unable to obtain a Daguerreotype plate in the country, he cut up a silver salver and worked away on a solid silver plate until he succeeded in making a Daguerreotype picture. Mr. Baynham Jones was not the first photographer in this country, for the Rev. J. B. Beade preceded him by about two years; but I have not the slightest doubt of his being the first *Daguerreotypist* in England, and in that jubilee year of 1889 he was working with gelatine plates and films, and enthusiastic enough to come all the way from Cheltenham to London to attend the meetings of the Jubilee Convention of Photography.

With this brief allusion to the doings and attractions of the Jubilee Convention, I fear I must bring my reminiscences of photography to a close; but before doing so I feel it incumbent on me to call attention to the fact that *two years* after celebrating the jubilee of photography we should, paradoxical as it may appear, celebrate its centenary, for in 1791 the first photographic *picture* that ever was made, seen, or heard tell of, was produced by Thomas Wedgwood, and though he was unable to fix it and enable us to look upon *that* wonder *to-day*, the honour of being the first photographer, in its truest sense, is unquestionably due to an Englishman. Thomas Wedgwood made photographic pictures on paper, and there they remained until light or time obliterated them; whereas J. H. Schulze, a German physician, only obtained impressions of letters on a semi-liquid chloride of silver in a bottle, and at every shake of the hand the meagre impression was instantly destroyed. If we consider such men as Niepce, Reade, Daguerre, and Fox Talbot the fathers of photography, we cannot but look upon Thomas Wedgwood as the Grand Father, and the centenary of his first achievement should be celebrated with becoming honour as the English centenary of photography.

CHRONOLOGICAL RECORD

OF

INVENTIONS, DISCOVERIES, PUBLICATIONS, AND APPLIANCES, FORMING FACTORS IN THE INCEPTION, DISCOVERY, AND DEVELOPMENT OF PHOTOGRAPHY.

1432 B.C. Iron said to have been first discovered.

424 B.C. Lenses made and used by the Greeks. And a lens has been found in the ruins of Nineveh.

79 A D. Glass known and used by the Romans.

697 Glass brought to England.

1100 Alcohol first obtained by the alchemist, Abucasis.

1287. Nitric acid first obtained by Raymond Lully. Present properties made known by Dr Priestley, 1785.

1297. Camera-obscura constructed by Roger Bacon.

1400 Chloride of gold solution known to Basil Valentine.

1500. Camera-obscura improved by Baptista Porta.

1555. Chloride of silver blackening by the action of light. Doubtless it was the knowledge of this that induced Thomas Wedgwood and Sir Humphrey Davy to make their experiments.

1590. Paper first made in England, at Dartford, Kent, by Sir John Speilman It is said that the Chinese made paper 170 years B.C.

1646. Magic lantern invented by Athanasius Kircher.

1666. Sir Isaac Newton divided a sunbeam into its seven component parts, and re-constructed the camera-obscura.

1670. Salt mines of Staffordshire discovered.

1727. J. H. Schulze, a German physician, observed that light blackened chalk impregnated with nitrate of silver solution and gold chloride.

1737. Solution of nitrate of silver applied to paper, by Hellot.

1739. Chloride of mercury made by K. Neumann.

1741. Platinum first known in Europe: M. H. St. Claire Deville's new method of obtaining it from the ore, 1859.

1750. J. Dollond, London, first made double achromatic compound lenses.

1757. Chloride of silver made by J. B. Beccarius.

1774. Dr. Priestley discovered ammonia to be composed of nitrogen and hydrogen; but ammonia is as old as the first decomposition of organic matter.

1777. Charles William Scheele observed that the violet end of the spectrum blackened chloride of silver more rapidly than the red end. Chlorine discovered.

1779. Oxalate of silver made by Bergmann.

1789. Uranium obtained from pitch-blende by Klaproth.

1791. Thomas Wedgwood commenced experiments with a solution of nitrate of silver spread upon paper and white leather, and obtained impressions of semi-transparent objects and cast shadows. Sir Humphry Davy joined him later.

1797. Nitrate of silver on silk by Fulhame.

1799. Hyposulphite of soda discovered by M. Chaussier.

1800. John William Ritter, of Samitz, in Silesia, observed that chloride of silver blackened beyond the violet end of the spectrum, thus discovering the action of the ultra violet ray.

1801. Potassium discovered by Sir Humphry Davy.

1802. Examples of Heliotypes, by Wedgwood and Davy, exhibited at the Royal Institution, and the process published.

1803. Palladium discovered in platinum by Dr. Wollaston.

1808. Strontium obtained from carbonate of strontia by Sir Humphry Davy.

1812. Iodine discovered by M. D. Curtois, of Paris.

— Nitrate of silver and albumen employed by D. Fischer.

1813. Ditto investigated by M. Clement.

1814. Joseph Nicephore de Niepce commenced experiments with the hope of securing the pictures as seen in the camera-obscura.

— Iodide of silver made by Sir H. Davy.

1819. Sir John Herschel published the fact that hyposulphite of soda dissolved chloride and other salts of silver.

1824. Niepce obtained pictures in the camera-obscura upon metal plates coated with asphaltum, or bitumen of Judea.

— L. G. M. Daguerre commenced his researches.

— Permanganate of potash. Fromenkerz.

1826. Bromine discovered in sea-water by M. Balard.

— Bromine of silver made.

1827. Niepce exhibited his pictures in England, and left one or more, now in the British Museum.

1829. Niepce and Daguerre entered into an alliance to pursue their researches mutually.

1832. Evidence of Daguerre employing iodine.

1837. Rev. J. B. Reade, of Clapham, London, obtained a photograph in the solar microscope, and employed tannin as an accelerator and hyposulphite of soda as a fixer for the first time in photography.

1838. Reflecting stereoscope exhibited by Charles Wheatstone.

— Mungo Ponton observed that light altered and hardened bichromate of potash, and produced yellow photographs with that material. This discovery led to the invention of the Autotype, Woodburytype, Collotype, and other methods of photo-mechanical printing.

1839. Daguerre's success communicated to the Academy of Science, Paris, by M. Arago, January 7th.

— Electrotype process announced.

— Professor Faraday described Fox Talbot's new method of photogenic drawing to the members of the Royal Institution, January 25th.

— Fox Talbot read a paper, giving a full description of] his process, before the Royal Society, January 31st.

— Sir John Herschel introduced hyposulphite of soda as a fixing agent, February 14th.

— Dr. Alfred Swaine Taylor employed ammonia-nitrate of silver in preference to chloride of silver for making photogenic drawings, and employed hyposulphite of lime in preference to hyposulphite of soda for fixing.

— Daguerre's process published in August, and patent, for England, granted to Mr. Beard, London, August 14th.

— "History and Practice of Photogenic Drawing"; L. S. M. Daguerre. Published September.

— First photographic portrait taken on a Daguerreotype plate by Professor J. W. Draper, New York, U.S., in the autumn of this year.

1840. "On the Art of Photogenic Drawing," by Alfred S. Taylor, lecturer on chemistry, &c., at Guy's Hospital. Published by Jeffrey, George Yard, Lombard Street, London.

— The Handbook of Heliography, or the Art of Writing or Drawing by the Effect of Sunlight, with the Art of Dioramic Painting, as practised by M. Daguerre." Anon.

— Wolcott's reflecting camera brought from America to England and secured by Mr. Beard, patentee of the Daguerreotype process.

— The moon photographed for the first time by Dr. J. W. Draper, of New York, on a Daguerreotype plate.

— John Frederic Goddard, of London, inventor of the polariscope and lecturer on chemistry, employed chlorine added to iodine, and afterwards bromine, as accelerators in the Daguerreotype process.

1840. Antoine F. J. Claudet, F.R.S., of London, employed chlorine for the same purpose.

— M. Fizeau, of Paris, deposited a film of gold over the Daguerreotype picture after the removal of the iodine, which imparted increased brilliancy and permanency.

— Chloride of platinum employed by Herschel.

— Fox Talbot's developer published September 20th.

1841. Calotype process patented by Fox Talbot, September 20th.

— First photographic compound portrait lens made by Andrew Ross, London.

— Towson, of Liverpool, noted that chemical and visual foci did not coincide. Defect corrected by J. Petzval, of Vienna, for Voightlander.

— "A Popular Treatise on the Art of Photography, including Daguerreotype and all the New Methods of Producing Pictures by the Chemical Agency of Light," by Robert Hunt, published by R. Griffin, Glasgow.

— Daguerre announced an instantaneous process, but it was not successful.

1842. Sir John Herschel exhibited blue, red, and purple photographs at the Royal Institution.

— "Photography Familiarly Explained," by W. R. Baxter, London.

1843. "Photogenic Manipulation," by G. T. Fisher Knight, Foster Lane.

— Treatise on Photography by N. P. Lerebours, translated by J. Egerton.

1844. Fox Talbot issued "The Pencil of Nature," a book of silver prints from calotype negatives.

— C. Cundell, of London, employed and published the use of bromide of potassium in the calotype process.

1844. "Researches on Light and its Chemical Relations," by Robert Hunt. First edition; second ditto, 1854.

— Robert Hunt recommended proto-sulphate of iron as a developer for Talbot's calotype negatives; also oxalate of iron and acetate of lead for other purposes.

— A. F. J. Claudet patented a red light for "dark-room," but at that date a red light was not necessary, so the old photographers continued the use of yellow lights.

1845. "Photogenic Manipulations:" Part 1, Calotype, &c.; Part 2, Daguerreotype. By George Thomas Fisher, jun. Published by George Knight and Sons, London.

— "Manual of Photography," including Daguerreotype, Calotype, &c., by Jabez Hogg. First edition. Second ditto, including Archer's collodion process, bichloride of mercury bleaching and intensifying, and gutta-percha transfer process, 1856

1845. "Practical Hints on the Daguerreotype; Willat's Scientific Manuals."

— "Plain Directions for Obtaining Photographic Pictures by the Calotype and other processes, on paper; Willat's Scientific Manuals." Published by Willats, 98, Cheapside; and Sherwood, Gilbert, and Piper, Paternoster Row.

1846. Gun-cotton made known by Professor Schonbein, of Basel.

1847. Collodion made by dissolving gun-cotton in ether and alcohol, by Mr. Maynard, of Boston, U.S.

1848. "Photogenic Manipulation:" Part II., Daguerreotye, by Robert Bingham. Published by George Knight and Sons, London.

— Albumen on glass plates first employed for making negatives by M. Niépce de Saint Victor. Process published June 13th.

— Frederick Scott Archer experimented with paper pulp, tanno-gelatine, and iodised collodion, and made collodion negatives in the autumn.

1849. Collodion *positive* of Hever Castle, Kent, made by Frederick Scott Archer *early* in the year.

— M. Gustave Le Gray *suggested* the application of collodion to photography.

1850. "A Practical Treatise on Photography upon Paper and Glass," by Gustave Le Gray. Translated from the French by Thomas Cousins, and published by T. and R. Willats. This book is said to contain the first printed notice of collodion being used in photography.

— R. J. Bingham, London, suggested the use of collodion and gelatine in photography.

— M. Poitevin's gelatine process, published January 25th.

1851. Frederick Scott Archer published his collodion process in the March number of *The Chemist*, and introduced pyrogallic acid as a developer December 20th.

— Fox Talbot announced his instantaneous process, and obtained, at the Royal Institution, a copy of the *Times* newspaper, while revolving rapidly, by the light of an electric spark.

— Niepce de St. Victor's heliochromic process, published June 22nd. Examples sent to the judges of the International Exhibition of 1862. See Jurors' Report thereon, pp. 88-9.

— Sir David Brewster's improved stereoscope applied to photography.

1851. "Photography, a Treatise on the Chemical Changes produced by Solar Radiation, and the Production of Pictures from Nature, by the Daguerreotype, Calotype, and other Photographic Processes," by Robert Hunt. Published by J. J. Griffin and Co., London and Glasgow.

1852. "Archer's Hand-Book of Collodion Process." Published May 14th. Second edition, enlarged; published 1854.

— "Archer's Collodion *Positive* Process." Published July 20th.

— Fox Talbot's photo-engraving on steel process, patented October 29th.

1853. A Manual of Photography, by Robert Hunt, published.

— Photographic Society of London founded. Sir Charles Eastlake, P.R.A., President; Roger Fenton, Esq., Secretary. First number of the Society's Journal published March 3rd.

— Cutting's American patent for use of bromides in collodion obtained June 11th, and his Ambrotype process introduced in America.

— "The Waxed-Paper Process," by Gustave Le Gray. Translated from the French with a supplement, by James How. Published by G. Knight and Co., Foster Lane, Cheapside.

— Frederick Scott Archer introduced a triple lens to shorten the focus of a double combination lens.

1854. E. R., of Tavistock, published directions for the use of isinglass as a substitute for collodion.

— First series of photographic views of Kenilworth Castle, &c., from collodion negatives, published by Frederick Scott Archer.

— Liverpool Photographic Journal, first published by Henry Greenwood, bi-monthly.

— First roller-slide patented by Messrs. Spencer and Melhuish, May 22nd.

— Fox Talbot first applied albumen to paper to obtain a finer surface for photographic printing.

— Photo-Enamel process; first patent December 13th.

— Dry collodion plates first introduced.

1855. M. Poitevin's helioplastic process patented February 20th.

— Dr. J. M. Taupenot's dry plate process introduced.

— Photo-galvanic process patented June 5th.

— "Hardwich's Photographic Chemistry." First edition, published March 12th.

— Ferrotype process introduced in America by Mr. J. W. Griswold.

1856. "Photographic Notes." Edited by Thomas Sutton. Commenced January 1st; bi-monthly.

1856. Sutton's Calotype process, published March.

1856 Dr. Hill Norris's dry plate process. Patented September 1st.

1856. Caranza published method of toning silver prints with chloride of platinum.

1857. Moule's photogen, artificial light for portraiture. Patented February 18th.

— Carte-de-visite portraits introduced by M. Ferrier, of Nice.

— Kinnear Camera introduced. Made by Bell, Edinburgh.

1858. Pouncy's Carbon process patented April 10th.

— Skaife's Pistolgraph camera intotroduced.

1858. J. C. Burnett exposed the back of the carbon paper and obtained half-tones.

— Fox Talbot's photo-etching process, patented April 20th.

— Paul Pretsch's photo-engraving process introduced.

— "Sutton's Dictionary of Photography," published August 17th.

— *The Photographic News*, founded, weekly. First number published September 10th, by Cassell, Petter, and Galpin, London.

— "Fothergill Dry Process," by Alfred Keene, published August.

1859. Sutton's panoramic camera patented, September 28th.

— Photo-lithographic Transfer process patented by Osborne, in Melbourne, Australia.

— Wm. Blair, of Perth, secured half-tone in carbon printing by allowing the light to pass through the back of the paper on which the pigment was spread.

— Asser, of Amsterdam, also invented a photo-lithographic transfer process about this time.

1860. "Principles and Practice of Photography," by Jabez Hughes. First edition published; fourteenth edition, 1887.

— Fargier coated carbon surface with collodion, exposed, and transferred to glass to develop.

— Spectroscope invented by Kertchoff and Bunsen.

1860. "Year-Book of Photography," edited by G. Wharton Simpson, first published.

— Improved Kinnear camera with swing front and back by Meagher.

1861. Captain Dixon's iodide emulsion process patented, April 29th.

— M. Gaudin, of Paris, employed gelatine in his photogene, and published in *La Lumière* his collodio-iodide and collodio-chloride processes.

— H. Anthony, New York, discovered that Tannin dry plates could be developed by moisture and ammonia vapour.

1862. "Alkaline Development," published by Major Russell.

— Meagher's square bellows camera, with folding bottom board, exhibited at the International Exhibition. Noticed in Jurors' Report

— Parkesine, the forerunner of celluloid films, invented by Alexander Parkes, of Birmingham.

1863. Pouncy's fatty ink process; patented January 29th.

— Toovey's photo-lithographic process; patented June 29th.

— "Tannin Process," published by Major Russell.

— "Popular Treatise on Photography," by D. Van Monckhoven. Translated from the French by W. H. Thornthwaite, London.

1864. Swan's improved carbon process; patented August 27th.

— "Collodio-Bromide Emulsion," by Messrs. B. J. Sayce and W. B. Bolton; published September 9th.

— Collodio-Chloride Emulsion," by George Wharton Simpson; published in *The Photographic News*, October 28th.

— Willis's aniline process; patented November 11th.

— Obernetter's chromo-photo process; published.

— Instantaneous dry collodion processes by Thomas Sutton, B.A. Sampson, Low, Son, and Marston, London.

1865. Paper read on "Collodio-Chloride Emulsion," by George Wharton Simpson, at the Photographic Society, March 14th.

1865. Photography, a lecture, by the Hon. J. W. Strutt, now Lord Rayleigh, delivered April 18th; and afterwards published.

— Eburneum process; published by J. Burgess, Norwich, in *The Photographic News*, May 5th.

— Bromide as a restrainer in the developer; published by Major Russell.

1865. Interior of Pyramids of Egypt, photographed by Professor Piazzi Smyth with the magnesium light.

— W. H. Smith patented a gelatino-bromide or gelatino-chloride of silver process for wood blocks, &c.

1866. Magic photographs revived and popularised.

— Woodburytype process patented by Walter Bentley Woodbury, of Manchester, July 24th.

— Photography reviewed, in *British Quarterly Review*, by George Wharton Simpson, October 1st.

1867. M. Poitevin obtained the balance of the Duc de Luyne's prize for permanent printing.

— Cabinet portraits introduced by F. R. Window, photographer, Baker Street, London.

1868. W. H. Harrison experimented with gelatino-bromide of silver and obtained results, though somewhat rough and unsatisfactory.

1869. John Robert Johnson's carbon process double transfer patented.

— "Pictorial Effect in Photography," by H. P. Robinson, first edition. London: Piper and Carter.

1870. Thomas Sutton described Gaudin's gelatino-iodide process.

— Jabez Hughes toned collodion transfers with chloride of palladium.

— John Robert Johnson's single transfer process for carbon printing patented.

1871. Dr. R. L. Maddox, of Southampton, published his experiments with gelatino-bromide of silver in the *British Journal of Photography*, September 8th.

1872. "Emaux Photographiques" (photographic enamels), second edition, by Geymet and Alker, Paris.

1873. J. Burgess, of Peckham, advertised his gelatino-bromide of silver emulsion, but it would not keep, so had to be withdrawn.

— Ostendo non Ostento published a gelatino-bromide of silver formula with alcohol.

— Platinotype process patented by W. Willis, junior, June 1st.

1873. R. Kennet's gelatino-bromide of silver pellicle patented November 20th.

— "The Ferrotypers' Guide" published by Scovill Manufacturing Company, New York.

1874. R. Kennett issued his gelatino-bromide of silver dry plates in March.

— Gelatino-bromide of silver paper first announced by Peter Mawdsley, of Liverpool Dry Plate Company.

— "Backgrounds by Powder Process" published by J. Werge, London.

— Flexible supports in carbon printing patented by John Robert Sawyer, of the Autotype Company.

— Leon Lambert's carbon printing process patented.

1875. Demonstrations in carbon printing by L. Lambert given in London and elsewhere.

— Eder and Toth intensified collodion negatives and toned lantern slides with chloride of platinum.

1876. "Practical Treatise on Enamelling and Retouching," by P. Piquepé. Piper and Carter, London.

1877. Ferrous oxalate developer published June 29th.

— Wratten precipitated the gelatine emulsion with alcohol, and so avoided the necessity of dialysing.

1878. Improvement in platinotype patented by W. Willis, junior, July.

— Abney's "Treatise on Photography" published.

— Abney's "Emulsion Process" published.

1879. J. Werge's non-actinic developing tray introduced at the South London Photographic Society.

1880. "Principles and Practice of Photography," by Jabez Hughes, comprising instructions to make and manipulate gelatino dry plates, by J. Werge. London: Simpkin and Marshall, and J. Werge.

— Gelatino-bromide of silver paper introduced by Messrs. Morgan and Kidd.

— Platinotype improvement patent granted.

— Iodides added to gelatino-bromide of silver emulsions by Captain W. de W. Abney.

1880. Warnerke's sensitometer introduced.

— "The Argentic Gelatino-Bromide Workers' Guide," by John Burgess W. T. Morgan and Co., Greenwich.

— "Photography; its Origin, Progress, and Practice," by J. Werge. London: Simpkin, Marshall, and Co.

— Hydroquinone developer introduced by Dr. Eder and Captain Toth.

1881 Stannotype process introduced by Walter Woodbury.

— Photographers in Great Britain and Ireland 7,614 as per census returns.

— "Modern Dry Plates; or Emulsion Photography," by Dr. J. M. Eder, translated from the German by H. Wilmer, edited by H. B. Pritchard. London: Piper and Carter.

— "Pictorial Effect in Photography," by H. P. Robinson (cheap edition). Piper and Carter.

— "The Art and Practice of Silver Printing," by H P. Robinson and Captain Abney. Piper and Carter.

1882. Herbert B. Berkely recommended the use of sulphite of soda with pyrogallic acid to prevent discolouration of film.

— "Recent Advances in Photography" (Cantor Lectures, Society of Arts), Captain Abney. London : Piper and Carter.

1882. "The A B C of Modern Photography," comprising practical instructions for working gelatine dry-plates, by W. K. Burton. London : Piper and Carter.

1882. "Elementary Treatise on Photographic Chemistry," by A. Spiller. London: Piper and Carter.

1883. Translation of Captain Pizzighelli and Baron A. Hubl's booklet on "Platinotype;" published in *The Photographic Journal*.

— Orthochromatic dry plates; English patent granted to Tailfer and Clayton, January 8th.

— "The Chemical Effect of the Spectrum," by Dr. J. M. Eder. (Translated from the German by Captain Abney). London: Harrison and Sons.

1883. "The Chemistry of Light and Photography," by Dr. H. Vogel. London: Kegan Paul.

1884. "Recent Improvements in Photo-Mechanical Printing Methods," by Thomas Bolas, Society of Arts, London.

— "Picture-Making by Photography," by H. P. Robinson. London: Piper and Carter.

1885. "Photography and the Spectroscope," by Capt. Abney, Society of Arts.

— "The Spectroscope and its Relation to Photography," by C. Ray Woods. London: Piper and Carter.

— "Photo-Micrography," by A. C. Malley; second edition. London: H. K. Lewis.

1886. Orthochromatic results exhibited by Dixon and Sons at the photographic exhibition in October.

— English patent rights of Tailfer and Clayton's orthochromatic process secured by B. J. Edwards and Co., Nov. 18th.

1887. Platinotype improvements; two patents.

1888. Pizzighelli's visible platinotype printing paper put on the market in June.

1889. Eikonogen developer patented by Dr. Andresen, of Berlin, Germany, March 26th.

— Wire frames and supports in camera extensions patented by Thomas Rudolph Dallmeyer and Francis Beauchamp, November 6th.

CONTRIBUTIONS TO PHOTOGRAPHIC LITERATURE.
BY
JOHN WERGE.

Originally published in the "Photographic News," "British Journal of Photography," Photographic Year-Book, and Photographic Almanac.

PICTURES OF NIAGARA.
TAKEN WITH CAMERA, PEN, AND PENCIL.

MANY very beautiful and interesting photographic views of Niagara Falls, and other places of romantic and marvellous interest, have been taken and exhibited to the world. Indeed, they are to be seen now in almost every print-seller's window; and in the albums, stereoscopes, or folios of almost every private collector. But I question very much if it ever occurred to the mind of anyone, while looking at those pictures, what an amount of labour, expense, and danger had to be endured and encountered to obtain them—"the many hairbreadth 'scapes by flood and field," of a very "positive" character, which had to be risked before some of the "negatives" could be "boxed." Doubtless Mr. England, Mr. Stephen Thompson, and Mr Wilson have many very vivid recollections of the critical situations they have been in while photographing the picturesque scenery of the Alpine passes of Switzerland, and the Highlands and glens of Scotland.

Mr. Stephen Thompson has narrated to me one or two of his "narrow escapes" while photographing his "Swiss scenes," and I am sure Mr. England did not procure his many and beautiful "points of view" of Niagara Falls without exposing himself to considerable risk.

I had the good fortune to be one of the earliest pioneers, in company with a Yankee friend, Mr. Easterly, in taking photographs of the Falls; and my recollections of the manner in which we "went about," poised ourselves and cameras on "points of rock" and "ledges of bluffs," and felled trees, and lopped off branches overhanging precipices, to "gain a point," even at this distant date are somewhat thrilling. To take a photograph of what is called "Visitors' View" is safe and easy enough. You might plant a dozen cameras on the open space at the brink of the "American Fall," and photograph the scene, visitors and all, as they stand, "fixed" with wonder, gazing at the Falls, American, Centre, and Horseshoe, Goat Island, and the shores of Canada included, for this point embraces in one view all those subjects. But to get at the out-of-the-way places, to take the Falls in detail, and obtain some of the grandest views of them, is a very different matter.

I remember, when we started, taking a hatchet with us, like backwoodsmen, to take a view of Prospect Tower, on the American side of the great Horseshoe Fall, how we had to hew down the trees that obstructed the light; how we actually hung over the precipice, holding on to each other's hands, to lop off a branch still in sight where it was not wanted. The manner in which we accomplished this was what some bystanders pronounced "awful." I hugged a sapling of a silver birch, growing on the brink of the precipice, with my left arm, while friend Easterly, holding my right hand with one of the Masonic grips —I won't say which—*hung over* the precipice, and stretching out as far as he could reach, lopped off the offending branch. Yet in this perilous position my lively companion must crack his joke by punning upon my name, and a Cockney weakness at the same time, for he "guessed he was below the *w*erge of the precipice." The branch down, and we had resumed our perpendicular positions, he simply remarked, if that was not holding on to a man's hand in *friendship*, he did not know what was.

But the *work* was not done yet; to get the view of the Tower we wanted, we had to make a temporary platform over the precipice. This we managed by laying a piece of "lumber" across a fallen tree, and, unshipping the camera, shoved it along the plank until it was in position, balancing the shore end of the plank with heavy stones. When all was ready for exposure, I went round and stood on the point of a jutting rock to give some idea of the great depth of the Fall, but I very nearly discovered, and just escaped being myself the plummet. In the excitement of the moment, and not thinking that the rock would be slimy and slippery with the everlasting spray, I went too rapidly forward, and the rock having a slight decline, I slipped, but was fortunately brought up by a juniper bush growing within a foot of the edge. For a second or two I lay on my back wondering if I could slide out of my difficulty as easily as I had slidden into it. In a moment I determined to go backwards on my back, hands, and feet, until I laid hold of another bush, and could safely assume a perpendicular position. After giving the signal that "all was right," the plate was exposed, and I *cautiously* left a spot I have no desire to revisit. But it is astonishing how the majesty and grandeur of the scene divest the mind of all sense of fear, and to this feeling, to a great extent, is attributed the many accidents and terrible deaths that have befallen numerous visitors to the Falls.

The Indians, the tribe of the Iroquois, who were the aboriginal inhabitants of that part of the country, had a tradition that the "Great Spirit" of the "Mighty Waters" required the sacrifice of two human lives every year. To give rise to such a tradition, doubtless, many a red man, in his skiff, had gone over the Falls, centuries before they were discovered by the Jesuit missionary, Father Hennepin, in 1678; and, even in these days of Christian civilization, and all but total extirpation of the aboriginals, the "Great Spirit" does not appear to be any less exacting.

Nearly every year one or more persons are swept over those awful cataracts, making an aveiage of at least one per annum. Many visitors and local residents have lost their lives under the most painful and afflicting circumstances, the most remarkable of which occurred just before my visit One morning, at daylight, a man was discovered in the middle of the rapids, a little way above the brink of the American Fall. He was perched upon a log which was jammed between two rocks. One end of the log was out of the water, and the poor fellow was comparatively dry, but with very little hope of being rescued from his dreadful situation. No one could possibly reach him in a boat. The foaming and leaping waters were rushing past him at the rate of eighteen or twenty miles an hour, and he knew as well as anyone that to attempt a rescue in a boat or skiff would be certain destruction, yet every effort was made to save him. Rafts were made and let down, but they were either submerged, or the ropes got fast in the rocks. The life-boat was brought from Buffalo, Lake Erie, and that was let down to him by ropes from the bridge, but they could not manage the boat in that rush of waters, and gave it up in despair. One of the thousands of agonized spectators, a Southern planter, offered a thousand dollars reward to anyone that would save the "man on the log." Another raft was let down to him, and this time was successfully guided to the spot. He got on it, but being weak from exposure and want, he was unable to make himself fast or retain his hold, and the doomed man was swept off the raft and over the Falls almost instantly, before the eyes of thousands, who wished, but were powerless and unable, to rescue him from his frightful death. His name was Avery. He and another man were taking a pleasure sail on the Upper Niagara river, their boat got into the current, was sucked into the rapids, and smashed against the log or the rock. The other man went over the Falls at the time of the accident; but Avery clung to the log, where he remained for about eighteen hours in such a state of mind as no one could possibly imagine. None could cheer him with a word of hope, for the roar of the rapids and thunder of the cataracts rendered all other sounds inaudible. Mr. Babbitt, a resident photographer, took several Daguerreotypes of the "man on the log," one of which he kindly presented to me. Few of the bodies are ever recovered. One or two that went over the Great Horse Shoe Fall were found, their bodies in a state of complete nudity. The weight or force of the water strips them of every particle of clothing; but that is not to be wondered at, considering the immense weight of water that rolls over every second, the distance it has to fall, and the depth of the foaming cauldron below. The fall of the Horse Shoe to the surface of the lower river is 158 feet, and the depth of the cauldron into which the Upper Niagara leaps about 300 feet, making a total of 458 feet from the upper to the lower bed of the Niagara River at the Great Horse Shoe Fall. It has been computed that one hundred million, two hundred thousand tons of water pass over the Falls every hour. The depth of the American Fall is 164 feet; but that falls on to a mass of broken rocks a few feet above the level of the lower river.

Our next effort was to get a view of the Centre Fall, or "Cave of the Winds," from the south, looking at the Centre and American Falls, down the river as far as the Suspension Bridge, about two miles below, and the Lower or Long Rapids, for there are rapids both above and below the Falls. In this we succeeded tolerably well, and without any difficulty. Then, descending the "Biddle Stairs" to the foot of the two American cataracts, we tried the "Cave of the Winds" itself; but, our process not being a "wet" one, had no sympathy with the blinding and drenching spray about us. However, I secured a pencil sketch of the scene we could not photograph, and afterwards took one of the most novel and fearful shower-baths to be had in the world. Dressed—or, rather, undressed—for the purpose, and accompanied by a guide, I passed down by the foot of the precipice, under the Centre Fall, and along a wet and slippery pole laid across a chasm, straddling it by a process I cannot describe—for I was deaf with the roar and blind with the spray—we reached in safety a flat rock on the other side, and then stood erect between the two sheets of falling water. To say that I saw anything while there would be a mistake; but I know and felt by some demonstrations, other than ocular, that I was indulging in a bath of the wildest and grandest description. Recrossing the chasm by the pole, we now entered the "Cave of the Winds," which is immediately under the Centre Fall The height and width of the cave is one hundred feet, and the depth sixty feet. It takes its name from the great rush of wind into the cave, caused by the fall of the waters from above. Standing in the cave, which is almost dry, you can view the white waters, like avalanches of snow, tumbling over and over in rapid succession. The force of the current of the rapids above shoots the water at least twenty feet from the rock, describing, as it were, the segment of a circle. By this circumstance only are you able to pass under the Centre Fall, and a portion of the Horse Shoe Fall on the Canadian side. To return, we ascended the "Biddle Stairs," a spiral staircase of 115 steps, on the west side of Goat Island, crossed the latter, and by a small bridge passed to Bath Island, which we left by the grand bridge which crosses the rapids about 250 yards above the American Fall Reaching the American shore again in safety, after a hard day's work, we availed ourselves of Mr. Babbitt's kindness and hospitality to develop our plates in his dark room, and afterwards developed ourselves, sociably and agreeably, refreshing the inner man, and narrating our day's adventures.

I shall now endeavour to describe our next trip, which was to the Canadian side—how we got there, what we did, and what were the impressions produced while contemplating those wonderful works of nature. In the first place, to describe how we descended to the "ferry" and crossed the river. On the north side of the American Fall a railway has been constructed by an enterprising American, where the "cars" are let down a steep decline by means of water-power, the proprietor of the railway having utilized the very smallest amount of the immense force so near at hand. Placing our "traps" in the car, and seating ourselves therein, the lever was moved by the "operator," and away we went down the decline as if we were going plump into the river below; but at the proper time the water was turned off, and we were brought to a standstill close by the boat waiting to ferry us across. Shifting our traps and selves into the boat and sitting down, the ferryman bent to the oars and off we dashed into the dancing and foaming waters, keeping her head well to the stream, and drawing slowly up until we came right abreast of the American Fall; then letting her drop gently down the stream, still keeping her head to the current, we gained the Canadian shore; our course on the river describing the figure of a cone, the apex towards the "Horse Shoe." Ascending the banks by a rather uphill road, we reached the Clifton Hotel, where we took some refreshments, and then commenced our labours of photographing the Grand Rapids and the Falls, from Table Rock, or what remained of it. On arriving at the spot, we set down our traps and looked about bewildered for the best point. To attempt to describe the scene now before us would be next to folly, nor could the camera, from the limited angle of our lens, possibly convey an adequate idea of the grandeur and terrific beauty of the Grand Rapids, as you see them rushing and foaming, white with rage, for about two and a half miles before they make their final plunge over the precipice. Many years ago an Indian was seen standing up in his canoe in the midst of these fearful rapids. Nearing the brink of the terrible Fall, and looking about him, he saw that all hope was lost, for he had passed Gull

Island, his only chance of respite; waving his hand, he was seen to lie down in the bottom of his canoe, which shot like an arrow into the wild waters below, and he was lost for ever. Neither he nor his canoe was ever seen again. In 1829 the ship *Detroit*, loaded with a live buffalo, bear, deer, fox, &c., was sent over the Falls. She was almost dashed to pieces in the rapids, but many persons saw the remains of the ship rolled over into the abyss of waters. No one knew what became of the animals on board. And in 1839, during the Canadian Rebellion, the steamer *Caroline* was set fire to in the night and cast adrift. She was drawn into the rapids, but struck on Gull Island, and was much shattered by the collision. The bulk of the burning mass was swept over the Falls, but few witnessed the sight. Doubtless no fire on board a ship was ever extinguished so suddenly. The view from Table Rock is too extensive to be rendered on one plate by an ordinary camera; but the pantascopic camera would give the very best views that could possibly be obtained.

Taking Table Rock as the centre, the entire sweep of the Fall is about 180 degrees, and stretching from point to point for nearly three-quarters of a mile—from the north side of the American Fall to the termination of the Horse Shoe Fall on the west side. The American and Centre Falls present a nearly straight line running almost due north and south, while the Great Horse Shoe Fall presents a line or figure resembling a sickle laid down with the left hand, the convex part of the bow lying direct south, the handle lying due east and west, with the point or termination to the west; the waters of the two American Falls rushing from east to west, and the waters of the Canadian Fall bounding towards the north. By this description it will be seen that but for the intervention of Goat and Luna Islands the three sheets of water would embrace each other like mighty giants locked in a death struggle, before they fell into the lower river. The whole aspect of the Falls from Table Rock is panoramic. Turning to the left, you see the American rapids rushing down furiously under the bridge, between Bath Island and the American shore, with a force and velocity apparently great enough to sweep away the bridge and four small islands lying a little above the brink, and pitch them all down on to the rocks below. Turning slowly to the right, you see the Centre Fall leaping madly down between Luna and Goat Islands, covering the Cave of the Winds from view. A little more to the right, the rocky and precipitous face of Goat or Iris Island, with the "Biddle Stairs" like a perpendicular line running down the precipice; and to the extreme right the immense sweeps of the Great Horse Shoe.

Doubtless this fall took its name from its former resemblance to the shape of a horse shoe. It is, however, nothing like that now, but is exactly the figure of a sickle, as previously described. Looking far up the river you observe the waters becoming broken and white, and so they continue to foam and rush and leap with increasing impetuosity, rushing madly past the "Three Sisters"—three islands on the left—and "Gull Island" in the middle of the rapids, on which it is supposed no man has ever trodden, until, with a roar of everlasting thunder, which shakes the earth, they fall headlong into the vortex beneath. At the foot of this Fall, and for a considerable distance beyond, the river is as white as the eternal snows, and as troubled as an angry sea. Indeed, I never but once saw the Atlantic in such a state, and that was in a storm in which we had to "lay to" for four days in the Gulf Stream.

The colours and beauty of Niagara in sunlight are indescribable. You may convey *some* idea of its form, power, and majesty, by describing lines and giving figures of quantity and proportion, but to give the faintest impression of its beauty and colours is almost hopeless. The rich, lovely green on the very brink of the Horse Shoe Fall is beyond conception. All the emeralds in the world, clustered together and bathed in sunlight, would fall far short of the beauty and brilliancy of that pure and dazzling colour. It can only be compared to an immense, unknown brilliant of the emerald hue, in a stupendous setting of the purest frosted, yet sparkling silver. Here, too, is to be seen the marvellous beauty of the prismatic colours almost daily. Here you might think the "Covenant" had been made, and set up to shine for ever and ever at the Throne of the Most Mighty, and here only can be seen the complete *circle* of the colours of the rainbow. I saw this but once, when on board the *Maid of the Mist*, and almost within the great vortex at the foot of the Falls. A brilliant sun shining through the spray all round, placed us in a moment as it were in the very centre of that beautiful circle of colour, which, with the thunder of the cataract, and the sublimity of the scene, made the soul feel as if it were in the presence of the "Great Spirit," and this the sign and seal of an eternal compact. Here, also, is to be seen the softer, but not the less beautiful Lunar Rainbow. Whenever the moon is high enough in the heavens, the lunar bow can be seen, not fitful as elsewhere, but constant and beautiful as long as the moon is shedding her soft light upon the spray. On one occasion I saw two lunar bows at once, one on the spray from the American Fall, and the other on the spray of the great Horse Shoe Fall. This I believe is not usual, but an eddy of the wind brought the two clouds of spray under the moon's rays. Yet these are not all the "beauties of the mist." One morning at sunrise I saw one the most beautiful forms the spray could possibly assume. The night had been unusually calm, the morning was as still as it could be, and the mist from the Horse Shoe had risen in a straight column to a height of at least 300 feet, and then spread out into a mass of huge rolling clouds, immediately above the cataracts. The rising sun shed a red lustre on the under edges of the cloud, which was truly wonderful. It more resembled one huge, solitary column supporting a canopy of silvery grey cloud, the edges of which were like burnished copper, and highly suggestive of the Temple of the Most High, where man must bow down and worship the great Creator of all these wondrous works. It is not in a passing glance at Niagara that all its marvellous beauties can been seen. You must stay there long enough to see it in all its aspects—in sunshine and in moonlight, in daylight and in darkness, in storm and in calm. No picture of language can possibly convey a just conception of the grandeur and vastness of these mighty cataracts. No poem has ever suggested a shadow of their majesty and sublimity. No painting has ever excited in the mind, of one that has not seen those marvellous works of God, the faintest idea of their dazzling beauties. Descriptive writers, both in prose and verse, have failed to depict the glories of this "Sovereign of the World of Floods." Painters have essayed with their most gorgeous colours, but have fallen far short of the intense beauty, transparency, and purity of the water, and the wonderful radiance and brilliancy of the "Rainbow in the Mist." And I fear the beauties of Niagara in natural colours can never be obtained in the camera; but what a glorious triumph for photography if they were. Mr. Church's picture, painted a few years ago, is the most faithful exponent of nature's gorgeous colouring of Niagara that has yet been produced. Indeed, the brilliant and harmonious colouring of this grand picture can scarcely be surpassed by the hand and skill of man.

After obtaining our views of the Grand Rapids and the Falls from Table Rock, we put up our traps, and leaving them in charge of the courteous proprietor of the Museum, we prepared to go *under* the great Horse Shoe Fall. Clothing ourselves in india-rubber suits, furnished by our guide, we descended the stairs near Table Rock, eighty-seven steps, and, led by a negro, we went under the great sheet of water as far as we could go to Termination Rock, and standing there for a while in that vast cave of watery darkness, holding on to the negro's hand, we felt lost in wonder and amazement, but not fear. How long we might have remained in that bewildering situation it would be impossible to say, but being gently drawn back by our sable conductor, we returned to the light and consciousness of our position. The volume of water being much greater here than at the Cave of the Winds, and the spray being all around, we could not see anything but darkness visible below, and an immense moving mass before, which we knew by feeling to be water. There is some fascination about the place, for after coming out into the daylight I went back again alone, but the guide, hurrying after me, brought me back, and held my hand until we reached the stairs to return to the Museum On our way back our guide told us that more than "twice-told tale" of Niagara and Vesuvius. If I may be pardoned for mixing up the ridiculous with the sublime, I may as well repeat the story, for having just come from under the Falls we were prepared to believe the truth of it, if the geographical difficulty could have been overcome. An Italian visiting the Falls and going under the Horse Shoe, was asked, on coming out, what he thought of the sight. The Italian replied it was very grand and wonderful, but *nothing* to the sight of Mount Vesuvius in a grand eruption. The guide's retort was, "I guess if you bring *your* Vesuvius here, *our* Niagara will soon put his fires out." I do not vouch for the truth of the story, but give it as nearly as possible as I was told. Returning to the Museum and making ourselves "as we were," and comforting ourselves with something inside after the wetting we had got out, we took up our traps, and wending our way back to the ferry, recrossed the river in much the same manner that we crossed over in the morning; and sending our "baggage" up in the cars we thought we would walk up the "long stairs," 290 steps, by the side of the railway. On nearing the top, we felt as if we must "cave in," but having trodden so far the back of a "lion," we determined to see the end of his tail, and pushing on to the top, we had the satisfaction of having accomplished the task we had set ourselves. Perhaps before abandoning the Canadian side of Niagara, I should have said something about Table Rock, which, as I have said, is on the Canadian side, and very near to the Horse Shoe Fall. It took its name from the table-like form it originally presented. It was formerly much larger than it is now, but has, from time to time, fallen away. At one time it was very extensive and projected over the precipice fifty or sixty feet, and was about 240 feet long and 100 feet thick. On the 26th of June, 1850, this tremendous mass of rock, nearly half an acre, fell into the river with a crash and a noise like the sound of an earthquake. The whole of that immense mass of rock was buried in the depths of the river, and completely hidden from sight. No one was killed, which was a miracle, for several persons had been standing on the rock just a few minutes before it fell. The vicinity is still called Table Rock, though the projecting part that gave rise to the name is gone. It is, nevertheless, the best point on the Canada side for obtaining a grand and comprehensive view of Niagara Falls.

The next scenes of our photographic labours were Suspension Bridge, the Long Rapids, The Whirlpool, and Devil's Hole. These subjects, though not so grand as Niagara, are still interestingly and closely associated with the topographical history and legendary interest of the Falls. And we thought a few "impressions" of the scenes, and a visit to the various places, would amply repay us for the amount of fatigue we should have to undergo on such a trip under the scorching sun of *August in America*. Descending to the shore, and stepping on board the steamer *Maid of the Mist*, which plies up and down the river for about two miles, on the tranquil water between the Falls and the Lower Rapids, we were "cast off," and in a little time reached the landing stage, a short distance above the Long Rapids. Landing on the American side, we ascended the steep road, which has been cut out of the precipice, and arriving at

Suspension Bridge, proceeded to examine that wonderful specimen of engineering skill. It was not then finished, but the lower level was complete, and foot passengers and carriages could go along. They were busy making the railway "track" overhead, so that, when finished (which it is now), it would be a bridge of two stories—the lower one for passengers on foot and carriages, the upper one for the "cars." I did not see a "snorting monster" going along that spider's-web-like structure, but can very well imagine what must be the sensations of "railway passengers" as they pass along the giddy height. The span of the bridge, from bank to bank, is 800 feet, and it is 230 feet from the river to the lower or carriage road. The estimated cost was two hundred thousand dollars, about £40,000. A boy's toy carried the first wire across the river. When the wind was blowing straight across, a wire was attached to a kite, and thus the connecting thread between the two sides was secured, and afterwards by means of a running wheel, or traveller, wire after wire was sent across until each strand was made thick enough to carry the whole weight of the bridge, railway trains, and other traffic which now pass along. We went on to the bridge, and looked down on the rapids below, for the bridge spans the river at the narrowest point, and right over the commencement of the Lower Rapids. It was more of a test to my nerves to stand at the edge of the bridge and look down on those fearful rapids than it was to go under the Falls. To us, it seemed a miracle of ingenuity and skill how, from so frail a connection, a mere wire, so stupendous a structure could have been formed; and yet, viewing it from below, or at a distance, it looked like a bridge of threads. During its erection several accidents occurred. On one occasion, when the workmen were just venturing on to the cables to lay the flooring, and before a plank was made fast, one of those sudden storms, so peculiar to America, came up and carried away all the flooring into the Rapids. Four of the men were left hanging to the wires, which were swaying backwards and forwards in the hurricane in the most frightful manner. Their cries for help could scarcely be heard, from the noise of the Rapids and the howling of the wind, but the workmen on shore, seeing the perilous condition of their comrades, sent a basket, with a man in it, down the wire to rescue them from death. Thus, one by one, they were saved. Leaving the Bridge, and proceeding to the vicinity of the Whirlpool, still keeping the American side of the river, we pitched the camera, not *over* the precipice, as I heard of one brother photographer doing, but on it, and took a view of the Bridge and the Rapids looking up towards the Falls, but a bend in the river prevented them being seen from this point. Not very far above the angry flood we saw the *Maid of the Mist* lying quietly at her moorings.

We next turned our attention to the great Whirlpool, which is about a mile below Suspension Bridge. Photographically considered, this is not nearly of so much interest as the Falls; but it is highly interesting, nevertheless, as a connecting link between their present and past history. It is supposed that ages ago—probably before the word went forth, "Let there *be* light, and there *was* light"—the Falls were as low down as the Whirlpool, a distance of over three miles below where they now are, or even lower down the river still. Geological observation almost proves this; and, that the present Whirlpool was once the great basin into which the Falls tumbled. In fact, that this was, in former ages, what the vortex at the foot of the Great Horse Shoe Fall is now. There seems to be no doubt whatever that the Falls are gradually though slowly receding, and they were just as likely to have been at the foot of the Long Rapids before the deluge, as not; especially when it is considered that the general aspect of the Falls has changed considerably, by gradual undermining of the soft shale and frequent falling and settling of the harder rocks during the last fifty years. Looking at the high and precipitous boundaries of the Long Rapids, it is difficult to come to any other conclusion.

than that, ages before the red man ever saw the Falls of Niagara, they rolled over a precipice between these rocky barriers in a more compact, but not less majestic body. The same vast quantity of water had to force its way through this narrower outlet, and it doubtless had a much greater distance to fall, for the precipices on each side of the river at this point are nearly 250 feet high, and the width of the gorge for a mile above and below the Whirlpool is not more than 700 feet. Considering that the Falls are now spread over an area of nearly three-quarters of a mile, and that this is the only outlet for all the superfluous waters of the great inland seas of Canada and America—Lakes Superior, Michigan, Huron, and Erie—and the hundreds of tributaries thereto, it may easily be conceived how great the rush of waters through so narrow a defile must necessarily be ; their turbulence and impatience rather aptly reminding you of a spoilt child—not in size or form, but in behaviour. They have so long had their own way, and done as they liked on the upper river and at the Falls, they seem as if they could not brook the restraint put upon them now by the giant rocks and lofty precipices that stand erect, on either side, hurling them back defiantly in tumultuous waves, seething, and hissing, and roaring in anger, lashing themselves into foam, and swelling with rage, higher in the middle, as if they sought an unpolluted way to the lake below, where they might calm their angry and resentful passions, and lay their chafed heads on the soft and gently heaving bosom of their lovely sister Ontario. It is a remarkable circumstance that the waters of the Rapids, both above and below the Whirlpool, in this defile are actually higher in the middle, by eight or nine feet, than at the sides, as if the space afforded them by their stern sentinels on each side were not enough to allow them to pass through in order and on a level. They seem to come down the upper part of the gorge like a surging and panic stricken multitude, until they are stopped for a time by the gigantic precipice forming the lower boundary of the Whirlpool, which throws them back, and there they remain whirling and whirling about until they get away by an under current from the vortex ; and, rising again in the lower part of the gorge, which runs off at right angles to the upper, they again show their angry heads, and rush madly and tumultuously away towards Lake Ontario. The bed of these rapids must be fearfully rugged, or the surface of the waters could not possibly be in such a broken state, for the water is at least 100 feet deep, by measurement made above and below the Rapids. But nobody has ventured to "heave the lead" either in the Rapids themselves or in the Whirlpool, the depth of which is not known. There is not much picturesque beauty at this point. Indeed, the Whirlpool itself is rather of a fearful and horrible character, with little to see but the mad torrent struggling and writhing in the most furious manner, to force its way down between its rocky boundaries. I saw logs of wood and other "wreck," probably portions of canal boats that had come down the river and been swept over the Falls, whirling around but not coming to the centre. When they are seen to get to the vortex they are tipped up almost perpendicularly and then vanish from sight, at last released from their continually diminishing and circular imprisonment. It has sometimes happened that the dead bodies of people drowned in the upper part of the river have been seen whirling about in this frightful pool tor many days. In 1841, three soldiers, deserters from the British army, attempting to swim across the river above these rapids, were drowned. Their bodies were carried down to the Whirlpool, where they were seen whirling about for nearly a fortnight. Leaving *this* gloomy and soul-depressing locality we proceeded for about half a mile further down the river, and visited that frightful chasm called Devil's Hole, or Bloody Run. The former name it takes from a horrible deed of fiendish and savage ferocity that was committed there by the Indians, and the latter name from the circumstance of that deed causing a stream of human blood to run through the ravine and mingle with the fierce water of the Rapids. Exactly one hundred years ago, during the French and Canadian wars, a party of 250 officers, men, women, and children, were retreating from Fort Schlosser, on the Upper Niagara River, and, being decoyed into an ambush, were driven over into this dreadful chasm, and fell to the bottom, a distance of nearly 200 feet. Only two escaped. A drummer was caught by one of the trees growing on the side of the precipice, and the other, a soldier named Steadman, escaped during the conflict, at the commencement of the treacherous onslaught He was mounted, and the Indians surrounding him, seized the bridle, and were attempting to drag him off his horse, but, cutting the reins, and giving his charger the "rowels deep," the animal dashed forward, and carried him back in safety to Fort Schlosser. The Indians afterwards gave him all the land he encircled in his flight, and he took up his abode among them In after years he put the goats on Goat Island—hence its name—by dropping carefully down the middle of the upper stream in a boat After landing the goats he returned to the main land, pushing his boat up the stream where the Rapids divide, until he reached safe water. The events of the foregoing episode occurred in 1765, and it is to be hoped that the Indians were the chief instigators and perpetrators of the massacre of Bloody Run

While we were looking about the chasm to see if there were any fossil remains in the place, an unlooked-for incident occurred. I saw two men coming up from the bottom of the ravine carrying *fish*—and the oddest fish and the whitest fish I ever saw. The idea of anyone fishing in those head-long rapids had never occurred to us; but probably these men knew some *fissures* in the rocks where the waters were quiet, and where the fish put into as a place of refuge from the stormy waters into which they had been drawn. No wonder the poor finny creatures were white, for I should think they had been frightened almost out of their lives before they were seized by their captors. I don't think I should have liked to have partaken of the meal they furnished, for they were very "shy-an'-hide" looking fishes. But soon we were obliged to give up both our geological studies and piscatorial speculations, for black clouds were gathering over head, shutting off the light, and making the dark ravine too gloomy to induce us to prolong our stay in that fearful chasm, with its melancholy associations of dark deeds of bloodshed and wholesale murder. Before we gained the road the rain came down, the lightning flashed, and the thunder clapped, reverberating sharp and loud from the rocks above, and we hurried away from the dismal place. On reaching the landing-stage, we took refuge from the storm and rain by again going on board the *Maid of the Mist*. She soon started on her last trip for the day, and we reached our hotel, glad to get out of a "positive bath," and indulge in a "toning mixture" of alcohol, sugar, and *warm* water. We had no "*gold*," but our "paper" being *good*, we did not require any.

After a delightful sojourn of three weeks at the Falls, and visiting many other places of minor interest in their neighbourhood, I bade adieu to the kind friends I had made and met, with many pleasant recollections of their kindness, and a never-to-be-forgotten remembrance of the charms and beauties, mysteries and majesty, power and grandeur, and terror and sublimity of Niagara —*Photographic News*, 1865.

PICTURES OF THE ST. LAWRENCE.
Taken in Autumn.

Photographs of the River St. Lawrence conveying an adequate idea of its extent and varied aspects, could not be taken in a week, a month, or a year. It is only possible in this sketch to call attention to the most novel and striking features of this great and interesting river, passing them hurriedly, as I did, in the "express boat," by which I sailed from the Niagara River to Montreal. Lake Ontario being the great head waters of the St. Lawrence, and the natural connection between that river and Niagara, I shall endeavour to illustrate, with pen and pencil, my sail down the Niagara River, Lake Ontario, and the St. Lawrence. Stepping on board the steamer lying at Lewiston, seven miles below Niagara, and bound for Montreal, I went to the "clerk's office," paid seven and a half dollars—about thirty shillings sterling—and secured my bed, board, and passage for the trip, the above small sum being all that is charged for a first class passage on board those magnificent steamers. I don't remember the name of "our boat," but that is of very little consequence, though I dare say it was the *Fulton*, that being in steam-boat nomenclature what "Washington" is to men, cities, and towns, and even territory, in America. But she was a splendid vessel, nevertheless, with a handsome dining saloon, a fine upper saloon running the whole length of the upper deck, about two hundred feet, an elegant "ladies' saloon," a stateroom cabin as well, and a powerful "walking engine." "All aboard," and "let go;" splash went the paddle-wheels, and we moved off majestically, going slowly down the river until we passed Fort Niagara on the American side, and Fort George on the British, at the foot of the river, and near the entrance to the Lake. On Fort Niagara the "Star Spangled Banner" was floating, its bright blue field blending with the clear blue sky of an autumn afternoon, its starry representatives of each State shining like stars in the deep blue vault of heaven, its red and white bars, thirteen in number, as pure in colour as the white clouds and crimson streaks of the west. The mingled crosses of St. Andrew and St. George were waving proudly over the fort opposite. Brave old flag, long may you wave! These forts played their respective parts amidst the din of battle during the wars of 1812 and 1813; but with these we have neither time nor inclination to deal; we, like the waters of the Niagara, are in a hurry to reach the bosom of Lake Ontario. Passing the forts, we were soon on the expanse of waters, and being fairly "at sea," we began to settle ourselves and "take stock," as it were, of our fellow travellers. It is useless to describe the aspect of the Lake; I might as well describe the German Ocean, for I could not see much difference between that and Lake Ontario, except that I could not sniff the iodine from the weeds drying in the sun while we "hugged the shore," or taste salt air after we were out in mid ocean—" the land is no longer in view."

To be at sea is to be at sea, no matter whether it is on a fresh water ocean or a salt one. The sights, the sensations, and consequences are much the same. There, a ship or two in full sail; here, a passenger or two, of both sexes, with the "wind taken out of their sails." The "old salts" or "old freshes" behave themselves much as usual, and so do the "green" ones of both atmospheres—the latter by preparing for a "bath" of perspiration and throwing everything down the "sink," or into the sea; and the former by picking out companions for the voyage. Being myself an "old salt," and tumbling in with one or two of a "fellow feeling wondrous kind," we were soon on as good terms as if we had known each other for years. After "supper," a sumptuous repast at 6 p.m., we went on to the "hurricane deck" to enjoy the calm and pleasant evening outside. There was a "gentle swell" on the Lake—not much, but enough to upset a few. After dark, we went into the "ladies' cabin"—an elegant saloon, beautifully furnished, and not without a grand piano where the "old freshes" of the softer sex—young and pretty ones too—were amusing themselves with playing and singing. An impromptu concert was soon formed, and a few very good pieces of music well played and sung. All went off very well while nothing but English, or, I should more properly say, American and Canadian, were sung, but one young lady, unfortunately, essayed one of the sweetest and most plaintive of Scotch songs—"Annie Laurie." Now fancy the love-sick "callant" for the sake of Annie Laurie lying down to *die*; just fancy Annie Laurie without the Scotch; only fancy Annie Laurie in a sort of mixture of Canadianisms and Americanisms; fancy "toddy" without the whisky, and you have some idea of "Annie Laurie" as sung on board the *Fulton* while splashing away on Lake Ontario, somewhere between America and Canada. There being little more to induce us to remain there, and by the ship's regulations it was getting near the time for "all lights out" in the cabins, we took an early "turn in," with the view of making an early "turn out," so as to be alive and about when we should enter the St. Lawrence, which we did at 6 o'clock a m., on a fine bright morning, the sun just rising to light up and "heighten" all the glorious tints of the trees on the Thousand and One Islands, among which we were now sailing.

It is impossible to form a correct idea of the width of the St. Lawrence at the head of the river. The islands are so large and numerous, it is difficult to come to a conclusion whether you are on a river or on a lake. Many of these islands are thickly wooded, so that they look more like the main land on each side of you as the steamer glides down "mid channel" between them. The various and brilliant tints of the foliage of the trees of America in autumn are gorgeous, such as never can be seen in this country; and their "chromotones" present an insurmountable difficulty to a photographer with his double achromatic lens and camera. Imagine our oaks clothed with leaves possessing all the varieties of red tints, from brilliant carmine down to burnt sienna—the brightest copper bays that grow in England are cool in tone compared with them; fancy our beeches, birches, and ashes thick with leaves of a bright yellow colour, from gamboge down to yellow ochre; our pines, firs, larches, and spruces, carrying all the varieties of green, from emerald down to terra verte; in fact, all the tints that are, can be seen on the trees when they are going into "the sere and yellow leaf" of autumn, excepting *blue*, and even that is supplied by the bluebirds (sialia Wilsonii) flitting about among the leaves, and in the deep cool tint of the sky, repeated and blended with the reflection of the many coloured trees in the calm, still water of the river. Some of the trees—the maples, for instance—exhibit in themselves, most vividly, the brightest shades of red, green, and yellow; but when the wind blows these resplendent colours about, the atmosphere is like a mammoth kaleidoscope that is never allowed to rest long enough to present to the eye a symmetrical figure or pattern, a perfect chaos of the most vivid and brilliant colours too gorgeous to depict. Long before this we had got clear of the islands at the foot of the lake and head of the river, and were steaming swiftly down the broad St. Lawrence. It is difficult to say how broad, but it varied from three to five or six miles in width; indeed, the river very much resembles the Balloch End, which is the broadest of Lochlomond; and some of the passages between the islands are very similar to the straits between the " Pass of Balmaha " and the island of Inchcailliach. The river is not hemmed in with such mountains as Ben Lomond and Ben Dhu, but, in many respects, the St. Lawrence very much resembles parts of our widest lakes, Lochlomond and Windermere. Having enjoyed the sight of the bright, beautiful scenery and the fresh morning air for a couple of hours, we were summoned to breakfast by the sound of the steward's "Big Ben." Descending to the lower cabin, we seated ourselves at the breakfast table, and partook of a most hearty meal All the meals on board these steamers are served in the most sumptuous style. During the repast some talked politics, some dollars and cents, others were speculating on how we should get down the Rapids, and when we should make them. Among the latter was myself, for I had seen rapids which I had not the slightest desire to be in or on; and, what sort of rapids we were coming to was of some importance to all who had not been on them. But everybody seemed anxious to be "on deck," and again "look out" for the quickening of the stream, or when the first "white lippers," should give indication of their whereabouts. My fellow passengers were from all parts of the Union ; the Yankee "guessed," the Southerner "reckoned," and the Western man "calculated" we should soon be among the "jumpers." Each one every now and then strained his eyes "a-head," down stream, to see if he could descry "broken water." At last an old river-man sung out, "There they are." There are the Longue Sault Rapids, the first we reach. Having plenty of "daylight," we did not feel much anxiety as we neared them, which we quickly did, for "the stream runs fast." We were soon among the jumping waters, and it is somewhat difficult to describe the sensation, somewhat difficult to find a comparison of a suitable character. It is not like being at sea in a ship in a "dead calm." The vessel does not "roll" with such solemn dignity, nor does she "pitch" and rise again so buoyantly as an Atlantic steamer (strange enough, I once crossed the Atlantic in the steamship *Niagara*), as she ploughs her way westward or eastward in a "head wind," and through a head sea. She rather kicks and jerks, and is let "down a peg" or two, with a shake and a fling. Did you ever ride a spavined horse down a hill? If so, you can form some idea of the manner in which we were let down the Longue Sault and Cedar Rapids and the St. Louis Cascades. One of our fellow passengers—a Scotchman—told that somewhat *apropos* and humorous story of the "Hielandman's" first trip across the Frith of Forth in a "nasty sea." Feeling a little uneasy about the stomach, and his bile being rather disturbed, the prostrate mountaineer cried out to the man at the "tiller" to "stop tickling the beast's tail—what was he making the animal kick that way for?" And so, telling our stories, and cracking our jokes, we spent the time until our swift vessel brought us to a landing, where we leave her and go on board a smaller boat, one more suitable for the descent of the more dangerous rapids, which we have yet to come to.

"All aboard," and away we go again as fast as steam and a strong current can take us, passing an island here and there, a town or a village half French and English, with a sprinkling of the Indian tribes, on the banks of the river now and then. But by this time it is necessary to go below again and dine. Bed, board, and travelling, are all included in the fare, so everyone goes to dinner. There is, however, so much to see during this delightful trip, that nobody likes to be below any longer than can be avoided. Immediately after dinner most are on deck again, anxious to see all that is to be seen on this magnificent river. The sights are various and highly interesting to the mind or "objectives" of either artist or photographer. Perhaps one of the most novel subjects for the camera and a day's photographing would be "Life on a Raft," as you see them drifting down the St. Lawrence. There is an immense raft—a long, low, flat, floating island, studded with twenty or thirty sails, and half a dozen huts, peopled with men, women, and children, the little ones playing about as if they were on a "plank road," or in a garden. It is "washing day," and the clean clothes are drying in the sun and breeze—indicative of the strictest domestic economy, and scrupulous cleanliness of those little huts, the many-coloured garments giving the raft quite a gay appearance, as if it were decked with the "flags of all nations." But what a life of tedious monotony it must be, drifting down the river in this way for hundreds of miles, from the upper part of Lake Ontario to Montreal or Quebec. How they get down the rapids of the St. Lawrence I do not know, but I should think they run considerable risk of being washed off; the raft seems too low in the water, and if not extremely well fastened, might part and be broken up. We passed two or three of these rafts, one a very large one, made up of thousands of timbers laid across and across like warp and weft; yet the people seemed happy enough on these "timber island;" we passed them near enough to see their faces and hear their voices, and I regretted I could not "catch their shadows," or stop and have an hour or two's work among them with the camera or the pencil; but we passed them by as if they were a fixture in the river, and they gave us a shout of "God speed," as if they did not envy our better pace in the least.

There is abundance of work for the camera at all times of the year on the St. Lawrence; I have seen it in summer and autumn, and have attempted to describe some of its attractions. And I was told that when the river—not the rapids—is ice-bound, the banks covered with snow, and the trees clad in icicles, they present a beautiful scene in the sunshine. And in the spring, when the ice is breaking up, and the floes piling high on one another, it is a splendid sight to see them coming down, hurled about and smashed in the rapids, showing that the water in its liquid state is by far the most powerful. But now we are coming to the most exciting part of our voyage. The steam is shut off, the engine motionless, the paddlewheels are still, and we are gliding swiftly and noiselessly down with the current. Yonder speck on the waters is the Indian coming in his canoe to pilot us down the dangerous rapids. We near each other, and he can now be seen paddling swiftly, and his canoe shoots like an arrow towards us. Now he is alongside, he leaps lightly on board, his canoe is drawn up after him, and he takes command of the "boat." Everybody on board knows the critical moment is approaching. The passengers gather "forward," the ladies cling to the arms of their natural protectors, conversation is stopped, the countenances of everyone exhibit intense excitement and anxiety, and every eye is "fixed ahead," or oscillating between the pilot and the rushing waters which can now be seen from the prow of the vessel. The Indian and three other men are at the wheel in the "pilot house," holding the helm "steady," and we are rushing down the stream unaided by any other propelling power than the force of the current, at a rate of twenty miles an hour. Now we hear the rushing and plunging sound of the waters, and in a moment the keen eye of the Indian catches sight of the land mark, which is the signal for putting the helm "hard a port;" the wheel flies round like lightning, and we are instantly dropped down a perpendicular fall of ten or twelve feet, the vessel careening almost on her "beam ends," in the midst of these wild, white waters, an immense rock or rocky island right ahead. But that is safely "rounded," and we are again in comparatively quiet water. The steam is turned into the cylinders, and we go on our course in a sober, sensible, and steamboat-like fashion. When we were safely past the rapids and round the rock, a gentleman remarked to me that "once in a lifetime was enough of that." It was interesting to watch the countenances of the passengers, and mark the difference of expression before and after the passage of the rapids. Before, it was all excitement and anxiety, mingled with a wish-it-was-over sort of look; and all were silent. After, everybody laughed and talked, and seemed delighted at having passed the *Lachine* Rapids in safety; yet most people are anxious to undergo the excitement and incur the risk and danger of the passage. You can, if you like, leave the boat above Lachine and proceed to Montreal by the cars, but I don't think any of our numerous passengers ever thought of doing such a thing. As long as ever this magnificent water way is free from ice, and the passage can be made, it is done. I don't know that more than one accident has ever occurred, but the risk seems considerable. There is a very great strain on the tiller ropes, and if one of them were to "give out" at the critical time, nothing could save the vessel from being dashed to pieces against the "rock ahead," and scarcely a life could be saved. No one can approach the spot except from above, and then there is no stopping to help others; you must go with the waters, rushing madly down over and among the rocks. The Indians often took these rapids, in their canoes, to descend to the lower part of the St. Lawrence; and one of them undertook to pilot the first steamer down in safety. His effort was successful, and he secured for his tribe (the Iroquois) a charter endowing them with the privileges and emoluments in perpetuity. I wish I could have obtained photographic impressions of these scenes and groups, but the only lens I could draw a "focus" with was the eye, and the only "plate" I had ready for use was the *retina*. However, the impressions obtained on that were so "vigorous and well defined," I can at any moment call them up, like "spirits from the vasty deep," and reproduce them in my mental camera.

The remaining nine miles of the voyage were soon accomplished. Passing the first abutment of the Victoria Bridge, which now crosses the St. Lawrence, at this point two miles wide, we quickly reached the fine quay and canal locks at Montreal, where we landed just as it was growing dark, after a delightful and exciting voyage of about thirty hours' duration, and a distance of more than four hundred miles. Quick work; but it must be borne in mind how much our speed was accelerated by the velocity of the current, and that the return trip by the canal, past the rapids, cannot be performed in anything like the time.

On reaching the quay I parted with my agreeable fellow travellers, and sought an hotel, where once more, after a long interval, I slept under a roof over which floated the flag which every Englishman is proud of—the Union Jack.

Next morning I rose early, and, with a photographic eye, scanned the city of Montreal. The streets are narrow, but clean, and well built of stone. Most of the suburban streets and villa residences are "frame buildings," but there are many handsome villas of stone about the base of the "mountain." I visited the principal buildings and the Cathedral of Notre Dame, ascended to the top of the Bell Tower, looked down upon the city, and had a fine view of its splendid quays and magnificent river frontage, and across the country southwards for a great distance, as far as the Adirondack Mountains, where the Hudson River bubbles into existence at Hendrick Spring, whence it creeps and gathers strength as it glides and falls and rushes alternately until it enters the Atlantic below New York, over three hundred miles south of its source. But the mountain at the back of Montreal prevented my seeing anything beyond the city in that direction. I afterwards ascended the mountain, from the summit of which I could see an immense distance up the river, far beyond Lachine, and across the St. Lawrence, and southwards into the "States." Being homeward bound, and having no desire at that time to prolong my stay in the western hemisphere, I did not wait to obtain any photographs of Montreal or the neighbourhood; but, taking ship for old England, I leave the lower St. Lawence and its beauties; Quebec, with its glorious associations of Wolfe and the plains of Abraham, its fortifications, which are now being so fully described and discussed in the House of Commons, and the Gulf of the St. Lawrence, where vessels have sometimes to be navigated from the "masthead," in consequence of the low-lying sea fog which frequently prevails there. A man is sent up "aloft" where he can see over the fog, which lies like a stratum of white cloud on the gulf, and pilot the ship safely through the fleet of merchantmen which are constantly sailing up and down while the river is open. The fog may not be much above the "maintop," but is so dense it is impossible to see beyond the end of the "bowsprit" from the deck of the ship you are aboard, but from the "masthead" the "look out" can see the high land and the masts and sails of the other ships, and avoid the danger of going "ashore" or coming into collision by crying out to the man at the wheel such sea phrases as "Port," "Starboard," "Steady," &c ; and when "tacking" up or down the gulf, such as "luff," "higher," "let her off." Indeed, the whole trip of the St. Lawrence—from Lake Ontario to the Atlantic—is intensely exciting. While off the coast of

Newfoundland, I witnessed one of those beautiful sights of nature in her sternest mood, which I think has yet to be rendered in the camera—icebergs in the sunlight. A great deal has been said about their beauty and colour, but nothing too much. Anyone who saw Church's picture of "The Icebergs," exhibited in London last year, may accept that as a faithful reflection of all their beautiful colours and dreadful desolation. All sailors like to give them as wide a "berth" as possible, and never admire their beauty, but shun them for their treachery. Sometimes their base extends far beyond their perpendicular lines, and many a good ship has struck on the shoal of ice under water, when the Captain thought he was far enough away from it. The largest one I saw was above a hundred feet above the water-line, and as they never exhibit more than one-third of their ponderous mass of frozen particles, there would be over two hundred feet of it below water, probably shoaling far out in all directions. We had a quick run across the Atlantic, and I landed in Liverpool, in the month of November, amid fog, and smoke, and gloom. What a contrast in the light! Here it was all fog and darkness, and photography impossible. There—the other side of the waters—the light is always abundant both in winter and summer, and it is only during a snow or rain storm that our transatlantic brother photographers are brought to a stand-still.—*Photographic News*, 1865.

PHOTOGRAPHIC IMPRESSIONS.

The Hudson, Developed on the Voyage.

"We'll have a trip up the Hudson," said a friend of mine, one of the best operators in New York; "we'll have a trip up the Hudson, and go and spend a few days with the 'old folk' in Vermont, and then you will see us 'Yankees'—our homes and hospitalities—in a somewhat different light from what you see them in this Gotham."

So it was arranged, and on the day appointed we walked down Broadway, turned down Courtland Street to the North River, and went on board the splendid river steamer *Isaac Newton*, named, in graceful compliment, after one of England's celebrities. Two dollars (eight and fourpence) each secured us a first-class passage in one of those floating palaces, for a trip of 144 miles up one of the most picturesque rivers in America.

Wishing for a thorough change of scene and occupation, and being tired of " posing and arranging lights " and " drawing a focus " on the faces of men, women, and children in a stifling and pent-up city, we left the camera with its " racks and pinions " behind, determined to revel in the beautiful and lovely only of nature, and breathe the fresh and exhilarating air as we steamed up the river, seated at the prow, and fanned by the breeze freshened by the speed of our swift-sailing boat.

Leaving New York, with its hundred piers jutting out into the broad stream, and its thousand masts and church spires on the one side, and Jersey City on the other, we are soon abreast of Hoboken and the "Elysian Fields," where the Germans assemble to drink "lager beer" and spend their Sundays and holidays. On the right or east side of the river is Spuyten Duyvil Creek, which forms a junction with the waters of the Sound or East River, and separates the tongue of land on which New York stands from the main, making the island of Manhattan. This island is a little over thirteen miles long and two and a-half miles wide. The Dutch bought the whole of it for £4 16s., and that contemptible sum was not paid to the poor, ignorant, and confiding Indians in hard cash, but in toys and trumpery articles not worth half the money. Truly it may be said that the " Empire City " of the United States did not cost a cent. an acre not more than two hundred and fifty years ago, and now some parts of it are worth a dollar a square foot. At Spuyten Duyvil Creek Henry Hudson had a skirmish with the Indians, while his ship, the *Half Moon*, was lying at anchor.

Now we come to the picturesque and the beautiful, subjects fit for the camera of the photographer, the pencil of the artist, and the pen of the historian. On the western side of the Hudson, above Hoboken, we catch the first glimpse of that singular and picturesque natural river wall called the "Palisades," a series of bold and lofty escarpments, extending for about thirty-five miles up the river, and varying in an almost perpendicular height from four to over six hundred feet, portions of them presenting a very similar appearance to Honister Craig, facing the Vale of Buttermere and Salisbury Craigs, near Edinburgh.

About two and a-half miles above Manhattan Island, on the east bank of the Hudson, I noticed a castellated building of considerable pretensions, but somewhat resembling one of those stage scenes of Dunsinane in *Macbeth*, or the Castle of Ravenswood in the *Bride of Lammermoor*. On enquiring to whom this fortified-looking residence belonged, I was told it was Fort Hill, the retreat of Edwin Forest, the celebrated American tragedian. It is built of blue granite, and must have been a costly fancy.

Now we come to the pretty village of Yonkers, where there are plenty of subjects for the camera, on Sawmill River, and the hills behind the village. Here, off Yonkers, in 1609, Henry Hudson came to the premature conclusion, from the strong tidal current, that he had discovered the north-west passage, which was the primary object of his voyage, and which led to the discovery of the river which now bears his name.

At Dobb's Ferry there is not much to our liking; but passing that, and before reaching Tarrytown, we are within the charming atmosphere of Sunnyside. where Washington Irving lived and wrote many of his delightful works. Tarrytown is the next place we make, and here, during the war for independence, the enthusiastic but unfortunate soldier, Major André, was captured; and at Tappan, nearly opposite, he was hung as a spy on the 2nd of October, 1780.

All the world knows the unfortunate connection between

Benedict Arnold, the American traitor, and Major André, the frank, gallant, and enterprising British officer; so I shall leave those subjects to the students of history, and pass on as fast as our boat will carry us to the next place of note on the east bank of the river, Sing Sing, which is the New York State prison, where the refractory and not over honest members of State society are sent to be "operated" upon by the salutary treatment of confinement and employment. Some of them are "doing time" in *dark rooms*, which are very unsuitable for photographic operations, and where *a little more light*, no matter how yellow or non-actinic, would be gladly received. The "silent cell" system is not practised so much in this State as in some of the others; but the authorities do their best to *improve the negative* or refractory character of the *subjects* placed under their care. It is, however, very questionable whether their efforts are not entirely *negatived*, and the bad character of the subject more *fully developed* and *intensified* by contact with the more powerful *reducing agents* by which they are surrounded. Their prison is, however, very pleasantly situated on the banks of the Hudson, about thirty-three miles above New York City.

Opposite Sing Sing is Rockland Lake, one hundred and fifty feet above the river, at the back of the Palisades. This lake is celebrated for three things—leeches and water lilies in summer, and ice in winter. Rockland Lake ice is prized by the thirsty denizens of New York City in the sultry summer months, and even in this country it is becoming known as a cooler and ' refresher."

Nearly opposite Sing Sing is the boldest and highest buttress of the Palisades; it is called "Vexatious Point," and stands six hundred and sixty feet above the water.

About eleven miles above Sing Sing we come to Peekskill, which is at the foot of the Peekskill Mountains. Backed up by those picturesque hills it has a pretty appearance from the river.

This was also a very important place during the wars. At this point the Americans set fire to a small fleet rather than let it fall into the hands of the British.

A little higher up on the west side is the important military station of West Point. This place, as well as being most charmingly situated, is also famous as the great military training school of the United States. Probably you have noticed, in reading the accounts of the war now raging between North and South, that this or that general or officer was a "West Point man." General George M'Clellan received his military education at West Point; but, whatever military knowledge he gained at this college, strengthened by experience and observation at the Crimea, he was not allowed to make much use of while he held command of the army of the Potomac. His great opponent, General Lee, was also a "West Point man," and it does not require much consideration to determine which of the "Pointsmen" was the smarter. Washington has also made West Point famous in the time of the war for independence. Benedict Arnold held command of this point and other places in the neighbourhood, when he made overtures to Sir Henry Clinton to hand over to the British, for a pecuniary consideration of £10,000, West Point and all its outposts.

A little higher up is Cold Spring, on the east side of the Hudson; but we will pass that by, and now we are off Newburg on the west bank. This is a large and flourishing town also at the foot of high hills—indeed, we are now in the highlands of the Hudson, and it would be difficult to find a town or a village that is not *backed up* by hills. At the time I first visited these scenes there was a large photographic apparatus manufactory at Newburg, where they made "coating boxes," "buff wheels," "Pecks blocks," &c., on a very extensive scale, for the benefit of themselves and all who were interested in the "cleaning," "buffing," and "coating" of Daguerreotype plates.

Opposite Newburg is Fishkill; but we shall pass rapidly up past Poughkeepsie on the right, and other places right and left, until we come to Hudson, on the east side of the river. Opposite Hudson are the Catskill Mountains, and here the river is hemmed in by mountains on all sides, resembling the head of Ullswater lake, or the head of Loch Lomond or Loch Katrine; and here we have a photographic curiosity to descant upon.

Down through the gorges of these mountains came a blast like the sound from a brazen trumpet, which electrified the photographers of the day. Among these hills resided the Rev. Levi Hill, who lately died in New York, the so-called inventor or discoverer of the Hillotype, or Daguerreotypes in natural colours. So much were the "Daguerreans" of New York startled by the announcement of this wonderful discovery, that they formed themselves into a sort of company to buy up the *highly-coloured* invention. A deputation of some of the most respectable and influential Daguerreotypists of New York was appointed to wait upon the reverend discoverer, and offer him I don't remember how many thousand dollars for his discovery as it stood; and it is said that he showed them specimens of "coloured Daguerreotypes,"—but refused to sell or impart to them the secret until he had completed his discovery, and made it perfect by working out the mode of producing the only lacking colour, chrome yellow. But in that he never succeeded, and so this wonderful discovery was neither given nor sold to the world. Many believed the truth of the man's statements— whether he believed it himself or not, God only knows. One skilful Daguerreotypist, in the State of New York, assured me he had seen the specimens, and had seen the rev. gentleman at work in his laboratory labouring and "buffing" away at a mass of something like a piece of lava, until by dint of hard rubbing and scrubbing the colours were said to "appear like spirits," one by one, until all but the stubborn chrome yellow showed themselves on the surface. I could not help laughing at my friend's statement and evident credulity, but after seeing "jumping Quakers," disciples of Joe Smith, and believers in the doctrine of Johanna Southcote, I could not be much surprised at any creed either in art or religion, or that men should fall into error in the Hillotype faith as easily as into errors of ethics or morality. I was assured by my friend (not my travelling companion) that they were beautiful specimens of colouring. Granted; but that did not prove that they were not done by hand. Indeed, a suspicion got abroad that the specimens shown by Mr. Hill were *hand-coloured* pictures brought from Europe. And from all that I could learn they were more like the beautifully coloured Daguerreotypes of M. Mansion, who was then colourist to Mr. Beard, than anything else I could see or hear of. Being no mean hand myself at colouring a Daguerreotype in those days, I was most anxious to see one of those wonderful specimens of "photography in natural colours," but I never could; and the inventor lived in such an out-of-the way place, among the Catskills, that I had no opportunity of paying him a visit. I have every reason to believe that the hand-coloured pictures by M. Mansion and myself were the only Hillotypes that were ever exhibited in America. Many of my coloured Daguerreotypes were exhibited at the State Fair in Castle Garden, and at the Great Exhibition at New York in 1853. But perhaps the late Rev. Levi Hill was desirous of securing a posthumous fame, and may have left something behind him after all; for surely, no man in his senses would have made such a noise about Daguerreotypes in "natural colours" as he did if he had not some reason for doing so. If so, and if he has left anything behind him that will lead us into nature's hidden mine of natural colours, now is the time for the "heirs and administrators" of the deceased gentlemen to secure for their deceased relative a fame as enduring as the Catskill Mountains themselves.

The Katzbergs, as the Dutch called the Catskill Mountains, on account of the number of wild cats they found among them, have more than a photographic interest. The late Washington Irving has imparted to them an attraction of a romantic character almost as bewitching as that conferred upon the mountains in the vicinity of Loch Lomond and Loch Katrine by Sir Walter Scott. It is true that the delicate fancy of Irving has not peopled the Katzbergs with such " warriors true " as stood

"Along Benledi's living side,"

nor has he "sped the fiery cross" over "dale, glen, and valley;" neither has he tracked

"The antler'd monarch of the waste"

from hill to hill; but the war-whoop of the Mohegans has startled the wild beasts from their lair, and the tawny hunters of the tribe have followed up the trail of the panther until with bow and arrow swift they have slain him in his mountain hiding place. And Irving's quaint fancy has re-peopled the mountains again with the phantom figures of Hendrick Hudson and his crew, and put Rip van Winkle to sleep, like a big baby, in one of nature's huge cradles, where he slept for *twenty years*, and slept away the reign of good King George III over the colonies, and awoke to find himself a bewildered citizen of the United States of America. And the place where he slept, and the place where he saw the solemn, silent crew of the "Half Moon" playing at ninepins, will be sought for and pointed out in all time coming And why should these scenes of natural beauty and charming romance not be photographed on the spot? It has not been done to my knowledge, yet they are well worthy the attention of photographers, either amateur or professional. We leave the Catskill Mountains with some regret, because of the disappointment of their not yielding us the promised triumph of chemistry, "photography in natural colours," and because of their beauty and varying effects of *chiaroscuro* not having been sufficiently rendered in the monochromes we have so long had an opportunity of obtaining in the camera.

Passing Coxackie, on the west bank of the Hudson, and many pleasant residences and places on each side of the river, we are soon at Albany, the capital of the State of New York, and the termination of our voyage on the board the *Isaac Newton*. And well had our splendid steamer performed her part of the contract. Here we were, in ten hours, at Albany, 144 miles from New York City. What a contrast, in the rate of speed, between the *Isaac Newton* and the first boat that steamed up the Hudson! The *Claremont* took over thirty-six hours, wind and weather permitting, to perform the voyage between New York and Albany; and we had done it in ten. What a contrast, too, in the size, style, and deportment of the two boats! The *Claremont* was a little, panting, puffing, half-clad, always-out-of-breath sort of thing, that splashed and struggled and groaned through the water, and threw its naked and diminutive paddle wheels in and out of the river—like a man that can neither swim nor is willing to be drowned, throwing his arms in and out of the water in agony—and only reached her destination after a number of stoppings-to-breathe and spasmodic start-agains. The *Isaac Newton* had glided swiftly and smoothly through the waters of the Hudson, her gigantic paddle-wheels performing as many revolutions in a minute as the other's did in twenty.

But these were the advanced strides and improvements brought about by the workings and experiences of half a century. If the marine steam engine be such a wonderfully-improved machine in that period of time, what may not photography be when the art-science is fifty years old? What have not the thousands of active brains devoted to its advancement done for it already? What have not been the improvements and wonderful workings of photography in a quarter of a century? What improvements have not been effected in the lifetime of any old Daguerreotypist? When I first knew photography it was a ghostly thing—a shimmering phantom—that was flashed in and out of your eyes with the rapidity of lightning, as you tried to catch a sight of the image between the total darkness of the black polish of the silvered plate, and the blinding light of the sky, which was reflected as from a mirror into your eyes.

But how these phantom figures vanished! How rapidly they changed from ghostly and almost invisible shadows to solid, visible, and all but tangible forms under the magical influence of Goddard's and Claudet's "bromine accelerator," and Fizeau's "fixing" or gilding process! How Mercury flew to the lovely and joint creations of chemistry and optics, and took kindly to the timid, hiding beauties of Iodine, Bromine, Silver, and Light, and brought them out, and showed them to the world, proudly, as "things of beauty," and " a joy for ever!" How Mercury clung to these latent beauties, and "developed" their charms, and became "attached" to them, and almost immovable, and consented, at last, to be tinted like a Gibson's Venus to enhance the charms and witcheries of his proteges! Anon was Mercury driven from Beauty's fair domain, and bright shining Silver, in another form, took up with two fuming, puffy fellows, who styled themselves Ether and Alcohol, with a villainous taint of methyl and something very much akin to gunpowder running through their veins. A most abominable compound they were, and some of the vilest of the vile were among their progeny; indeed, they were all a " hard lot," for I don't know how many rods—I may say tons—of iron had to be used before they could be brought into the civilised world at all. But, happily, they had a short life. Now they have almost passed away from off the face of the earth, and it is to be hoped that the place that knew them once will know them no more; for they were a dangerous set—fragile in substance, frightful abortions, and an incubus on the fair fame of photography. They bathed in the foulest of baths, and what served for one served for all. The poisonous and disgusting fluid was used over and over again. Loathsome and pestiferous vapours hovered about them, and they took up their abode in the back slums of our cities, and herded with the multitude, and a vast majority of them were not worth the consideration of the most callous officer of the sanitary commission. Everything that breathes the breath of life has its moments of agony, and these were the throes that agonised Photography in that fell epoch of her history.

From the ashes of this burning shame Photography arose, Phœnix-like, and with Silver, seven times purified, took her ethereal form into the hearts and *ateliers* of artists, who welcomed her sunny presence in their abodes of refinement and taste. They treated her kindly and considerately, and lovingly placed her in her proper sphere; and, by their kind and delicate treatment, made her forget the miseries of her degradation and the agonies of her travail. Then art aided photography and photography aided art, and the happy, delightful reciprocity has brought down showers of golden rain amidst the sunshine of prosperity to thousands who follow with love and devotion the chastened and purified form of Photography, accompanied in all her thoughts and doings by her elder sister— Art.

I must apologise for this seeming digression. However, as I have not entirely abandoned my photographic impressions, I take it for granted that I have not presumed too much on the good nature of my readers, and will now endeavour to further develop and redevelop the Hudson, and point out the many phases of beauty that are fit subjects for the camera which may be seen on the waters and highland boundaries of that beautiful river in all seasons of the year.

Albany is the capital of the State. It is a large and flourishing city, and one of the oldest, being an early Dutch settlement, which is sufficiently attested by the prevalence of such cognomens as "Vanderdonck" and "Onderdunk" over the doors of the traders.

About six or eight miles above Albany the Hudson ceases to be navigable for steamers and sailing craft, and the influence of the tide becomes imperceptible. Troy is on the east bank of the river; and about two miles above, the Mohawk River joins the Hudson, coming down from the Western part of the State of New York. For about two hundred miles the Hudson runs almost due north and south from a little below Fort Edward; but, from the Adirondack Mountains, where it takes its spring, it comes down in a north-westerly direction by rushing rapids, cascades, and falls innumerable for about two hundred miles more through some of the wildest country that can possibly be imagined.

We did not proceed up the Upper Hudson, but I was told it would well repay a trip with the camera, as some of the wildest and most picturesque scenery would be found in tracking the Hudson to its source among the Adirondack Mountains.

I afterwards sailed up and down the navigable part of the Hudson many times and at all periods of the year, except when it was ice-bound, by daylight and by moonlight, and a more beautiful moonlight sail cannot possibly be conceived. To be sailing up under the shadow of the Palisades on a bright moonlight night, and see the eastern shore and bays bathed in the magnesium-like light of a bright western moon, is in itself enough to inspire the most ordinary mind with a love of all that is beautiful and poetical in nature.

Moonlight excursions are frequently made from New York to various points on the Hudson, and Sleepy Hollow is one of the most favourite trips. I have been in that neighbourhood, but never saw the "headless horseman" that was said to haunt the place; but that may be accounted for by the circumstance of some superior officer having recently commanded the trooper without a head to do duty in Texas.

My next trip up the Hudson was in winter, when the surface of the river was in the state of "glacial," solid at 50° for two or three feet down, but the temperature was considerably lower, frequently 15° and 20° below zero—and that was nipping cold "and no mistake," making the very breath "glacial," plugging up the nostrils with "chunks" of ice, and binding the beard and moustache together, making a glacier on your face, which you had to break through every now and then to make a breathing hole.

On this arctic trip the whole aspect of the river and its boundaries is marvellously changed, without losing any of its picturesque attractions. Instead of the clear, deep river having its glassy surface broken by the splash of paddle wheels, it is converted into a solid highway. Instead of the sound of the "pilot's gong," and the cries of "a sail on the port bow," there is nothing to be heard but the jingling sound of the sleigh bells, and the merry laugh and prattle of the fair occupants of the sleighs, as they skim past on the smooth surface of the ice, wrapped cosily up in their gay buffalo robes.

The great excitement of winter in Canada or the States is to take a sleigh ride; and I think there is nothing more delightful, when the wind is still, than to skim along the ice in the bright, winter sunshine, behind a pair of spanking "trotters." The horses seem to enjoy it as much as the people, arching their necks a little more proudly than usual, and stepping lightly to the merry sound of the sleigh bells.

At this time of the year large sleighs, holding fifteen to twenty people, and drawn by four horses, take the place of steamers, omnibuses, and ferry boats. The steam ferries are housed, except at New York, and there they keep grinding their way through the ice "all winter," as if they would not let winter reign over their destinies if they could help it. Large sleighs cross and recross on the ice higher up the Hudson, and thus keep up the connection between the various points and opposite shores. As the mercury falls the spirits of the people seem to rise, and they shout and halloo at each other as they pass or race on the ice. These are animated scenes for the skill of a Blanchard or any other artist equally good in the production of instantaneous photographs.

Another of the scenes on the Hudson worthy of the camera is "ploughing the ice." It is a singular sight to an Englishman to see a man driving a team of horses on the ice, and see the white powder rising before the ice-plough like spray from the prow of a vessel as she rushes through the water, cutting the ice into blocks or squares, to stow away in "chunks," and afterwards, when the hot sulty weather of July and August is prostrating you, have them brought out to make those wonderful mixtures called "ice-creams," "sherry-cobblers," and "brandy-cocktails."

The Hudson is beautiful in winter as well as in summer, and I wonder its various and picturesque beauties have not been photographed more abundantly. But there it is. Prophets are never honoured in their own country, and artists and photographers never see the beauties of their country at home. I am sure if the Hudson were photographed from the sea to its source it would be one of the most valuable, interesting, and picturesque series of photographs that ever was published. Its aspects in summer are lovely and charming, and the wet process can then be employed with success. And in winter, though the temperature is low, the river is perfectly dry on the surface, the hills and trees are glistening with snow and icicles, the people are on the very happiest terms with one another, and frequently exhibit an abundance of dry, good humour. This is the time to work the "dry process" most successfully, and, instead of the "ammonia developers," try the "hot and strong" ones.

With these few hints to my photographic friends, I leave the beauties of the Hudson to their kind consideration.—*British Journal of Photography*, 1865.

PICTURES OF THE POTOMAC IN PEACE AND WAR.

When first I visited that lovely region which has so recently been torn and trampled down—blackened and defaced by the ruthlessness of war—peace lay in the valleys of the Potomac. Nothing was borne on the calm, clear bosom of the broad and listless river but the produce of the rich and smiling valleys of Virginia. Its banks were peaceful, silent, and beautiful. The peach orchards were white with the blossoms that promised a rich harvest of their delicious fruit. The neat and pretty houses that studded the sloping boundaries of the river were almost blinding with their dazzling whiteness as the full blaze of the sun fell upon them. Their inhabitants were happy, and dreamt not of the storm so soon to overtake them. The forts were occupied by only a few, very few soldiers. The guns were laid aside, all rusty and uncared for; and pilgrims to the tomb of Washington, the good and great, stopped on their return at Fort Washington to examine the fortifications in idleness and peaceful curiosity. The Capitol at Washington echoed nothing but the sounds of peace and good will. The senators of both North and South sat in council together, and considered only the welfare and prosperity of their great confederation.

The same harmonious fellowship influenced the appearance and actions of all, and at that happy conjuncture I made my first acquaintance with Washington, the capital of the United States. I shall not attempt a description of its geographical position: everybody knows that it is in the district of Columbia, and on the banks of the Potomac. It is a city of vast and pretentious appearance, straggling over an unnecessary amount of ground, and is divided into avenues and streets. The avenues are named after the principal States, and take their spring from the Capitol, running off in all directions in angular form, like the spokes of a wheel, the Capitol being the "angular point." The streets running between and across the avenues rejoice in the euphonious names of First, Second, and Third, and A, B, and C streets, the straight lines of which are broken by trees of the most luxurious growth all along the side-walks. These trees form a delightful sun-shade in summer, and have a very novel and pleasing effect at night, when their green and leafy arches are illuminated by the gas lamps underneath.

Excepting the Capitol, White House, Court House, Post Office, Patent Office, and Smithsonian Institute, there is nothing in the city of photographic interest. The "United States," the "National," and "Willards," are large and commodious hotels on Pennsylvania Avenue; but not worth a plate, photographically speaking, unless the landlords wish to illustrate their bar bills. The Capitol is out of all proportion the largest and most imposing structure in Washington—it may safely be said in the United States. Situated on an elevated site, at the top of Pennsylvania Avenue, it forms a grand termination to that noble thoroughfare at its eastern extremity. The building consists of a grand centre of freestone painted white, surmounted by a vast dome of beautiful proportions. Two large wings of white marble complete the grand façade. Ascending the noble flight of marble steps to the principal entrance, the great portico is reached, which is supported by about eighteen Corinthian columns. The pediment is ornamented with a statue of America in the centre, with the figures of Faith on her left, and Justice on her right. On each side of the entrance is a group of statuary. On one side an Indian savage is about to massacre a mother and her child, but his arm is arrested by the figure of Civilization. On the other side the group consists of a man holding up a globe, representing Columbus and the figure of an Indian girl looking up to it.

The large rotunda, immediately underneath the dome, is divided into panels, which are filled with paintings, such as the

"Landing of the Pilgrim Fathers," "The Baptism of the Indian Princess Pocahontas," and other subjects illustrative of American history. On either side of the Rotunda are passages leading to the House of Representatives on the one side, and the Senate Chamber on the other. Congress being assembled, I looked in to see the collective wisdom of the "States" during a morning sitting. In many respects the House of Representatives very much resembled our own House of Commons. There was a Mr. Speaker in the chair, and one gentleman had "the floor," and was addressing the House. Other members were seated in their desk seats, making notes, or busying themselves with their own bills. In one essential point, however, I found a difference, and that was in the ease of access to this assembly. No "member's order" was required. Strangers and "citizens" are at all times freely admitted. There is also a magnificent library, which is free to everyone.

During the Session there is Divine service in the Senate Chamber on Sunday mornings. On one occasion I attended, and heard a most excellent discourse by the appointed chaplain. The President and his family were there.

In some side offices, connected with the Capitol, I found a government photographer at work, copying plans, and photographing portions of the unfinished building, for the benefit of the architects and others whose duty it was to examine the progress of the works. From this gentleman I received much courteous attention, and was shown many large and excellent negatives, all of which were developed with the ordinary iron developer.

I next visited the Patent Office, and the museum connected therewith, which contains a vast collection of models of all kinds of inventions that have received protection—among them several things, in apparatus and implements, connected with photography. The American patent laws require a model of every new invention to be lodged in this museum, which is of immense value to inventors and intending patentees; for they can there see what has already been protected; and as the Patent Office refuses to grant protection to anything of a similar form, use, or application, much litigation, expense, and annoyance are saved the patentees. Our Government would do well to take a leaf out of "Brother Jonathan's" book on this subject; for not only is there increased protection given to inventors, but the fees are considerably less than in this country.

The presidential residence, called the White House, was the next interesting subject of observation. It is situated at the west end of Pennsylvania Avenue, and a good mile from the Capitol. The building is of white marble, and of very unpretending size and architectural attractions, but in every respect sufficient for the simple wants of the chief magistrate of the United States, whose official salary is only twenty-five thousand dollars per annum.

During congressional session the President holds weekly *levees;* and one of these I determined to attend, prompted as much by curiosity to see how such things were done, as desire to pay my respects. Accordingly, on a certain night, at eight o'clock precisely, I went to the White House, and was admitted without hesitation. On reaching the door of the reception room, I gave my card to the district marshal, who conducted me to President Pearce, to whom I was introduced. I was received with a hearty welcome, and a shake of the hand. Indeed, I noticed that he had a kindly word of greeting for all who came. Not having any very important communication to make that would be either startling or interesting to the President of the United States, I bowed, and retired to the promenade room, where I found numbers of people who had been "presented" walking about and chatting in groups on all sorts of subjects—political, foreign, and domestic, and anything they liked. Some were in evening dress, others not; but all seemed perfectly easy and affable one with another. There was no restraint, and the only passport required to these *levees* was decent behaviour and respectability. There was music also. A band was playing in the vestibule, and everyone evidently enjoyed the *reunion*, and felt perfectly at home. Never having been presented at court, I am not able to make any comparison *pro* or *con*.

There is also an observatory at Washington, which I visited; but not being fortunate enough to meet the—what shall I say? "astronomer-royal," comes readiest, but that is not correct: well, then, the—"astronomer republic," I did not see the large telescope and other astronomical instruments worked.

The photographic galleries were all situated on Pennsylvania Avenue, and they were numerous enough. At that time they rejoiced in the name of "Daguerrean Galleries," and the proprietor, or operator, was called a "Daguerrean." Their reception rooms were designated "saloons," which were invariably well furnished—some of them superbly—and filled with specimens. Their "studios" and workshops behind the scenes were fitted with all sorts of ingenious contrivances for "buffing" and "coating" and expediting the work. Although the greatest number of mechanical appliances were employed in the Daguerreotype branch of photography, art was not altogether ignored in its practice. One house made a business feature of very beautifully-coloured Daguerreotypes, tinted with dry colours, quite equal to those done in Europe. Another house made a feature of "Daguerreotypes painted in oil;" and the likeness was most admirably preserved. I saw one of the President, and several of the members of Congress, which I knew to be unmistakable portraits. Although the Daguerreotype was most tenaciously adhered to as the best means of producing photographic portraits, the collodion process—or the "crystaltype," as they then called it—was not neglected. It was used by a few for portraits, but chiefly for views.

Having seen all that was worth seeing in the city, I made

excursions into the country, in search of subjects for the camera or pencil.

Georgetown, a little way from Washington, and its picturesque cemetery, offer several pretty bits for the camera. Arlington Heights, the Long Bridge, and many nooks about there, are sufficiently tempting; but of all the excursions about Washington, Mount Vernon—a few miles down the Potomac, on the Virginia side—is by far the most interesting. Mount Vernon is the name of the place where General George Washington lived and died, and is the "Mecca" of the Americans. Nearly every day there are pilgrims from some or all parts of the States to the tomb of Washington, which is in the grounds of Mount Vernon. They visit this place with a kind of religious awe and veneration, and come from far and wide to say they have seen it. For, in truth, there is little to see but the strangest-looking and ugliest brick building I ever beheld, with open iron gates that allow you to look into the darkness of the interior, and see nothing. I took a view of the tomb, and here it is:—A red brick building, squat and low, of the most unsightly design and proportions imaginable—resembling one of our country "dead-houses" more than anything else I could compare it to. It was stuck away from the house among trees and brushwood, and in an advanced state of dilapidation—a disgrace to the nation that had sprung from that great man's honest devotion! Over the Gothic entrance is a white slab, with the following inscription on it:—

"Within this Enclosure
Rest
the remains of
GENERAL GEORGE WASHINGTON."

The remains of "Lady Washington" lie there also; and there are several white obelisks about to the memory of other members of the family.

The house itself is a "frame building" of two storeys, with a piazza running along the front of it, and is on the whole a mean-looking edifice; but was probably grand enough for the simple tastes of the man who dwelt in it, and has hallowed the place with the greatness and goodness of his life. The interior of the house looked as if it had once been a comfortable and cozy habitation. In the hall was put up a desk, with a "visitors' book," wherein they were expected to enter their names; and few failed to pay such a cheap tribute to the memory of the father of their country.

The grounds, which were full of natural beauties, had been allowed to run into a state of wild tangle-wood; and I had some trouble to pick my way over broken paths down to the river-side again, where I took the "boat," and returned to the city, touching at Fort Washington on the way. The day had been remarkably fine; the evening was calm and lovely ; the silence of the river disturbed only by the splash of our paddles, and the song of the fishermen on shore as they drew in their laden nets; and the moon shone as only she can shine in those latitudes. Nothing could denote more peace and quietude as I sailed on the Potomac on that lovely evening. There was such a perfect lull of the natural elements—such a happy combination of all that was beautiful and promising—it seemed impossible for such a hurricane of men's passions—such yells of strife and shouts of victory, such a swoop of death as afterwards rushed down those valleys—ever to come to pass.

Such sad reverse was, however, seen on my second visit to the Potomac. The narration of the stirring scenes then presented will form a picture less peaceful and happy, but unfortunately intensely real and painfully true.

My second visit to the Potomac was paid after the lapse of several years, and under very different circumstances. When the Capitol echoed loudly the fierce and deadly sentiments of the men of the North against the men of the South. When both had shouted—

> "Strike up the drums, and let the tongue of war
> Plead for our int'rest."

When the deliberations of the senators were "war estimates," arming of troops, and hurrying them to the "front" with all possible despatch. When the city of Washington presented all the appearance of a place threatened with a siege. When every unoccupied building was turned into barracks, and every piece of unoccupied land was made a "camp ground." When the inhabitants were in terror and dismay, dreading the approach of an invading host. When hasty earth-works were thrown up in front of the city, and the heights were bristling with cannon. When the woods and peach orchards on the opposite side of the Potomac were red with the glare of the camp fires at night, and the flashing of bayonets was almost blinding in the hot sun at noon. When the vessels sailing on the river were laden with armed men, shot, shell, and "villainous saltpetre." When the incessant roll of drums and rattle of musketry deadened almost every other sound. When sentinels guarded every road and access to the capital, and passports were required from the military authorities to enable you to move from one place to another. In short, when the whole atmosphere was filled with sounds of martial strife, and everything took the form of desolating war.

In spite of all these untoward events, I found photography actively engaged in the city, in the camp, and on the field, fulfilling a mission of mercy and consolation in the midst of carnage and tumult—fulfilling such a mission of holy work as never before fell to the lot of any art or art-science to perform. For what aspect of life is photography not called upon to witness? —what phase of this world's weal or woe is photography not required to depict? Photography has become a handmaiden to the present generation—a ministering angel to all conditions of life, from the cradle to the grave. An *aide-de-camp* of the loveliest character to the great "light of the world," humanizing and elevating the minds of all, administering consolation to the sorrowing, increasing the joy of the joyous, lessening the pangs of separation caused by distance or death, strengthening the ties of immediate fellowship, helping the world to know its benefactors, and the world's benefactors to know the world When grim death stalks into the gilded palaces of the great and powerful, or into the thatched cottages and miserable dwellings of the poor, photography is the assuager of the griefs of the sorrowing survivors, and the ameliorator of their miseries, by preserving to them so faithful a resemblance of the lost one. When the bride, in her youth and loveliness, is attired for the bridal, photography is the recorder of her trustful looks and April smiles, the fashion of her dress, the wreath and jewels that she wore; and, come what change in her appearance that may, the husband can look upon his bride whene'er he likes in after years, as vividly and as distinctly as on that day, connecting the present with the past with a kind of running chord of happy recollections. Photography is now the historian of earth and animated nature, the biographer of man, the registrar of his growth from childhood to "man's estate," the delineator of his physical, moral, and social progress, the book of fashion, and the mirror of the times. The uses and applications of photography are almost indescribable; scarcely an art, or a science, or a trade or profession that does not enlist photography into its service. Photography does not merely pander to the gratification of earthly vanity, but is an alleviator of human misery. Photography enters our hospitals and registers faithfully the progress of disease, its growth and change from day to day, until it is cured, or ripe for the knife of the surgeon; its pictures are lessons to the professor, and a book of study for the students, charts for their guidance through the painful and tedious cases of others similarly afflicted, teaching them what to do and what to avoid, to relieve the suffering of other patients. Photography is dragged into our criminal law courts, and sits on the right hand of Justice, giving evidence of the most undeniable character, without being under oath, and free from the suspicion of perjury, convicting murderers and felons, and acquitting the innocent without prejudice; and in our courts of equity, cases are frequently decided by the truth-telling evidence of photography.

Astronomers, geographers, and electricians freely acknowledge how much they are indebted to photography in making their celestial and terrestrial observations. Engineers, civil and military, employ photography largely in their plans and studies. Art, also, has recourse to photography, and is the only one of the liberal professions that is half ashamed to admit the aid it gains from the camera. If art admits it at all, it is done grudgingly, apologetically, and thanklessly. But there it is the old, old story of family quarrels and family jealousies. Old art might be likened to an old aunt that has grown withered and wrinkled, and peevish with disappointment, who, in spite of all her long-studied rules and principles of light and shade, harmony of colour, painting, "glazing," and "scumbling," has failed to win the first prize—that prize which a woman's ambition pants after from the moment she enters her teens until her dream is realised—that living model, moulded after God's own image, which, not having won in her mature age, she becomes jealous of the growing graces, the fresh and rollicking charms, the unstudied and ingenuous truthfulness of form exhibited by her niece. Old Art the aunt, Photography the niece. Readers, draw the moral for yourselves.

I have digressed, but could not help it. Photography is so young and lovely, so bewitchingly beautiful in all her moods, so fascinating and enslaving—and she has enslaved thousands since she first sprung from the source that gives her life. But to return to my theme.

The practice of photography, like the aspects of the country and condition of the people, was changed. " Old things had passed away, and all things had become new." The shining silver plates, buffing wheels, coating boxes, mercury pans, &c., of the old dispensation had given place to the baths, nitrate of silver solutions, and iron developers of the new. Ambrotypes, or glass positives, and photographs on paper, had taken the place of the now antiquated Daguerreotype. Mammoth photographs were the ambition of all photographers. The first full-length life-sized photograph I ever saw was in Washington, and was the work of Mr. Gardner, the manager of Mr. Brady's gallery. But a more republican idea of photography, which, strange to say, originated in an empire not remarkable for freedom of thought, soon became the dominant power. Cartes-de-visite, the many, ruled over mammoth, the few. The price of mammoth photographs was beyond the reach of millions, but the prices of cartes-de-visite were within the grasp of all; and that, combined with their convenient size and prettiness of form, made them at once popular, and created a mania.

The carte-de-visite form of picture became the "rage" in America about the time the civil war commenced, and as the young soldiers were proud of their new uniforms, and those who had been "in action" were prouder still of their stains and scars, the photographers did a good business among them, both in the city and in the camp. I saw a little of this "camp work" and "camp life" myself, and some of the havoc of war as well. Photographers are adventurous, and frequently getting into odd kinds of "positions," as well as their "sitters."

It was my destiny, under the guidance of the Great Source of Light, to witness the results of the first great conflict between the opposing armies of the Federals and Confederates; to hear the thunder of their artillery, and see the clouds of smoke hovering over the battle field, without being in the battle itself. To see the rout and panic of the Northern troops, who had so recently marched proudly on to fancied victory; to witness the disgraceful and disastrous stampede of the Northern army from the field of Bull Run; to listen to the agonized groans of the "severely wounded" as they were hurried past to the temporary hospitals in Washington and Georgetown; to be an eye-witness to the demoralized condition of men who, naturally brave, were under the influence of a panic caused by the vague apprehension of a danger that did not exist; to hear the citizens exclaim, "What shall we do?" and "For God's sake don't tell your people at home what you have seen!" and comparing the reverse of their national arms to a "regular Waterloo defeat," which was anything but a happy simile. To see the panic-stricken men themselves, when they discovered their error, and began to realize their shame, weeping like women at the folly they had committed. But they atoned for all this, afterwards, by deeds of glorious valour which were never surpassed, and which ended in restoring their country to peace and reunion.

The 21st of July, 1861, was a Sunday, and as calm and beautiful a day as could be wished for. From its associations it ought to have been a day of rest and peace to all; but it was not. There was terrible slaughter among men that Sunday in Virginia. During the morning, I took advantage of an opportunity offered me to go down to Alexandria, in Virginia, about five or six miles below Washington, which was then occupied by a portion of the Federal Army. Everything in the place had the appearance of war. There were more soldiers than civilians about. Hotels were turned into barracks and military storehouses. The hotel where Colonel Ellsworth, of the New York Fire Zouaves, was shot by the proprietor for hauling down the Confederate flag—which the latter had hoisted over his house—had been taken possession of by the military authorities, and the whole place was under martial law. It was there I first heard rumours of a battle being fought in the neighbourhood of Manassas Junction. These rumours were soon confirmed by the roar of cannon in the distance, and the hurrying of fresh troops from Washington to the field of battle. But they were not needed. Before they could reach the field the "stampede" had commenced, and the retreating hosts came like a rushing tide upon the advancing few, and carried them back, absorbed in the unshapen mass of confusion.

The night came, and little was known by the inhabitants of Washington of the rout and rush of terrified men towards the city; but the next morning revealed the fact.

Wet and wretched was the morning after the battle. The heavens seemed to weep over the disgrace as the men poured into the city, singly and in groups, unofficered, and without their firearms, which many had lost, or thrown away in their flight. The citizens gathered round them, anxious to learn all about the defeat, and the whereabouts of the Confederate army, and invited them into their houses to take refreshment and rest. Several instances of this impromptu hospitality and sympathy I witnessed myself; and many of the weary and wounded soldiers I talked to. They that were only slightly wounded in the hands and arms had their wounds washed and dressed by the wives and daughters of many of the residents. The hotels were crowded, and the "bars" were besieged by the drenched and fatigued soldiers, whom the curious and sympathizing citizens invited to "liquor." The men all told wonderful stories of the fight and of their own escape, but none could tell satisfactorily what had created the panic. Some said that a few "teamsters" took the alarm, and, riding to the rear in hot haste, conveyed the impression that an exterminating pursuit by the Confederates had commenced.

In a day or two the majority of the men were mustered

together again, and occupied their old camping grounds, where I visited them, and heard many of their stories, and got some of the relics of the battle field. Fresh troops were raised, and placed under the command of another general. But it was long before another "onward march to Richmond" was attempted. The North had learned something of the strength and prowess of the South, and began to prepare for a longer and fiercer struggle with "Secession."

Such are the two pictures of the Potomac which I have endeavoured to reproduce, and which fell under my observation during my professional peregrinations in connection with the practice of photography.

RAMBLES AMONG THE STUDIOS OF AMERICA.
Boston.

My impressions of America, from a photographic point of observation, were taken at two distinct periods—which I might call the two epochs of photographic history—the dry and the wet; the first being the Daguerreotype, and the second what may be termed the present era of photography, which includes the processes now known and practised.

I take Boston as my starting point for several reasons. First, because it was the first American city I visited; secondly, it was in Boston that the change first came over photography which wrought such a revolution in the art all over the United States; thirdly and severally, in Boston I noticed many things in connection with photography which differed widely from what I had known and practised in England.

Visiting the gallery of Mr. Whipple, then in Washington Street, the busiest thoroughfare in Boston, I was struck with the very large collection of Daguerreotype portraits there exhibited, but particularly with a large display of Daguerreotypes of the moon in various aspects. I had heard of Mr. Whipple's success in Daguerreotyping the moon before I left Europe, but had no idea that so much had been achieved in lunar photography at that early date until I saw Mr. Whipple's case of photographs of the moon in many phases. Those Daguerreotypes were remarkable for their sharpness and delicacy, and the many trying conditions under which they were taken. They were all obtained at Cambridge College under the superintendance of Professor Bond, but in what manner I had better allow Mr. Whipple to speak for himself, by making an extract from a letter of his, published in *The Photographic Art Journal* of America, July, 1853. Mr. Whipple says: "My first attempt at Daguerreotyping the moon was with a reflecting telescope; the mirror was five feet focus, and seven inches diameter. By putting the prepared plate directly in the focus of the reflector, and giving it an exposure of from three to five seconds, I obtained quite distinct impressions; but owing to the smallness of the image, which was only about five-eighths of an inch in diameter, and the want of clockwork to regulate the motion of the telescope, the results were very far from satisfactory.

"Having obtained permission of Professor Bond to use the large Cambridge reflector for that purpose, I renewed my experiments with high hopes of success, but soon found it no easy matter to obtain a clear, well-defined, beautiful Daguerreotype of the moon. Nothing could be more interesting than its appearance through that *magnificent* instrument : but to transfer it to the silver plate, to make something tangible of it, was quite a different thing. The "governor," that regulates the motion of the telescope, although sufficiently accurate for observing purposes, was entirely unsuitable for Daguerreotyping; as when the plate is exposed to the moon's image, if the instrument does not follow exactly to counteract the earth's motion, even to the nicety of a hair's-breadth, the beauty of the impression is much injured, or entirely spoiled. The governor had a tendency to move the instrument a little too fast, then to fall slightly behind. By closely noticing its motion, and by exposing my plates those few seconds that it exactly followed between the accelerated and retarded motion, I might obtain one or two perfect proofs in the trial of a dozen plates, other things being right. But a more serious obstacle to my success was the usual state of the atmosphere in the locality—the sea breeze, the hot and cold air commingling, although its effects were not visible to the eye; but when the moon was viewed through the telescope it had the same appearance as objects when seen through the heated air from a chimney, in a constant tremor, precluding the possibility of successful Daguerreotyping. This state of the atmosphere often continued week after week in a greater or less degree, so that an evening of perfect quiet was hailed with the greatest delight. After oft-repeated failures, I finally obtained the Daguerreotype from which the crystallotypes I send for your journal were copies; it was taken in March, 1851. The object glass only of the telescope was used. It is fifteen inches in diameter, and about twenty-three feet focal length; the image it gives of the moon varies but little from three inches, and the prepared plate had an exposure of thirteen seconds."

Copies of several of these "crystallotypes" of the moon I afterwards obtained and exhibited at the Photographic Exhibition in connection with the British Association which met in Glasgow in 1855. The "crystallotypes" were simply enlarged photographs, about eight or nine inches in diameter, and conveyed to the mind an excellent idea of the moon's surface. The orange-like form and the principal craters were distinctly marked. Indeed, so much were they admired as portraits of the moon, that one of the *savans* bought the set at the close of the exhibition.

Mr. Whipple is still a successful practitioner of our delightful art in the "Athens of the Western World," and has reaped the reward of his continuity and devotion to his favourite art. The late decision of the American law courts on the validity of Mr. Cutting's patent for the use of bromides in collodion must have laid Mr. Whipple under serious liabilities, for he used bromo-iodized negative collodion for iron development as far back as 1853.

There were many other professional photographers in the chief city of Massachusetts; but I have described the characteristics of the principal and oldest concerns. Doubtless there are many new ones since I visited the city where Benjamin Franklin served his apprenticeship as a printer; where the "colonists" in 1773, rather than pay the obnoxious "tea tax," pitched all the tea out of the ships into the waters of Boston Bay, and commenced that long struggle against oppression and unjust taxation which eventually ended in severing the North American Colonies from the mother country. With the knowledge of all this, it is the more surprising that they should now so quietly submit to what must be an obnoxious and troublesome system of taxation; for, not only have photographers to pay an annual licence of about two guineas for carrying on their trade, but also to affix a government stamp on each picture sent out, which is a further tax of about one penny on each. Surely the patience of our brother photographers on the other side of the Atlantic must be sorely tried, what with the troubles of their business, the whims and eccentricities of their sitters, Mr. Cutting's unkind cut, and the prowling visitations of the tax-collector.

NEW YORK.

WHAT a wonderful place New York is for photographic galleries! Their number is legion, and their size is mammoth. Everything is "mammoth." Their "saloons" are mammoth. Their "skylights" are mammoth. Their "tubes," or lenses, are mammoth. Their "boxes," or cameras, are mammoth; and *mammoth* is the amount of business that is done in some of those "galleries." The "stores" of the dealers in photographic "stock" are mammoth; and the most mammoth of all is the "store" of Messrs. E. & H. T. Anthony, on Broadway. This establishment is one of the many palaces of commerce on that splendid thoroughfare. The building is of iron, tall and graceful, of the Corinthian order, with Corinthian pilasters, pillars, and capitals. It is five storeys high, with a frontage of about thirty feet, and a depth of two hundred feet, running right through the "block" from Broadway to the next street on the west side of it. This is the largest store of the kind in New York; I think I may safely say, in either of the two continents, east or west, containing a stock of all sorts of photographic goods, from "sixpenny slides" to "mammoth tubes," varying in aggregate value from one-hundred-and-fifty thousand to two hundred thousand dollars. The heads of the firm are most enterprising, one taking the direction of the commercial department, and the other the scientific and experimental. Nearly all novelties in apparatus and photographic requisites pass through this house into the hands of our American *confrères* of the camera, and not unfrequently find their way to the realms of Queen Victoria on both sides of the Atlantic.

When the carte-de-visite pictures were introduced, the oldest and largest houses held aloof from them, and only reluctantly, and under pressure, took hold of them at last. Why, it is difficult to say, unless their very small size was too violent a contrast to the mammoth pictures they were accustomed to handle. Messrs. Rockwood and Co., of Broadway, were the first to make a great feature of the carte-de-visite in New York. They also introduced the "Funnygraph," but the latter had a very short life.

In the Daguerreotype days there was a "portrait factory" on Broadway, where likenesses were turned out as fast as coining, for the small charge of twenty-five cents a head. The arrangements for such rapid work were very complete. I had a dollar's worth of these "factory" portraits. At the desk I paid my money, and received four tickets, which entitled me to as many sittings when my turn came. I was shown into a waiting room crowded with people. The customers were seated on forms placed round the room, sidling their way to the entrance of the operating room, and answering the cry of "the next" in much the same manner that people do at our public baths. I being "the next," at last went into the operating room, where I found the operator stationed at the camera, which he never left all day long, except occasionally to adjust a stupid sitter. He told the next to "Sit down" and "Look thar," focussed, and, putting his hand into a hole in the wall which communicated with the "coating room," he found a dark slide ready filled with a sensitised plate, and putting it into the camera, "exposed," and saying "That will dew," took the dark slide out of the camera, and shoved it through another hole in the wall communicating with the mercury or developing room. This was repeated as many times as I wanted sittings, which he knew by the number of tickets I had given to a boy in the room, whose duty it was to look out for "the next," and collect the tickets. The operator had nothing to do with the preparation of the plates, developing, fixing, or finishing of the picture. He was responsible only for the "pose" and "time, the "developer," checking and correcting the latter occasionally by crying out "Short" or "Long" as the case might be. Having had my number of "sittings," I was requested to leave the operating room by another door which opened into a passage that led me to the "delivery desk," where, in a few minutes, I got all my four portraits fitted up in "matt, glass, and preserver,"—the pictures having been passed from the developing room to the "gilding" room, thence to the "fitting room" and the "delivery desk," where I received them. Thus they were all finished and carried away without the camera operator ever having seen them. Three of the four portraits were as fine

Daguerreotypes as could be produced anywhere. Ambrotypes, or "Daguerreotypes on glass," as some called them, were afterwards produced in much the same manufacturing manner.

There were many other galleries on Broadway: Canal Street; the Bowery; the Avenues, 1, 2 and 3; A, B, and C, Water Street; Hudson Street, by the shipping, &c., the proprietors of which conducted their business in the style most suited to their "location" and the class of customers they had to deal with; but in no case was there any attempt at that "old clothesman" —that "Petticoat Lane"—style of touting and dragging customers in by the collar. All sorts of legitimate modes of advertising were resorted to—flags flying out of windows and from the roofs of houses, handsome show cases at the doors; glowing advertisements in the newspapers, in prose and verse; circulars freely distributed among the hotels, &c; but none of that "have your picture taken," annoying, and disreputable style adopted by the cheap and common establishments in London.

Unhappily, "Sunday trading" is practised more extensively in New York than in London. Nearly all but the most respectable galleries are open on Sundays, and evidently do a thriving trade. The authorities endeavoured to stop it frequently, by summoning parties and inflicting fines, but it was no use. The fines were paid, and Sunday photography continued.

The "glass houses" of America differ entirely from what we understand by the name here; indeed, I never saw such a thing there, either by chance, accident, or design—for chance has no "glass houses" in America, only an agency; there are no accidental glass houses, and the operating rooms built by design are not "glass houses" at all.

The majority of the houses in New York and other American cities are built with nearly flat roofs, and many of them with lessening storeys from front to back, resembling a flight of two or three steps. In one of these roofs, according to circumstances, a large "skylight" is fixed, and pitched usually at an angle of 45°, and the rooms, as a rule, are large enough to allow the sitter to be placed anywhere within the radius of the light, so that any effect or any view of the face can easily be obtained.

The light is not any more actinic there than here in good weather, but they have a very great deal more light of a good quality *all the year round* than we have

The operators work generally with a highly bromized collodion, which, as a rule, they make themselves, but not throughout. They buy the gun-cotton of some good maker— Mr Tomlinson, agent for Mr. Cutting, generally supplied the best—then dissolve, iodize, and biomize to suit their working

Pyrogallic acid as an intensifier is very little used by the American operators, so little that it is not kept in stock by the dealers. Requiring some once, I had quite a hunt for it, but found some at last, stowed away as "Not Wanted," in Messrs Anthony's store. The general intensifier is what they laconically call "sulph," which is sulphuret of potassium in a very dilute solution, either flowed over the plate, or the plate is immersed in a dipping bath, after fixing, which is by far the *pleasantest* way to employ the "sulph solution." Throwing it about as some of them do is anything but agreeable. In such cases, "sulph." was the first thing that saluted my olfactories on putting my head inside one of their "dark rooms."

Up to 1860 the American photographic prints were all on plain paper, and obtained by the ammonia-nitrate of silver bath, and toned and fixed with the hyposulphite of soda and gold. The introduction of the cartes-de-visite forced the operators to make use of albumenized paper; but even then they seemed determined to adhere to the ammonia process if possible, for they commenced all sorts of experiments with that volatile accelerator, both wet and dry, some by adding ammonia and ether to an 80-grain silver bath, others by fuming, and toning with an acetate and gold bath, and fixing with hypo afterwards.

With the following "musings" on "wrappers" (not "spirit rappers," nor railway wrappers, but "carte-de-visite wrappers"). I shall conclude my rambles among the galleries of New York. Wrappers generally afford an excellent opportunity for ornamental display. Many of the wrappers of our magazines are elegantly and artistically ornamented. Nearly every pack of playing cards is done up in a beautiful wrapper. The French have given their attention to the subject of "carte-de-visite wrappers," and turned out a few unique patterns, which, however, never came much into use in this country. The Americans, more alive to fanciful and tasteful objects of ornamentation, and close imitators of the French in these matters, have made more use of carte-de-visite wrappers than we have. Many wrappers of an artistic and literary character are used by the photographers in America—some with ornamental designs; some with the address of the houses tastefully executed; others with poetical effusions, in which the cartes-de-visite are neatly wrapped up, and handed over to the sitter.

Surely a useful suggestion is here given, for wrappers are useful things in their way, and, if made up tastefully, would attract attention to the photographic establishments that issue them. Photography is so closely allied to art that it is desirable to have everything in connection with it of an elegant and artistic description The plain paper envelopes—gummed up at the ends, and difficult to get open again—are very inartistic, and anything but suitable to envelop such pretty little pictures as cartes-de-visite. Let photography encourage art and art manufactures, and art will enter into a treaty of reciprocity for their mutual advancement.—*Photographic News*, 1865.

TO DUBLIN AND BACK, WITH A GLANCE AT THE EXHIBITION.

THE bell rings; a shrill shriek; puff, puff goes the engine, and we dart away from the station at Euston Square, provided with a return ticket to Dublin, issued by the London and North Western Railway, available for one month, for the very reasonable charge of £3, first class and cabin; £2 7s. 6d. second class and cabin; or forty shillings third class and steerage, viâ Holyhead. These charges include steamboat fare and steward's fee The Exhibition Committee have made arrangements with the railway companies to run excursion trains once a fortnight at still lower rates; twenty-one shillings from London to Dublin and back, and from other places in proportion. This ticket will be good for a fortnight, and will entitle the holder to another ticket, giving him two admissions to the Exhibition for one shilling. With the ordinary monthly ticket, which is issued daily, it is quite optional whether you go by the morning or evening train; but by all means take the morning train, so that you may pass through North Wales and the Island of Anglesea in daylight. Passing through England by Rugby, Stafford, Crewe, and Chester, nothing remarkable occurs during our rapid run through that part of the country. But an "Irish Gentleman," a fellow traveller, learning our destination, kindly volunteered to enlighten us how we could best see Dublin and its lions in the shortest possible time, and advised us by all "manes" not to "lave" Dublin without seeing "Faynix Park," and taking a car drive to Howth and other places round the "Bee of Dublin." Accordingly we agreed to take his advice; but as our primary object in visiting Dublin is to see the Exhibition, we will first attend to that on our arrival in the Irish capital; and if, after that, time will permit, the extraneous lions will receive our attention. First of all, we must describe how we got there, what we saw on the way, and what were our impressions on entering Dublin Bay.

As we said before, nothing particular occurred during our journey through England to excite our attention or curiosity; but on passing into Wales—Flintshire—our attention is at once arrested by the difference of the scenery through which we pass. Soon after leaving Chester, we get a sight of the river Dee on our right, and continue to run down by its side past Flint, Bagillt, Holywell, and Mostyn, then we take a bend to the left and skirt a part of the Irish Channel past Rhyl, Abergele, and Colwyn to Conway, with its extensive ruins of a once vast and noble castle, through, under, and about the ruins of which the double lines of iron rails twist and twine and sinuously encoil themselves like a boa constrictor of civilisation and demolisher of wrecks, ruins, and vestiges of the feudal ages and semi-barbarism Our iron charger dashes up to the very walls of the ancient stronghold, close past the base of a tower, and right under the hanging ruins of another, which is in truth a "baseless fabric," but no "vision," for there it is suspended in mid air, a fabric without a base, holding on to its surroundings by the cohesive power of their early attachments. We rush into the very bowels of the keep itself, snorting and puffing defiance to the memoried sternness of the grim warriors who once held the place against all intruders Anyone who has not had an opportunity before of visiting North Wales should keep a sharp look-out right and left, and they will get a peep at most of the principal places on the route: the Welsh mountains on the left, their summits illuminated by the sun sinking towards the west, and the mass of them thrown into shadow in fine contrast.

Now we are at Penmænmawr, that pretty little watering place, with its neat-looking houses snugly nestling in the laps of the hills, and we pass along so close to the sea, we can feel the spray from the waves as they break on the shore.

Passing Llanfairfechan and Aber we are at Bangor, and almost immediately afterwards make a dive into the long, dark chamber of the Tubular Bridge, with a shriek and rumbling rattle that is almost startling. In a few seconds we are out into the daylight again, and get a view of the Straits of Menai, and on the right-hand side, looking back, get an excellent sight of the Tubular Bridge. At the moment of our passing, a ship in full sail was running before the wind through the Straits, which added considerably to the picturesque beauty of the scene. On the left a fine view of the "Suspension Bridge" is obtained. We are soon past Llanfair, and across that bleak and desolate part of the island of Anglesea between the Menai Straits and the Valley. Arriving at Holyhead, we go on board the steamer which is to carry us across the Channel to Dublin. The boat not starting immediately, but giving us a little time to look around, we go on shore again, and saunter up and down the narrow hilly streets of Holyhead, listening in vain for the sound of a word spoken in our mother tongue. Not a word could we hear, not a word of English could we get without asking for it. The most of the people can speak English with a foreign-like accent, but you seldom hear it unless you address them in English. Even the urchins in the streets carry on their games and play in the Welsh and unintelligible sounds resembling language.

We also had time to examine the stupendous breakwater which the Government is building at Holyhead to form a harbour of refuge. The wall is a mile and three-quarters in length, and of immense thickness, in the form of three terraces, the highest towards the sea. At one place we noticed that the solid slatey rocks were hewn and dressed into shape, and thus formed part of the wall itself, a mixture of Nature's handiwork and the work of man.

Time to go on board again, and as the wind was blowing rather strong, we expected to have a rough voyage of it; and sure enough we had, for we were scarcely clear of the sheltering kindliness of the sea wall and the "north stack" till our vessel began to "pitch and toss," and roll and creak, and groan in agony; and so highly sympathetic were we that we did the same, and could not help it, do what we could. Strong tea, brandy and water, were all no use. Down we went, like prostrate sinners as we were, on our knees, with clasped hands, praying for the winds and the waves "to be still;" but they did not heed our prayer in the least, and kept up their inhumane howling, dancing, and jumbling until, by the time we reached the middle of the Channel, we began to think that the captain had lost his course, and that we were somewhere between Holyhead and purgatory, if not in purgatory itself, being purged of our sins, and becoming internally pure and externally foul. But we discovered that we, and not the captain, had lost the course and the even tenour of our way, for we fancied—perhaps it was only fancy—that we could hear him humming snatches of old song, among them "Oh ! steer my bark to Erin's Isle!" and soon the mountains of Wicklow are in sight. As we near, and get under the lee of the land—for it was a stiff "sou'-wester" that bothered us—our sensations and feelings begin to improve, and we pick ourselves up out of the mire, and turn our eyes eagerly and hopefully towards the Emerald Isle, and Dublin Bay more particularly.

As we approach the Bay, the Carlingford Hills can be seen on the right, and a little more southwards Lambay and Ireland's Eye. The latter island is rugged and precipitous, seaward, in the extreme—a barren and desolate-looking spot, possessing an unenviable notoriety on account of the murder of a lady by her husband having been committed there a few years ago : Howth, the light-house, and the Bailey Rock, where the *Queen Victoria* steamer was wrecked, now attract our attention. And, as nearly as we can remember, these are the most striking features on the north side of the Bay. On the south the Harbour of Kingstown is distinctly visible, and we saw the mail steamer which crosses from Holyhead to Kingstown, a distance of sixty miles, in three and a-half hours, blowing off her steam. By paying a little extra you can cross in the mail steamers, if you wish, but it is not worth while paying the difference, as the ordinary steamers cross from Holyhead to Dublin in about five and a-half hours. All round the south side of the Bay we could trace the Kingstown and Dublin railway, which is the oldest line but one in the United Queendoms of Great Britain and Ireland. An obelisk commemorates the visit of the last of the four Georges to Ireland in 1821. Right over Kingstown the Killinny Hills are to be seen, and all along the water line the Bay is studded with pretty little villas, and the scene is truly beautiful. If possible, arrange your entrance into the Bay of Dublin in the early morning, for then the sun, rising in the east, lights up the subjects to the very best advantage, and throws a charm about them which they do not exhibit at any other time of the day. By waiting at Holyhead for the early morning boat you can easily manage this. But now we are at the North Wall, and on landing are besieged by carmen to have a "rowl," and jumping on to one of those light, odd-looking, jaunting cars which are one of the institutions of the country, we are "rowled" up the North Wall for nearly a mile, past the Docks, over the drawbridges, and past the Custom House—a large stone building, too large for the business of the port—along Carlisle Bridge, down Westmoreland Street, past the Bank of Ireland—once the Houses of Parliament—and up Dame Street, leaving the College on our left, and passing King William's statue, representing a mounted Roman with *gilded* laurels and ornamental toga, we arrive at Jury's Hotel, a commercial and family house of superior arrangements which was well recommended to us before we left London; and here we rest.

After breakfast, and having made ourselves internally and externally comfortable, we start for the Exhibition, which is within easy walking distance of the hotel; but the car fares are so very moderate that we prefer a "rowl." The fare is sixpence a "set down," that is, you may ride from one end of the city to the other for sixpence, but if you get off to post a letter, or buy an umbrella to keep the rain off—for the cars have no covering—that is a "set down;" and so every time you get down and get up again you have sixpence to pay, no matter how short the distance you are taken each time. So we hailed a car at the door of the hotel, determined to be "rowled" to the Exhibition for sixpence each. We go down Dame Street, across College Green, up Grafton Street, along the west and south sides of St. Stephen's Green or Square to Earlsfort Terrace and the principal entrance to the Dublin Exhibition, which occupies the site of what was formerly Coburg Gardens.

Arriving at the entrance-hall, we pay our admission fee, and on passing the registering turnstiles we are at once in the sculpture hall on the ground floor, the contents of which we shall notice more particularly by-and-by. Passing through the Sculpture Hall we are within the western transept, or winter garden portion of the Exhibition. This transept is 500 feet long and of lofty proportions, with galleries on each side, and tastefully hung with the banners and flags of the nations exhibiting. The northern court is about 300 feet long, also of iron and glass, with galleries running round both sides similar to the western transept. The ground floor and part of the galleries of the northern court are devoted to the productions of the United Kingdom. On the north side of the northern court is the machinery department, both at rest and in motion. Here machines of the most delicate and ponderous nature are at work. There a forge-hammer daintily cracking nuts, or coming down with a crushing force at the will of the attendant. In another place a delicate curving-machine is at work; and another can be seen making steel pens. There are high pressure engines, sewing machines, and photographic rolling-presses. Indeed, there is almost everything to be seen and everything going on that is instructive, edifying, and amusing. The Exhibition building is small, but well arranged and compact, and partakes of the character of an art and industrial exhibition and place of amusement and recreation, like our Crystal Palace at Sydenham, with ornamental gardens and archery grounds attached. The gardens are small—a little larger than the area of the building itself—but most tastefully laid out. And there are fountains and grottoes, and rockeries and cascades, with flowers growing about them, which give the whole place a pleasant, healthy, and delightful appearance. Stepping out of the western transept into the gardens, we found the band of the 78th Highlanders playing in the centre, and their pipers walking about the grounds ready to take up the strains of music in another key, for presently we saw them marching about, playing "Hielan' Skirls," and sounding the loud pibroch, with a five-bag power that was more stunning than the nocturnal wailings of a dozen or two Kilkenny cats. The directors furnish music and offer other inducements to secure a good attendance, and their efforts ought to be successful, and it is to be hoped they will be so.

On the first day of our visit there was a grand archery meeting, and the turn-out of Dublin belles was double in numbers. There was a large attendance of bowmen, too, and belles and beaux were banging away at the targets most unmercifully in keen contest for the prize; whether it was a medal, a ring, or an heiress, we could not learn; but if nothing more than the privilege of entering the lists against such lovely competitors, the bowmen ought to have been satisfied; but we don't suppose they were, for men are both ambitious and avaricious, and probably some of them hoped to win a prize medal, kill a beauty, and catch an heiress all at once, with one swift arrow sent whizzing and quivering into the very heart and gilded centre of the gaily-painted target.

Perched up on the top of the cascades we noticed a double sliding-front stereoscopic camera, and doubtless Mr. York was busy photographing the scene we have been describing—impressions of which the London Stereoscopic Company will probably issue ere long. We must, however, leave this gay scene and turn our attention to other things, certainly not more attractive; but duty calls us away from beauty, and we must submit.

Re-entering the Exhibition building, we seek the photographic department, which we readily find on the ground-floor, between the music hall and the first class refreshment-room. Entering from the Belgian department in the western transept, we find three rooms in the main building devoted to the exhibition of photographs, and a lobby between the rooms pretty well filled with apparatus To Sir J. Jocelyn Coghill are photographers indebted for obtaining so much space for their works, and in such a get-at-able situation; but it is a pity the rooms are not better lighted. Many of the pictures on the screens are very indistinctly seen, and some are in dark corners scarcely to be seen at all.

The foreign department, which is the first room we enter, is mainly made up of reproductions of old and modern engravings, and copies of drawings and paintings. One very remarkable photograph on the wall of this room is an immense magnification of a flea, by A. Duvette. What a subject for the camera!—one that suggests in sporting phraseology something more than the "find," the "chase," and the "death"

A panoramic view of Rome, by M. Petagna, is a great achievement in panoramic photography. There are seven impressions from 15 by 12 plates, all carefully joined, and of equal tone. The point of view is "Tasso's Oak," and the panorama gives us an excellent idea of Rome at the present day.

The British part of the Photographic Exhibition in Dublin might be very properly denominated an enlargement of the Society's exhibition now open in Conduit Street, London. Nearly all the principal exhibitors there have sent duplicates of their chief works to the Dublin Exhibition. There is Robinson's beautiful picture of "Brenda," his "May Gatherers," "Sunshine," " Autumn," " Somebody Coming," " Bringing home the May," &c., all old and familiar pictures, every one of which we have seen before. Robinson himself in his study—a beautiful piece of photography, even to his black velvet coat. Blanchard also repeats his " Zealot," and other subjects, and sends a frame full of his exquisite stereographs. England also sends some of his charming stereoscopic pictures of Switzerland and Savoy. Bedford's contribution is much the same as his pictures in the London exhibition Among them are his lovely Warwickshire pictures. Wet-plate photography is well represented, both in landscape, portraiture, and composition. Among the latter, Rejlander is most prominent. One frame containing some pictures showing the "expression" of the hands, illustrates Rejlander's artistic knowledge and ability more than many of his other pictures. None but a thoughtful and accomplished artist could have disposed of those members in such a skilful manner. His pictures of "Grief," "The Mote," "The Wayfarer," "'Tis Light within—Dark without," and his "Home, Sweet Home," reveal exquisite feeling in his treatment of such subjects. Thurston Thompson also exhibits some of his fine reproductions of Turner. There is "Crossing the Brook," and "Childe Harold's Pilgrimage;" but a much larger collection of these beautiful copies of Turner's pictures are now on view at Marion's, in Soho Square.

Dry-plate photography is exemplified in all its phases, from the oldest form of albumen alone, to the latest modifications with collodion, collodio-albumen, Fothergill, tannin, malt, &c The most prominent and largest contributor to this department is Mr. Mudd. In addition to the duplicates in the London Exhibition, he sends a few others, the most remarkable of which is a large view of "Borrowdale," a noble picture, exquisitely treated, showing masses of light and shade and pleasing composition which stamp it at once as a work of art.

Mr. G. S. Penny exhibits some very fine examples of the

tannin and malt process. They are soft and delicate, and possess sufficient force to give powerful contrasts when necessary. Mr. Bull's tannin and malt pictures are also very good; his "Menai Bridge" particularly so.

The amateur photographers, both wet and dry, make a good show. And among the Irish followers of our delightful art are Sir J. J. Coghill, who exhibits twelve very pretty views of the neighbourhood of Castletownsend. Dr. Hemphill, of Clonmel, also exhibits a variety of subjects, many of them pretty compositions and excellent photography.

Dr. Bailey, of Monaghan, contributes both landscapes and portraits of very good quality. Mr. T. M. Brownrigg shows seventeen photographs all excellent examples of the wet collodion process. Many of them are exquisite bits of photography, and evince an amount of thought and care in selecting the best point of view, arranging the lines of the subject, and catching the best effect of light so as to make them pictures, which is seldom attended to by professional photographers.

Amongst the Irish professional photographers in landscape work, Mr. F. Mares, of Dublin, stands pre-eminent. His pictures of Killarney, and views in the county of Wicklow, are very beautiful, and give evidence of a cultivated eye and artistic taste in the selection of his subjects and points of view. There are other excellent views and architectural subjects by Irish photographers; but we are sorry to observe some that really ought not to have been admitted. They are not even average photography, being utterly destitute of manipulative skill, and as deficient in art-excellence as they can well be.

One branch of landscape, or, we should say, marine photography, is without competition. We refer to those exquisite and charming transparencies by Mr. C. S. Breese. His moonlight effect is wonderfully managed; the water looks "alive," and the moonlight is dancing on the waves just as we have seen it far away upon the sea. His "Breaking Wave" is marvellous, coming to shore with its cavernous curl; we almost fancy we hear its angry howl as it dashes itself into foam on the beach. We have seen such a wave sweep the deck of a ship before now, and know well with what a ponderous weight and velocity it comes; and we wonder the more at Mr. Breese's success in catching the wave in such a position. We cannot, however, speak so highly of the "Sunlight" effects by the same artist. The transparencies as photographs are inimitable; but there is colour introduced into the skies which ought to have been taken up by the rocks, and so carried into the foregrounds of the pictures, to be natural. Such warm skies and cold middle distances and foregrounds are too antagonistic for the harmony of nature.

In portraiture our Irish brethren of the camera contribute somewhat liberally. In that branch we noticed the works of Messrs. Robertson and Co, S. Lawrence, and G. Schroeder, of Grafton Street; Millard and Robinson, Nelson and Marshall, and S. Chancellor, of Sackville Street, Dublin. T. Cranfield, Grafton Street, also exhibits some photographs beautifully coloured in oil.

The most eminent English photographers also show up well. We saw the well-known works of Mayall, Silvy, Claudet, Maull and Co, and others, eminent in plain photography. Messrs. Lock and Whitfield exhibit a Royal case of exquisitely coloured photographs of the Prince and Princess of Wales, and Prince Albert Victor. Mr G. Wharton Simpson also exhibits a few specimens of his beautiful collodio-chloride of silver printing process. There are some lovely specimens of that process with such a frightfully ugly name, but which, in plain parlance, are pictures on opal glass, though Mr. Helsby has christened them "Helioaristotypia miniatures." As a set-off to this, the next dry process that is discovered should be called "Hydrophobiatypia."

In amateur portraiture, Mr. H. Cooper, Jun., exhibits a large number of his clever life studies, as well as those quiet and charming representations of his friends in their habits as they live.

Solar camera enlargements are very numerously contributed. Mr. Claudet sends some good pictures enlarged by solar camera, and developed with gallic acid. Mr. Solomon also has some very good examples of enlarging. Dr. D. Van Monckhoven is an exhibitor of the capabilities of his direct printing camera. Mr. Mayall exhibits two series of very interesting enlargements by the Monckhoven camera, printed direct on albumenized paper; one is Tennyson, in eight different sizes, from a one-ninth to a life-size head on a whole sheet of paper ; of the other, Captain Grant, there are seven similar pictures. These photographs are all bold and vigorous and uniform in colour, and come nearer to our idea of what an enlargement should be than anything we have yet seen. Of the two, that of the Poet-Laureate is the best; the other is harsher, which is in all probability due to the difference in the subjects themselves. We can easily imagine that the face of Captain Grant, bronzed and weather-beaten as it must be, will present more obstacles to the obtaining of a soft negative than that of Tennyson. Specimens of photo-sculpture are also to be seen at the Dublin Exhibition, many of which are very pretty and life-like statuettes ; but some of the figures seem much too large in the *busts*, and the plinths on which the figures of ladies stand are in very bad taste ; being diminishing beads of a circular form, they suggest the idea of a huge crinoline just dropped.

Nearly all the denominations of photography have their representative forms and impressions in this Exhibition ; and the history of the art, from the early days of the Daguerreotype to the latest vagary of the present day, may be traced in the collection of photographs spread before you on the walls and screens of the Dublin International Exhibition. There is the Daguerreotype, the Ambrotype, and the collodiotype, which ought to have been known as the Archertype; for the wet collodion process, although it is the most important of all the discoveries in photography that have been made since the first pictures were obtained by Wedgwood, is without a name conferring honour on the man who first applied collodion to photography. Archer's name is generally associated with it, but without taking that definite and appellative form it ought to. We know that another claimant has been "cutting in" for the honour, but unless that claim can be "backed up" by data, we are not disposed to believe that it was anterior to 1851—the year of the first exhibition; at that date we know that Mr. Archer took photographs on collodionized glass plates. Then why should we not honour Archer as the French honoured Daguerre, and call the wet collodion process the Archertype?

In printing and toning, there are samples of nearly all the formulæ that have been discovered since the days of printing on plain salted paper and fixing in "hypo" only. There are prints on plain paper and on albumenized paper, toned and fixed in every conceivable way. There are prints on glass, porcelain, and ivory; prints in carbon, from the negative direct; and impressions in printer's ink from plates, blocks, and lithographic stones, which have had the subjects transferred to them by the aid of photography. There are Wothlytypes, and Simpsontypes, and Tooveytypes, and all the other types that have sprung from a desire to introduce novelties into the art.

In graphs and the various forms and fanciful applications of photography to portraiture, &c., there are stereographs and micrographs, and the old-fashioned "sit-on-a-chair" graphs, the "stand-not-at-ease" graphs, the "small carte" graph, the "large carte" graph, the "casket gem" graph, the "magnesium" graph, the "cameo" graph, the "double-stupid" graph, and the latest of all novelties, the "turn-me-round" graph. The latter is a great curiosity, and must have been suggested by a recollection of that "scientific toy" of ancient manufacture with which we used to awaken the wonder of our little brothers and sisters at Christmas parties when we were boys, by twirling before their astonished eyes a piece of cardboard with a bird painted on one side and a cage on the other, both pictures being seen at the same time during the rapid revolution of the card.

In apparatus there is not much to talk about, the Pantascopic camera being the chief novelty. There are several of the manufacturers exhibiting in the photographic department, but we could not reconcile ourselves to the circumstance of Mr. Dallmeyer not exhibiting in the right place. His name is honoured by photographers, and he should have honoured Photography by going in under her colours. If he must go to the "scientific department," he ought to have gone there with his scientific instruments alone, and shown his photographic apparatus in the place assigned for that purpose. True, he makes a handsome show, but that does not atone for his mistake. Photographers are queer animals—jealous of their rights, and as sensitive to slight as their plates are to light, and we fear we are ourselves not much better. A large majority of photographers stand by Mr. Dallmeyer, and very justly believe in his 1 and 2 B's as shippers do in A 1's at Lloyd's; and *his* stand should have been in the photographic department.

In other parts of the Exhibition building there are various subjects highly interesting to photographers.

The chemical department has its attractions in samples of collodio-chloride of silver, prepared by Messrs. Mawson and Swan, for the opal printing process and the Simpsontype. Specimens of each type are also to be seen there; and there are other chemicals used in photography, even to dextrine and starch: the purity of the latter is known by the size and length of its crystals.

In metallurgy there is also something to interest photographers. Messrs. Johnson and Sons exhibit some very fine samples of nitrate of silver, double and treble crystallized, silver dippers, chloride of gold, nitrate of uranium, and other scarce metals.

Messrs. Johnson, Matthey, and Co. also exhibit some fine samples of nitrate of silver and chloride of gold, and some wonderful specimens of magnesium, in various forms, in wire and ribbon. One coil of ribbon is 4,800 feet long, and weighs 40 ounces; and there is an obelisk of magnesium about 20 inches high, and weighing 162 ounces.

There are many other things in this case of great value which have a photographic bearing—amongst these a platinum boiler, valued at £1,500, for the concentration and rectification of sulphuric acid; a platinum alembic, value £350, for the separation and refining of gold and silver; also an ingot of platinum, weighing 3,200 ounces, and valued at £3,840. The exhibitors say that "such a mass of fused platinum is never likely to be again produced." The whole of the contents of Messrs. Johnson, Matthey, and Co.'s case of precious metals, most of which have a direct or indirect application to photography, are estimated at the enormous value of £16,000!

Mining, too, has its attractions for us; and as we near the Nova Scotia division of the Exhibition building the needle of our observation dips towards a bar of pure gold, weighing 48 pounds, and valued at £2,200 sterling.

By the gentlemanly courtesy of the Rev. Dr. Honeyman, Honorary Secretary and Commissioner in Dublin, from the province of Nova Scotia, we were favoured with a "lift" of this valuable lump of gold, and we could not help exclaiming, "What a lot of chloride this would make!" But we had to "drop it" very quickly, for the muscles of our fingers could not bear the strain of holding it more than a few seconds. This bar of gold was obtained from very rich quartz, specimens of which are to be seen near it; and Dr. Honeyman informed us that the average daily remuneration from such quartz was thirty shillings sterling per man.

It is not generally known that the province of Nova Scotia is so rich in gold; but, from statistics by the Chief Commissioner of Mines for the province, we find that the average yield of the Nova Scotia quartz is over 19 dwt. per ton, and richer than the quartz of Australia; and the deeper the shafts are sunk the richer the quartz becomes. In 1864 the total yield from all the gold districts of Nova Scotia was 20,022 ounces, 18 dwts., 13 grs. Gold dust and scales have also been found in the sands on the sea coast of the province, and in the sands of Sable Island, which is eighty miles distant, in the Atlantic Ocean. Having in our own colonies such an abundance of one of the precious metals so extensively used in the practice of our art, photographers need not be under any apprehension of having their supplies cut off.

Continuing our general survey, we stumble upon many things of considerable interest. But, as our space will only allow us to particularize those articles which have a photographic attraction, direct or indirect, we must as far as possible imagine ourselves something like animated photometers for the time being, registering the aspects, changes, and remarkable phenomena connected with our art, and whatever can be applied to photography and the use of photographers; or whatever photography can be applied to, artistically or commercially considered.

Of some things non-photographic, but of interest to photographers as well as others, we may be induced to say a little; but of most subjects foreign to our profession we shall simply say to our readers, "We have seen such wondrous things, go ye and do likewise."

We finished our last paper with a few comments on what was photographically interesting in the province of Nova Scotia. Passing from that to the provinces of the Lower and Upper Canadas, which are very properly placed next door to each other, we are struck with some very good and interesting photographs of Canadian scenery, both plain and in colours, and a frame of portraits of the delegates of the British North American Confederation. Samples of all kinds of native and Indian manufactures, and specimens of mineral ores, chiefly iron and copper, are also displayed here.

Pursuing our way southwards from the Colonial division of the galleries, we come to China and Japan. The geographical and relative positions of the countries exhibiting are not strictly adhered to in the plan of the Exhibition, so we must, of necessity, make some "long legs," and experience some imaginary transitions of temperature during our journey of observation. In Japan we stop to look at a life-size group of female figures, representing a princess at her toilette, attended by four female slaves, books illustrated with wood-cuts, plain and coloured, bronzes, and many other articles of art and manufacture, by the Japanese, of much interest.

In China, there is a State bedstead of great beauty, books of paintings upon rice-paper, and many beautiful bronzes, carvings, and other specimens of Chinese art.

We pass through Turkey, and next come to Siam, but the latter country does not exhibit much, except of a "seedy" character. We admit we are sometimes addicted to making puns, but the Siamese send puns for exhibition. There is an article called "pun," which is "prepared lime, coloured pink with turmeric," but to what use it is applied we have not been enlightened.

Passing through France, Austria, Prussia, Belgium, and Holland, without stopping to notice anything particularly, and turning into the south corridor, we enter the Water Colour Gallery, which we quickly leave, sighing, "How unlike that beautiful and attractive section of the Art Treasure Exhibition at Manchester in 1857!" Hastening into the Central Picture Gallery, we are much struck with the different appearance it presents, and find numbers of ladies and gentlemen admiring the numerous productions by painters belonging to the various foreign schools. Among these works are some grand subjects, both in historical and ideal composition, and landscape representations. This gallery has a particularly noble and handsome appearance. It is oblong, well-lighted, and open in the middle, by which means the Sculpture Hall, which is underneath, is lighted. The sides of the gallery next the open space are handsomely railed round, and pedestals, with marble busts and statuettes on them, are tastefully arranged at intervals, leaving room enough for you to look down into the Sculpture Hall below. What with the fine pictures on the walls and staircase, and the noble statues in marble about and below, you cannot but come to the conclusion that this is a noble temple of art.

We next enter the east front room, which contains the works of the Belgian artists. Many of these paintings are very finely conceived and executed. The largest and most striking of them is the "Defeat of the Duke of Alençon's Troops by the Citizens of Antwerp," painted by A. Dillens.

Now we enter the Great Picture Gallery, which is devoted to the painters belonging to the British school. Here we find many of the well-known works from the National Gallery and Kensington Museum. There are examples of the works of Callcott, Collins, Wilkie, Wilson, Turner, Landseer, Mulready, Etty, Egg, Ward, Leslie, and a host of others. Her Majesty the Queen also sends several pictures from her private collection, as examples of the works of Winterhalter, Thomas, and Stanfield. Nearly all the British artists are creditably represented in the Dublin International Art Exhibition.

We next come to the Collection of Ancient Masters in the North Gallery, which we enter from the North Corridor. To this part of the Fine Art Exhibition the Earl of Portarlington is the most liberal contributor. He sends examples of Titian, Rubens, Carlo Dolci, Tintorette, Canalette, Claude, Watteau, Rembrandt, Gerard Dow, Schneiders, Vandevelde, Sir Joshua Reynolds, Sir Peter Lely, and others. The Marquis of Drogheda also sends several examples of the same masters, some of them very fine ones. Sir Charles Coote sends a great many paintings; among them a Murillo, a Guido, and a Gainsborough.

Thence we pass into the Mediæval Court, where we find nothing but croziers, sacramental cups and plates, carved panels for pulpits and clerks' desks, reminding us of "responses" and "amens." These we leave to Churchmen, enthusiastic Puseyites, and devotees of Catholicism. And we wend our way round the galleries, passing through Switzerland and Italy into the United Kingdom, where we stop to examine some of the art manufactures peculiar to Ireland, and are particularly interested in the specimens of Irish bog oak, carved most tastefully into various ornaments, such as brooches, pins, paper-knives, &c., and sculptured into humorous and characteristic statuettes. The most noticeable of that class of Irish art and industry is a clever group, entitled, "Where's the man that dare tread on my coat?" This really humorous and artistic statuette is one of a group of two. One is a rollicking Irishman brandishing his shillelah over his head and trailing his coat on the ground, which is the Irishman's challenge for a fight at such places as Donnybrook Fair. The other Irishman, who is equally ready for a "row," is in the act of treading on the coat, as an acceptance of the challenge. The story is so cleverly told, that we almost fancy we see the fight begin, and hear the shillelahs cracking crowns in a genuine Irish row.

Pushing on through India to the British Colonies again, whence we started, we descend to the ground floor, and resume our survey of Sweden, Norway, Italy, and Rome, and turn into the Music Hall, which is on the south side of the entrance and Statuary Hall. Here we find the organ builders at work on the grand organ, blowing up one pipe after another, and producing such volumes of inharmonious sounds that we are glad to leave them to the full and hearty enjoyment of their pipes, choids, discords, and bellows-blowing. The walls of the Music Hall are nearly covered with cartoons and paintings of a high class, some of them so high that we require an opera-glass to bring them within the range of our visual organs.

We next enter the Sculpture Hall with a view of examining the statues and describing them carefully. But they are so numerous that we can only find space to call attention to the most striking. There are over three hundred pieces of sculpture from various countries, comprising colossal and life-size figures, groups, busts, statuettes, and alto-relievos in marble and bronze. The most attractive of the marble statues are "Michael Angelo, when a child, sculpturing the head of a Faun" (his first work), by Emilio Zocchi, of Florence. The earnestness of purpose and devotion to his task are wonderfully expressed in the countenance of the boy-sculptor. Plying the hammer and chisel actively and vigorously, every part of the figure betokens a thorough abandonment to his occupation. A very remarkable work by a lady sculptor—Miss Harriett Hosmer—entitled "The Sleeping Faun," is the very opposite to the other, in its complete abandonment to repose. This fine statue has been purchased by Mr. Guiness, and we were told he had given a munificent sum for it. Another piece of exquisite beauty and daring skill in marble working is "The Swinging Girl," by Pietro Magni, of Milan, the sculptor of "The Reading Girl," which attracted so much attention in the International Exhibition of 1862. The figure of the girl swinging is beautifully modelled, and entirely free from contact with the base; and is supported only by the swing attached to the branch of a tree, and the hand of a boy giving action to the subject. "Ophelia," by W. C. Marshall, is perhaps the most poetic conception of the loveliest and most mournful of Shakespeare's creations that has ever been sculptured. It is almost impossible to look at this touching representation of Ophelia in her madness without exclaiming, in a modified quotation of her own description of Hamlet—

"O, what a gentle mind is here o'erthrown."

But we must stop. To go on in this way describing all the beautiful works of art in the Dublin Exhibition would fill a volume. Already we have allowed our admiration to carry us beyond the limits we had assigned ourselves. We have been tempted to describe more than photographic works, but none that have not a value artistically or otherwise to photographers. We recommend all our readers that possibly can to go and see for themselves. The trip is a very pleasant one, and need not be expensive; nor need much time be spent unnecessarily. A week's absence from business will give you five clear days in Dublin, the other two only being occupied in travelling. Five days will be amply sufficient to see the Exhibition and the "extraneous lions" of Dublin also. If your time is limited, give a carman a job to "rowl" you to the principal places of interest. But "by all means" select a rough, ragged, red-headed, laughing-faced Irishman for your jarvey, and depend upon it he will keep you in good humour during the whole of your trip. And every time you come to a public-house he will say his "horse wants a dthrink," and "Won't yer honours have a dthrop?" as if he was going to stand treat; but of course you know what he means; besides, the idea of allowing a carman to treat his fare is not to be entertained for a moment, nor can you resist the good-humoured intimation of his desire to drink your health, for which honour, as a matter of course, you pay costs.

Having endeavoured to conduct our readers to Dublin, and give them a glance at the Exhibition, photographically and generally, we shall now take our leave of the capital of Ireland, and return to town in much the same manner as we went. We leave the Irish capital at 1.30 in the afternoon, and, after a pleasant and quiet run across the Channel, enter Holyhead harbour about seven o'clock. This arrangement gives you an opportunity of seeing the Welsh coast to the best advantage as you approach. Stepping into the train which is waiting our arrival, we are speedily on our way home. At Rugby we have to change, and wait a little; but before leaving there we pass the sign which only old masons and travellers know, and are provided with a first-class bed and *board*, and so make ourselves comfortable for the night. We know nothing more of the remainder of the journey. Old Somnus has charge of us inside, and an old kind-hearted guard takes care of us outside, until we are aroused by the guard's "Good morning, gentlemen!" about six o'clock, a.m., within a few miles of Euston Square. In conclusion, we sincerely recommend as many of our readers as can to take a trip " to Dublin and back," and a glance at the Dublin International Exhibition.

PHOTOGRAPHY IN THE NORTH.

On a recent journey northwards, I was tempted to stop at York, take a look at the Exhibition there, and see if there were anything worth notice in the Photographic Department. That part of the Exhibition is exceedingly scanty, but the best Yorkshire photographers are well represented, both in landscape and portraiture. Among the contributors are the names of Sarony, Glaisby, Holroyd, Gowland, and other well-known names. Mr. Sarony exhibits a couple of frames containing several "new photo-crayons," cartes-de-visite vignettes, which are very sketchy and effective, exhibiting those free and "dashy lines" and "hatchings" so characteristic of the "softening off" of artistic crayon drawings. This effect may be produced by a process of double printing, but it is more likely to have been obtained direct in the camera from a screen, having the edges of the aperture "softened off" with some free touches, the screen, in all probability, being placed between the lens and the sitter. Mr. Sarony also exhibits some large photographs very beautifully finished in colours. Messrs. Gowland exhibit, in a revolving case, a very unique collection of medallions and vignettes, both plain and coloured, mounted on tinted grounds, which give the pictures a very chaste and delicate appearance. The photographs themselves are exquisite bits of artistic pose and careful manipulation. They also exhibit a charming vignette of twenty-nine young ladies, all cleverly arranged, each figure sharp and distinct, and evidently recognisable portraits. This picture reminds one of Watteau, for the figures are in the woods, only, instead of semi-nude nymphs, the sitters are all properly and fashionably dressed young ladies. Messrs. Holroyd contribute some very excellent cartes-de-visite and enlargements. Mr. E. C. Walker, of Liverpool, exhibits some very beautiful opalotypes, or "photographs on enamelled glass." Mr. Swan, Charing Cross, London, also sends specimens of his crystal cube portraits. Mr. A. H. Clarke, a deaf and dumb photographer, exhibits some very good groups of the Princess of Wales, Lady Wharncliffe, Lady Maud Lascelles, Countess Granville, and the Hon. Mrs. Hardinge, taken in the conservatory, when the Princess and suite were on a visit to Studley Royal, Yorkshire.

Amongst the landscape photographs are to be found some of Bedford's finest views of Egypt and Jerusalem, Devonshire and Warwickshire, the beauties of which are so well known to everyone interested in photography. Some of the local views by local artists are very fine; W. P. Glaisby's views of York Minster are capital, especially the interiors. Messrs. Jackson Brothers, of Oldham, exhibit some very fine views, and show what atmospheric effects the camera is capable of rendering. That view of "Birstall Church" is a perfect master-piece of photo-aerial perspective. There are also a considerable number of photographic productions from the South Kensington Museum. Mr. Gregson, of Halifax, exhibits some excellent photographs of machinery. In apparatus there is nothing novel or striking, there being but one case of cameras, &c., exhibited by a London maker. There is a "water agitator" in the machinery "annexe," for washing photographic prints, but the invention is more ingenious than effective, for the water is not agitated sufficiently, except in the immediate neighbourhood of the fan or "agitator," which moves backwards and forwards in the water, in a manner somewhat similar to the motion of the pendulum of a clock, and so laves the water to and fro; but the force is not sufficient to prevent the prints from lying close together at the extremities of the trough, and imperfect washing is sure to be the result. The motion is given to the "agitator" by the water falling on a small wheel, something like "Williams's revolving print washing machine."

To describe the Exhibition itself: It is rather like a "compound mixture" of the church, the shop, and the show. The "Great Hall" is something like the nave of a wooden cathedral, with galleries running all round, and a grand organ at the end, peeling forth, at intervals, solemn strains of long measure. Over the organ, in white letters on a red ground, is the quotation, "He hath made all things beautiful in his time."

The show cases on the floor of the Grand Hall are arranged as indiscriminately as the shops in Oxford Street. In one case there are exhibited samples of Colman's mustard, in that next to it samples of "Elkington and Co.'s plated goods," and in another close by are samples of saddlery, which give the place more the business aspect of a bazaar than the desirable and advantageous classification of an exhibition. Then you are reminded of the show by the frequent ringing of a loud bell, and cries of "This way to the fairy fountain, just going to begin, only twopence." Such things jar on the ears and nerves of quiet visitors, and are only expected in such a place as the Polytechnic in London.

The great features of the York Exhibition are the picture galleries; and here a better order of things prevails. The collections are classified; one gallery, or part of it, being devoted to the works of the old masters, another to the modern, and another to the water colours. Among the old masters are some fine portraits by Velasquez, Tintoretto, Rembrandt, Vandyke, Sir Joshua Reynolds, Gainsborough, Sir Peter Leley, and others. And some of those grand old landscapes by Salvator Rosa, Rubens, Claude, Wilson, the English Claude, and George Morland, such pictures as are rarely seen out of private collections. The modern masters are abundantly represented by Wilkie, Etty, Frith, Westall, Faed, Cope, E. Nicol, Stanfield, Linnell, and a host of others. Amongst the water colours are many fine examples of the works of Turner, the Richardsons (father and sons), Birket Foster, &c., &c.

Sculpture is very faintly represented, but there is a charming little Canova, Dirce, exhibited by Lord Wenlock; an antique bust of Julius Cæsar, which seems to have been found in fragments and carefully joined together. This bust is exhibited by the Hon. P. Downay, and was found in Rome amongst some rubbish, while some excavations were being made. There is also an interesting series of marble busts of the Twelve Cæsars, exhibited by Lord Londesborough. The Exhibition is open in the evening, and brilliantly lighted with gas till ten o'clock; and, taking it "all in all," it is a very creditable effort in the right direction, and does honour to York and Yorkshiremen.

Further north still, at Newcastle-on-Tyne, there is another exhibition of "Arts and Manufactures," the chief photographic feature of which is a considerable display of "Swan's Carbon Prints," from several well-known negatives by Bedford and Robinson. The promise of this process is very great, and its commercial advantages were singularly demonstrated to me when visiting the printing establishment of Mr. Swan, which I happened to do on a dark and unfavourable day—one totally unfit for silver printing; and yet I saw several very beautiful carbon prints that had been produced that day, the rate of production being about eight to one over silver printing. As a proof of the certainty and commercial application to which Mr. Swan has reduced his beautiful process, I need only mention that he has undertaken the printing of two thousand copies of the celebrated picture of "The First General Assembly of the Church of Scotland," painted by D. O. Hill. This historical picture contains four hundred and fifty portraits: the negatives were taken from the original painting by Mr. Annan, photographer, Glasgow, and are 32 by 14 inches, and 24 by 9 inches; and Mr. Swan has to turn off one thousand copies of each within a given time. The publishers of the work give a guarantee to their subscribers that every print shall be of a high standard, for each one has to pass the examination of two competent judges. They also very justly pride themselves on being the very first to translate and multiply such noble works of art by a process "so beautiful, and, at the same time, *imperishable.*" I saw several of the prints, both in process of development and complete; and anything more like rich, soft, and brilliant impressions of a fine mezzotint engraving I never saw, by any process of photography.

Mr. Swan's arrangements for conducting the various parts of his process are very extensive and complete; and his mode of "developing and transferring" seems to be the very acme of perfection. But, as Mr. Swan is about to publish a work containing a full description of the process, with a beautiful specimen print as frontispiece, I will not anticipate him, or mar his own comprehensive account of the details of a process which he has brought to such a state of beauty and perfection, by an amount of patient perseverance and thoughtful application rarely exhibited or possessed by one individual.

I also visited the photographic establishment of Messrs. Downey in Newcastle, and there saw some *cabinet pictures* of the Princess of Wales, taken recently at Abergeldie Castle. Messrs. Downey have just returned from Balmoral with upwards of two hundred negatives, including whole-plate, half-plate, and *cabinet* size, which will be published in one or all those sizes, as soon as the orders of Her Majesty have been executed. From the well-known reputation of the Messrs. Downey as photographers, it is, in all probability, a treat in store for the lovers of photography, to get a sight of their latest works at Balmoral and Abergeldie.

Mr. Parry, another excellent photographer in Newcastle, was also making arrangements to introduce the new cabinet size picture in a style that will insure its success.

Altogether, the movements of the best photographers in the North are highly commendable, and, with their notoriously practical minds, there is little doubt of their undertakings becoming a success. Let us hope that the same elements of energy and "push" will speedily impregnate the minds of all photographers, and create a combination that will develop a new form of popular beauty, and result in forming a salt that will savour their labours, produce deposits of gold, and create innumerable orders of merit.

ERRORS IN PICTORIAL BACKGROUNDS.

We have recently had a few papers on the necessity of art culture and art knowledge in relation to photography, but they have chiefly been of a theoretical and speculative character, few, if any, assuming a practical form. "Apply the rod to teach the child" is an old saying, and our artist friends and teachers *have* applied the rod and belaboured photography most unmercifully, but they have *not* taught the child. They have contented themselves with abusing photographers for not doing what was right, instead of teaching them how to avoid what was wrong.

It will be my endeavour to point out, in this paper, some errors that have crept into photographers' and artists' studios, and I hope to be able to suggest a remedy that will lessen these evils, and elevate photography in the scale of art. The faults in pictorial backgrounds that I invite your attention to, arise from the neglect of the principles of linear and aerial perspective. I do not speak of the errors in perspective that may exist in the backgrounds themselves, viewing them as pictures; but I refer to the manifest fault of depicting the sitter—the principal object—according to one condition of perspective, and the background that is placed behind him according to another. An unpardonable error in any work of art, whether photograph or painting, is to represent a natural object in an unnatural position. By this I do not mean an awkward and constrained attitude, but a false position of the principal subject in relation to the other objects by which it is surrounded. We frequently see portraits, both full-length and three-quarter size, with landscape backgrounds—or a bit of landscape to be seen through a painted or actual window—of the most unnatural proportions in relation to the figure itself. The head of the subject is stuck high in the heavens—sometimes so high that, in relation to the painted landscape, nothing shorter than a church steeple could attain such an altitude. The trees and castles of the pretty landscape, supposed to be behind the sitter, are like children's toys; the mountains are like footballs in size, and the "horizon" is not so much in relation to the figure as the width of a fishpond is to a man standing on one side of it. It must be admitted that artists themselves have set this bad example of departing from truth to give increased importance to their subjects by placing their figures against diminutive backgrounds; but that is a liberty taken with nature which photographers should neither imitate nor allow. Photography is, in all other respects, so rigidly truthful that it cannot consistently sanction such a violation of natural laws.

Pictorial backgrounds have usually been painted on the same principle as a landscape picture, and one of the earliest things the painter has to determine is, where he shall represent that line where the sky and earth appear to meet—technically, the *horizontal line*. This settled, all the lines, not vertical or horizontal in the picture, below this are made to appear to rise up to it, and those above descend, and if all these are in due proportion the perspective is correct, no matter whether this governing line is assumed to be in the upper, lower, or middle part of the picture. A painter can suppose this imaginary line to be at any height he pleases in his picture, and paint accordingly. In photography it is invariable, and is always on a level with the lens of the camera. To illustrate the relation of the horizontal line to the human figure, when a pictorial background is to be introduced, let us imagine that we are taking a portrait out of doors, with a free and open country behind the person standing for his carte-de-visite. The camera and the model are, as a matter of course, on the same level. Now focus the subject and observe the linear construction of the landscape background of nature. See how all the lines of the objects below the level of the lens run up to it, and the lines of the objects above run down to it. Right across the lens is the horizontal line, and the centre is the point of sight, where all the lines will appear to converge. Suppose the lens to be on a level with the face of the subject, the horizontal line of the picture produced on the ground glass will be as near as possible as high as the eyes of the subject. Trees and hills in the distance will be above, and the whole picture will be in harmony. This applies to interior views as well, but the ocular demonstration is not so conclusive, for the converging lines will be cut or stopped by the perpendicular wall forming the background. Nevertheless, all the converging lines that are visible will be seen to be on their way to the point of sight. Whether a natural background consisted of an interior, or comprised both—such as a portion of the wall of a room and a peep through a window on one side of the figure—the conditions would be exactly the same. All the lines above the lens must come down, and all that are below must go up. The following diagrams will illustrate this principle still more clearly.

Fig 1.

O Point of Observation. Base Line.

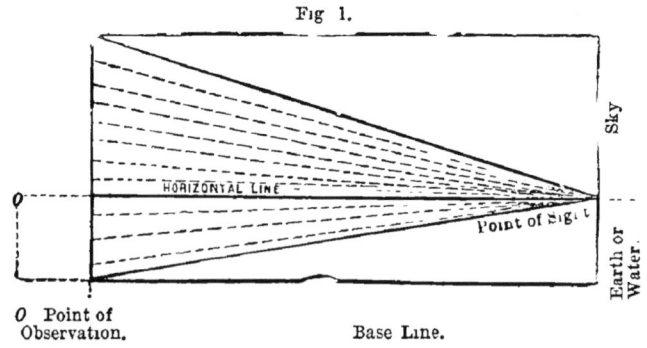

Fig. 1 is a section of the linear construction of a picture, and will show how the lines converge from the point of observation to the point of sight. Artists, in constructing a landscape of an ordinary form, allot to the sky generally about twice the space between the base and horizontal lines. But for portraits and groups, where the figures are of the greatest importance

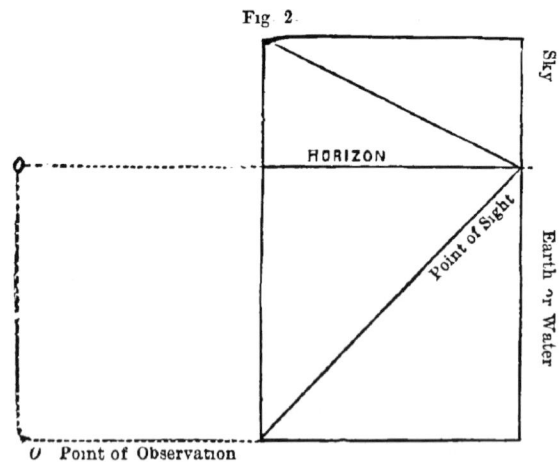

Fig 2.

O Point of Observation

and nearer to the eye, the proportion of sky and earth is reversed, so as to give increased value to the principal figures, by making them apparently larger, and still preserving the proper relation between them and the horizontal line (see fig. 2). This diagram represents the conditions of a full-length carte portrait, where the governing horizontal line is on a level with the camera. If a pictorial background, painted in the usual way, with the horizontal line low in the picture, is now placed behind the sitter, the resulting photograph will be incongruous and offensive. It will be seen, on referring to fig. 2, that all the lines below the horizon must of necessity run up to it, no matter how high the horizontal line may be, for it is impossible to have two horizons in one picture; that is, a visible horizon in the landscape background, and an imaginary one for the figure, with the horizontal line of the background far below the head of the figure, and the head far up in the sky. The head of a human figure can only be seen so far above the horizontal line under certain conditions; such as being elevated above the observer by being mounted on horseback, standing on higher ground, or otherwise placed considerably above the base line, none of which conditions are present in a studio. Whenever the observed and observer are on the same level, as must be the case when a photographer is taking the portrait of a sitter in his studio, the head of the subject could not possibly be seen so high in the sky, if the lens included a natural background instead of a painted one. As, for convenience, the painted background is intended to take the place of a natural one, care should be taken that the linear and aerial perspectives should be as true to nature as possible, and in perfect harmony with the size of the figures. The lens registers, on the prepared plate, the relative proportions of natural objects as faithfully as the retina receives them through the eye, and if we wish to carry out the illusion of pictorial backgrounds correctly, we *must* have the linear construction of the picture, which is intended to represent nature, as true in every respect as nature is herself.

Aerial perspective has not been sufficiently attended to by the painters of pictorial backgrounds. There are many other subjects in connection with art and photography that might be discussed with advantage—such as composition, arrangement of accessories, size, form, character, and fitness of the things employed; but I leave all these for another opportunity, or to some one more able to handle the subjects. For the present, I am content to point out those errors that arise from neglecting true perspective, and while showing the cause, distinctively supply a remedy.

It is not the fault of perspective in the background where the lines are not in harmony with each other—these too frequently occur, and are easily detected—but it is the error of painting a pictorial background as if it were an independent picture, without reference to the conditions under which it is to be used. The conditions of perspective are determined by the situation of the lens and the sitter. If the actual objects existed behind the sitter, and were photographed simultaneously with the sitter, the same laws of perspective would govern the two. What I urge is, that if, instead of the objects, a representation of them be put behind the sitter, that represenation be also a correct one. The laws of perspective teach how it may be made correctly, and the starting point is the position of the lens in relation to the sitter.

Some may say that these conditions of painting a background cannot be complied with, as the lens and sitter are never twice exactly in the same relation to each other. There is less force in this objection than at first appears. Each photographer uses the same lens for all his *carte* portraits—and pictorial backgrounds are very frequently used for these—and the height of his camera, as well as the distance from his sitter, are so nearly constant, that the small amount of errors thus caused need not be recognized. If the errors that exist were not far more grave, there would be no necessity for this paper. Exceptional pictures should have corresponding backgrounds.

When a "sitter" is photographed standing in front of a pictorial background, the photograph will represent him either standing in a natural scene, or before a badly-painted picture. Nobody should wittingly punish his sitter by doing the latter when he could do the former, and the first step to form the desirable illusion is pictorial truth. There is no reason why the backgrounds should not be painted truthfully and according to correct principles, for the one is as easy as the other. I daresay the reason is that artists have not intentionally done wrong—it would be too bad to suppose that—but they have treated the backgrounds as independent pictures, and it is for photographers to make what use of them they think proper. The real principles are, however, now stated, by which they can be painted so as to be more photographically useful, and artists and photographers have alike the key to pictorial truth.

In conclusion, I would suggest to photographers the necessity of studying nature more carefully—to observe her in their walks abroad, to notice the gradual decrease of objects both in size and distinctness, to remember that their lens is to their camera what their eye is to themselves, to give as faithful a transcript of nature as they possibly can, to watch the flow of nature's lines, as well as natural light and shade, and, by a constant study and exhibition of truth and beauty in their works, make photography eventually the teacher of art, instead of art, as is now the case, being the reviler of photography.

PERSPECTIVE.
To the Editors.

GENTLEMEN,—At the end of Mr. Alfred H. Wall's reply to Mr. Carey Lea's letter on *Artists and Photographers*, I notice that he cautions your readers not to receive the very simple rules of perspective laid down in my paper, entitled *Errors in Pictorial Backgrounds*, until they have acquired more information on the subject. Allow me to state that all I said on perspective in that paper only went to show that there should be but one horizon in the same picture; that the lines of all objects *below* that horizon should run up to it; that the lines of all objects *above* should run down, no matter where that *one* horizon was placed; and that the horizon of the landscape background should be in due relation to the sitter and on a level with the eye of the observer, the observer being either the lens or the painter.

If your correspondent considers that I was in error by laying down such plain and common-sense rules, which every one can see and judge for himself by looking down a street, then I freely admit that your correspondent knows a great deal more about *false* perspective than I do, or should like to do.

Again, if your correspondent cannot see why I " volunteered to instruct artists " or painters of backgrounds, perhaps he will allow me to inform him that I did so simply because background painters have hitherto supplied photographers with backgrounds totally unfit for use in the photographic studio.

In spite of Mr. Wall's assumption of superior knowledge on subjects relating to art, I may still be able to give him a hint how to produce a pictorial background that will be much more natural, proportionate, and suitable for the use of photographers than any hitherto painted.

Let Mr. Wall, or any other background painter, go *out* with the camera and take a *carte-de-visite* portrait out of doors, placing the subject in any well-chosen and suitable natural scene, and photograph the "sitter" and the natural scene at the same time. Then bring the picture so obtained into his studio and enlarge it up to "life size," which he can easily do by the old-fashioned system of "squaring," or, better still, by the aid of a magic lantern, and with the help of a sketch of the scene as well, to enable him to fill in correctly that part of the landscape concealed by the figure taken on the spot; so that, when reproduced by the photographer in *his* studio, he will have a representation of a natural scene, with everything seen in the background in correct perspective, and in natural proportions in relation to the "sitter." This will also show how *few* objects can naturally be introduced into a landscape background; and if the distant scenery be misty and undefined, so much the better. It is the sharpness, hardness, and superabundance of subjects introduced into pictorial backgrounds generally that I object to, and endeavoured to point out in my paper; and I consider it no small compliment to have had my views on that part of my subject so emphatically endorsed by so good an authority as Mr. Wallis, in his remarks on backgrounds at the last meeting of the South London Photographic Society.

I make no pretensions to the title of "artist," although I studied perspective, drawing from the flat and round, light and shade, and other things in connection with a branch of art which I abandoned many years ago for the more lucrative profession of a photographer. Were I so disposed, I could quote Reynolds, Burnett, and Ruskin as glibly as your correspondent; but I prefer putting my own views on any subject before my readers in language of my own.

I endeavour to be in all my words and actions thoroughly independent and consistent, which is more than I can say for your correspondent "A. H. W." In proof of which, I should like to call the attention of your readers to a passage in his "Practical Art Hints," in the last issue of *The British Journal of Photography*, where he says:—"It is perversion and degradation to an art like ours to make its truth and unity subservient to conventional tricks, shams, and mechanical dodges," while at the last meeting of the South London Photographic Society, when speaking of backgrounds, he admitted they were *all conventional.*

Now, that is just what we do not want, and which was the chief object I had in view when I wrote my paper. We have had too many of those art-conventional backgrounds, and want something more in accordance with natural truth and the requirements of photography.

In conclusion, allow me to observe that I should be truly sorry were I to mislead anyone in the pursuit of knowledge relative to our profession, either artistically or photographically. But let it be borne in mind that it is admitted on all sides, and by the best authorities, that nearly all the pictorial backgrounds now in use are quite unnatural, and totally unsuited for the purposes for which they are intended. Therefore the paper I read will have done the good I intended, and answered the purpose for which it was written, if it has been the means of calling attention to such glaring defects and absurdities as are now being perpetrated by background painters, and bringing in their place more natural, truthful, and photographically useful backgrounds into the studios of all photographers—I am, yours, &c., J. WERGE.

February 10*th*, 1866.

PERSPECTIVE IN BACKGROUNDS.
To the Editors.

GENTLEMEN,—I must beg of you to allow me to reply to Mr. Wall once more, and for the last time, on this subject, especially as that gentleman expects an answer from me.

To put myself into a fair position with regard to Mr. Wall and your readers, I will reply to the latter part of his letter first, by stating that I endeavour to avoid all personality in this discussion, and should be sorry to descend to anything of the kind knowingly. When I spoke of "independency and consistency," I had not in view anything relative to his private character, but simply that kind of independence which enables a man to trust to his own powers of utterance for the expression of his ideas, instead of that incessant quoting the language of others, to which your correspondent, Mr. Wall, is so prone. As to his inconsistency, I mean that tendency which he exhibits to advocate a principle at one time, and denounce it at another. I shall prove that presently. Towards Mr. Wall, personally, I have neither animosity nor pique, and would take him by the hand as freely and frankly as ever I did were I to meet him at this moment. With his actions as a private gentleman I have nothing to do. I look upon him now as a controvertist only. So far, I hope I have made myself clearly understood by Mr. Wall and all concerned.

I also should like to have had so important a question discussed without introducing so much of that frivolous smartness of style generally adopted by Mr Wall. But, as he has introduced two would-be-funny similes, I beg to dispose of them before going into more serious matter. Taking the "butcher" first (see the fifth paragraph in Mr. Wall's last letter), I should say that, if I were *eating* the meat, I should be able to judge of its quality, and know whether it was good or bad, in spite of all the butcher might say to the contrary; and surely, no man not an out-and-out vegetarian, or lacking one of the five senses—to say nothing of *common sense*—will admit that it is *necessary* to be a "butcher" to enable him to be a judge of good meat. On the same ground, I contend that it is *not* necessary for a man to be an artist to have a thorough knowledge of perspective; and I have known many artists who knew as little about perspective, practically, as their easel did. They had a vague and dreamy idea of some governing principles, but how to put those principles into practice they had not the slightest notion. I once met an artist who could not put a tesselated pavement into perspective, and yet he had some right to the title of artist, for he could draw and paint the human figure well. Perspective is based on geometrical principles, and can be as easily mastered by any man not an artist as the first book of Euclid, or the first four rules of arithmetic; and, for all that, it is astonishing how many artists know so little about the working rules of perspective.

Again: Mr. Wall is surely not prepared to advance the dictum that no one can know anything about art but a professional artist. If so, how does he reconcile that opinion with the fact of his great and oft-quoted authority, Ruskin, not being an artist, but simply, in his public character, a voluminous writer on art, not always right, as many artists and photographers very well know.

Mr. Wall objects to my use of the word "artist," but he seems to have overlooked the fact that I used the quotation marks to show that I meant to apply it to the class of self-styled artists, or men who arrogate to themselves a title they do not merit—not such men as Landseer, Maclise, Faed, Philips, Millais, and others of, and not of, the "Forty." Mr. Wall may be an artist. I do not say he is not. He also is, or was, a painter of backgrounds. So he can apply to himself whichever title he likes best; but whether he deserves either one or the other, depends on what he has done to merit the appellative.

Mr. Wall questions the accuracy of the principles I advocated in my paper. I contend that I am perfectly correct, and am the more astonished at Mr. Wall when I refer to vol. v., page 123, of the *Photographic News*. There I find, in an article bearing his own name, and entitled "The Technology of Art as Applied to Photography," that he says:—

"If you make use of a painted cloth to represent an interior or out-door view, the horizontal line must be at somewhere about the height which your lens is most generally placed at, and the vanishing point nearly opposite the spot occupied by the camera. * * * * I have just said that the horizon of a landscape background and the vanishing point should be opposite the lens; I may, perhaps, for the sake of such operators as are not acquainted with perspective, explain why. The figure and the background are supposed to be taken at one and the same time, and the camera has the place of the spectator by whom they are taken. Now, suppose we have a real figure before a real landscape : if I look up at a figure I obtain one view of it, but if I look down on it, I get another and quite a different view, and the horizon of the natural landscape behind the figure is always exactly the height of *my* eye. To prove this, you may sit down before a window, and mark on the glass the height of the horizon; then rise, and, as you do so, you will find the horizon also rises, and is again exactly opposite your eye. A picture, then, in which the horizontal line of the background represents the spectator as looking up at the figure from a position near the base line, while the figure itself indicates that the same spectator is at that identical time standing with his eyes on a level with the figure's breast or chin—such productions are evidently false to art, and untrue to nature. * * * * The general fault in the painted screens we see behind photographs arises from introducing too many objects."

Now, as I advanced neither more nor less in my paper, why does Mr. Wall turn round and caution your readers not to receive such simple truths uttered by me ? I was not aware that Mr. Wall had forestalled me in laying down such rules ; for at that date I was in America, and did not see the *News;* but, on turning over the volume for 1861 the other day, since this discussion began, I there saw and read, with surprise, the above in his article on backgrounds. I am perfectly aware that I did not say all that I might have said on perspective in my paper; but the little I did say was true in principle, and answered my purpose.

When Mr. Wall (in the second paragraph of his last letter) speaks of the "principal visual ray going from the point of distance to the point of sight, and forming a right angle to the perspective plane," it seems to me that he is not quite sure of the difference between the points of *sight, distance,* and *observation,* or of the relation and application of one to the other. However, his coming articles on perspective will settle that. It also appears to me that he has overlooked the fact that my diagrams were *sections,* showing the perspective inclination and declination of the lines of a parallelogram towards the point of sight. In my paper I said nothing about the *point of distance;* with that I had nothing to do, as it was not my purpose to go into all the dry details of perspective. But I emphatically deny that anything like a "bird's eye view" of the figure could possibly be obtained by following any of the rules I laid down. In my paper I contended for the camera being placed on a level with the head of the sitter, and that would bring the line of the horizon in a pictorial background also as high as the head of the sitter. And if the horizon of the pictorial background were placed anywhere else, it would cause the apparent overlapping of *two* conditions of perspective in the resulting photograph. These were the errors I endeavoured to point out. I maintain that my views are perfectly correct, and can be proved by geometrical demonstration, and the highest artistic and scientific testimony.

I wish it to be clearly understood that I do not advocate the use of pictorial backgrounds, and think I pretty strongly denounced them; but if they *must* be used by photographers, either to please themselves or their customers, let them, for the credit of our profession, be as true to nature as possible.

I think I have now answered all the points worth considering in Mr. Wall's letter, and with this I beg to decline any further correspondence on the subject.—I am, yours, &c.,

J. WERGE.

March 5th, 1866.

NOTES ON PICTURES IN THE NATIONAL GALLERY.

In the following notes on some of the pictures in the National Gallery, it is not my intention to assume the character of an art-critic, but simply to record the impressions produced on the mind of a photographer while looking at the works of the great old masters, with the view of calling the attention of photographers and others interested in art-photography to a few of the pictures which exhibit, in a marked degree, the relation of the horizon to the principal figures.

During an examination of those grand old pictures, two questions naturally arise in the mind: What is conventionality in art? and—In whose works do we see it? The first question is easily answered by stating that it is a mode of treating pictorial subjects by established rule or custom, so as to obtain certain pictorial effects without taking into consideration whether such effects can be produced by natural combinations or not. In answer to the second question, it may be boldly stated that there is very little of it to be seen in the works of the best masters; and one cannot help exclaiming, " What close imitators of nature those grand old masters were!" In their works we never see that photographic eye-sore which may be called a binographic combination of two conditions of perspective, or the whereabouts of two horizons in the same picture.

The old masters were evidently content with natural combinations and effects for their backgrounds, and relied on the rendering of natural truths more than conventional falsehoods for the strength and beauty of their productions. Perhaps the simplest mode of illustrating this would be to proceed to a kind of photographic analysis of the pictures of the old masters, and see how far the study of their works will enable the photographer to determine what he should employ and what he should reject as pictorial backgrounds in the practice of photography. As a photographer, then—for it is the photographic application of art we have to consider—I will proceed to give my notes on pictures in the National Gallery, showing the importance of having the horizontal line in its proper relation to the sitter or figure.

Perhaps the most beautiful example is the fine picture by Annibale Carracci of "Christ appearing to Peter." This admirable work of art as nearly as possible contains the proportions of a carte-de-visite or whole-plate picture enlarged, and is well worthy the careful attention and study of every photographer; not only for its proportions and the amount of landscape background introduced, showing the proper position of the horizon and the small amount of sky visible, but it is a wonderful example of light and shade, foreshortening, variety and contrast of expression, purity of colour, simplicity of design, and truthfulness to nature. Neither of the figures lose any of their force or dignity, although the horizontal line is as high as their heads, and the whole of the space between is filled in with the scene around them. In its linear perspective it is quite in keeping with the figures, and the scenery is in harmonious subjection, controlled and subdued by aerial perspective.

The large picture of "Erminia takes refuge with the Shepherds," by the same artist, is also a fine example of a horizon high in the picture. The figure of Erminia is separated from the other figures, and could be copied or reproduced alone without any loss of beauty and dignity, or any violation of natural laws.

Murillo's picture of "St. John and the Lamb" suggests an admirable background for the use of the photographer. It consists of dark masses of rock and foliage. Nothing distinct or painfully visible, the distant masses of foliage blend with the clouds, and there is nothing in the background but masses of light and shade to support or relieve the principal objects.

In the picture of "Christ appearing to Mary Magdalene," by Titian, the water-line is above the head of Christ, but if the figure were standing upright, the head of the Saviour would break the horizontal line.

Titian's "Bacchus and Ariadne" also has the water-line breast high, almost to the neck of Ariadne. The figure of Bacchus springing from the car, as a matter of course, is much higher in the sky. This picture presents the perspective conditions of the painter having been seated while painting such figures from nature, or similar to the results and effects obtained by taking a group with the lens on a level with the breast or lower part of the necks of figures standing.

In Titian's portrait of Ariosto there is a dark foliated background which gives great brilliancy to the picture, but no sky is visible. The "Portrait of a Lady," by Paris Bardone, has an architectural background in which no sky is to be seen. The picture is very brilliant, and the monotony of a plain background is skilfully overcome.

The picture of "St. Catharine of Alexandria," by Raphael, has a landscape background, with the horizon about as high as the breast, as if the artist had been seated and the model standing during the process of painting.

Raphael's picture of "The Vision of a Knight" is another example of the fearlessness of that artist in putting in or backing up his figures with a large amount of landscape background.

The proportions of Correggio's "Venus, Mercury, and Cupid," are as nearly as possible those of a carte-de-visite enlarged; and that picture has no sky in the background, but a very suitable dark, cool, rocky scene, well subdued, for the rocks are quite near to the figures. This background gives wonderful brilliancy to the figures, and contrasts admirably with the warm and delicate flesh tints.

Correggio's "Holy Family" has a landscape and architectural background, with a very little sky visible in the right-hand corner.

In the "Judgment of Paris," by Rubens, the horizontal line

of the background cuts the waist of the first female figure, showing that the artist was seated. The other two female figures are placed against a background of rocks and dark masses of foliage. Rubens' picture of the "Holy Family and St. George" is also a good example of the kind of picture for the photographer to study as to the situation of the horizontal line.

The picture of "The Idle Servent," by Nicolas Maas, is also an excellent subject for study of this kind. It shows the due relation of the horizon of an interior in a very marked degree, and its shape and subject are very suitable to the size and form of a carte-de-visite. So are his pictures of "The Cradle" and "A Dutch Housewife."

The picture of "John Arnolfini of Lucca and his Wife," painted by John Van Eyck in the fifteenth century, is an excellent specimen of an interior background, with a peep out of a window on one side of the room. This is a capital subject for the study of photographers who wish to use a background representing an interior.

"The Holy Family at a Fountain," a picture of the Dutch school, painted by Schoorel in the sixteenth century, has an elaborate landscape background with the horizon *above* the heads of the figures, as if the artist had been standing and the models sitting.

For an example of a portrait less than half-length, with a landscape background, look at the portrait of "An Italian Gentleman," by Andrea da Solario. This picture shows how very conscientiously the old masters worked up to the truth of nature in representing the right amount of landscape in proportion to the figure, but the background is much too hard and carefully worked out to be pleasing. Besides, it is very destructive to the force and power of the picture, which will be at once visible on going to the portraits by Rembrandt, which have a marvellous power, and seem to stand right before the dark atmospheric backgrounds which that artist generally painted in his portraits.

There are other examples of half-length portraits with landscape backgrounds, wherein the horizontal line passes right through the eyes of the principal figure, one of which I will mention. It is that of the "Virgin and Child," by Lorenzo di Credi. In this picture the horizontal line passes right through the eyes of the Virgin without interfering with the interest of the chief object.

Several examples of an opposite character are to be seen in the National Gallery, with the horizon of the landscape background much too low in the picture. It is needless to call special attention to them. After carefully examining the works already named, and comparing them with the natural effects to be observed daily, it will be quickly seen which is a truthful picture in this respect, and which is a false one.

SHARPNESS AND SOFTNESS *V.* HARDNESS.

THE discussion on "Sharpness: what is it?" at the meeting of the South London Photographic Society in May, 1861, and the more recent discussion on "Focussing" at the last meeting of the same Society, seem to me to have lost much of their value and importance to photographers for want of a better definition of the term *hardness* as applied to art, and as used by *artists* in an *artistic sense*. Webster, in his second definition of the word "hardness," gives it as "difficulty to be understood." In that sense Mr. Wall succeeded admirably when he gave the term *concentration*, in reply to Mr. Hughes, who asked Mr. Wall what he meant by *hardness*. Fairholt gives the *art meaning* of the word as "want of refinement; academic drawing, rather than artistic feeling." But even that definition would not have been sufficiently comprehensive to convey an adequate idea of the meaning of the term in contradistinction to the word *sharp-*

ness, and I cannot but think that Mr. Wall failed in his object in both papers, and lost considerable ground in both discussions, by not giving more attention to the nice distinctions of the two terms as used in art, and explaining their artistic meanings more clearly.

Sharpness need not be hardness; on the contrary, sharpness and softness can be harmoniously combined in the representation of any object desired. On the other hand, a subject may possess abundance of detail, and yet convey to the mind an idea of *hardness* which the artist did not intend. This kind of hardness I should attribute to a miscarriage of thought, or a failure, from want of manipulative skill, to produce the desired effect. For example: one artist will paint a head, model it carefully, and carry out all the gradations of light and shade, and for all that it will be *hard*—hard as stone, resembling the transcript of a painted statue more than flesh. With the same brushes and colours another artist will paint a head that may be no better in its drawing, nor any more correct in its light and shade, but it will resemble *flesh*, and convey to the mind of the observer a correct impression of the substance represented—its flexibility and elasticity—that it is something that would be warm and pleasant to the touch, and not make you recoil from it as if it were something cold, hard, and repulsive, as in the former case. Again, two artists will paint a fabric or an article of furniture (say a table) with the same brushes, pigments, and mediums: the one artist will render it so faithfully in every respect that it would suggest to the mind the dull sound peculiar to wood when struck, and not the sharp, clear ring of metal which the work of the other artist would suggest.

Another example: one artist paints a feather, and it appears to have all the feathery lightness and characteristics of the natural object; the other will paint it the same size, form, and colour, and yet it will be more like a painted chip, wanting the downy texture and float-in-the-air suggestiveness of the other.

Thus it will be seen that both artists had similar ideas, had similar materials and means at their disposal to render on canvas the same or similar effects. The one succeeded, and the other failed, in giving a faithful rendering of the same subjects ; but it was no fault in the materials with which they worked. The works of one artist will convey to the mind an idea of the thing itself; with its texture, properties, weight, and proportions; nothing undervalued ; nothing overrated, nothing softer, nothing harder, than the thing in nature intended to be portrayed. The other gives the same idea of form and size, light and shade, and colour, but not the texture ; it is something harder, as iron instead of wood, or hard wood instead of soft wood, or stone instead of flesh. This, then, is the artistic meaning of hardness (or concentration, as Mr. Wall said), and that is an apparent packing together, a compression or petrefaction of the atoms or fibre of which the natural materials are composed. This difference in the works of artists is simply the effects of *feeling*, of power over the materials employed, and ability to transfer to canvas effects that are almost illusious. And so it is with photographers in the production of the photographic image. There is the same difference in feeling and manipulative skill, the same difference of power over the materials employed, that enables one photographer to surpass another in rendering more truthfully the difference of texture. Photographers may and do use the same lenses and chemicals, and yet produce widely different results. One, by judgment in lighting and superior manipulation, will transfer to his plates more texture and suggestiveness of the different substances represented than the other. It is a fact well known to old photographers that in the best days of the Daguerreotype practice two widely different classes of pictures were produced by the most skilful *Daguerreotypists*, both sharp and full of exquisite detail ; yet the one was *hard*, in an artistic sense, not that it wanted half-tone to link the lights and shades together, but because it was of a bronzy hardness, unlike flesh from which it was taken, and suggested to the mind a picture taken from a bronze or iron statue of the individual, rather than a picture taken from the warm, soft flesh of the original. The other would be equally sharp as far as focussing and *sharp lenses* could make it, and possess as much detail, but it would be different in colour and texture; the detail would be soft, downy, and fleshy, not hony, if I may use that word in such a sense; and this difference of effect arose entirely from a difference of feeling, lighting, preparation of the plate, and development of the pictures. They might all use the best of Voigtlander's or C. C. Harrison's lenses, the favourite lenses of that day. They might all use the same make of plates, the same iodine, bromine, and mercury, yet there would be this difference in the character of the two classes of pictures. Both would be sharp and possess abundance of detail, still one would be *soft* and the other hard in an artistic acceptation of the word *hardness*.

Collodion positives exhibited a similar difference of character. The works of one photographer would be cold and metallic looking, while the works of another would be softer and less metallic, giving a better idea of the texture of flesh and the difference of fabrics, which many attributed to the superiority of the lens; but the difference was really due to manipulation, treatment, and intelligence. And so it is with the collodion negative. A tree, for instance, may be photographed, and its whole character changed by selecting a bad and unsuitable light, or by bad manipulation. The least over-development or "piling up" of a high light may give it a sparkling effect that would change it into the representation of a tree of cast iron, rather than a *growing tree*, covered with damp, soft, and moss-stained bark. Every object and every fabric, natural or manufactured, has its own peculiar form of "high light" or mode of reflecting light, and care must be taken by both artist and photographer not to exceed the amount of light reflected by each particular object, else a *hardness*, foreign to the natural object, will be represented. But not only should the artist and photographer possess this feeling for nature in all her subtle beauties and modes of expressing herself, to prevent a miscarriage in the true rendering of any object, the photographic printer should also have a sympathy for the work in hand, or he will, by over-fixing, or in various other ways, mar the successful labours of the photographer, and make a negative that is full of softness, and tenderly expresses the truth of nature, yield prints that are crude, and convey to the mind a sense of *hardness* which neither the natural objects nor the negative really possess.

Now, I think it will be seen that *hardness* in a painting or a photograph does not mean sharpness; nor is the artistic meaning of the word *hardness* confined to "rigid or severe drawing," but that it has a broader and more practical definition than concentration; and that the converse to the art meaning of *hardness* is softness, tenderness, truthfulness in expressing the varied aspects of nature in all her forms, all of which are coincident with sharpness.—J. WERGE (*Photographic News*).

UNION OF THE NORTH AND SOUTH LONDON PHOTOGRAPHIC SOCIETIES.
To the Editors, British Journal.

GENTLEMEN,—Allow me to express my opinion on the suggestion to unite the North and South London Societies, and to point out a few of the advantages which, I think, would accrue from a more extensive amalgamation.

Though I am a member of all the three London photographic societies, I have long been of opinion that there are too many, and that the objects of all are considerably weakened by such a diffusion of interests. If the furtherance of the art and the free and mutual interchange of thought and experience among the members were the only things considered, there would be but one society in London ; and with one society embodying all the members that now make the three, how much more good might be done!

In the first place, the amounts now paid for rent by the three would, if united, secure an excellent meeting room or chambers, in a central position, for the *exclusive* use of the society, where the ordinary and special meetings, annual exhibitions, and *soirees* could be held much more independently than now, and at a cost little or no more than what is now paid for the privilege of holding the ordinary meetings alone.

Secondly: If such a place of meeting were secured, then that laudable scheme of an art library, so strenuously advocated by Mr. Wall and Mr. Blanchard at the South London Photographic Society, might be successfully carried into effect. Then a library and a collection of works of art might be gradually gathered together, and one of the members could be chosen curator and librarian, to attend the rooms one evening in the week, or oftener, as circumstances might require, so as to give members access to the library to make exchanges, extracts from bulky books, &c.

Thirdly: If the union were effected, and the place of meeting more central, there would be a larger attendance of members, and more spirited and valuable proceedings would be the result. Papers to be read at the regular meetings would be much more certain, and the discussions would be more comprehensive and complete. The members would become personally acquainted with each other, and a much better feeling would pervade the whole photographic community.

These, gentlemen, are a few of the advantages which ought to accrue from a union of the three societies; but, if that cannot be effected, by all means let the triumvirate now existing be reduced to a biumvirate. If it be not possible for the "Parent Society" and her offspring to reunite their interests and affection for the common good, surely the other two can, and thereby strengthen themselves, and secure to their members a moiety of the advantages which would result from the triple alliance.

But, before proceeding further, let me ask—Has such a thing as a triple alliance ever been considered? Has it been ascertained that an amicable amalgamation with the Photographic Society of London is impossible? If so, what are the motives of the proposers of the union of the North and South London Societies? Do they wish to form a more powerful antagonism to the other society, or do they simply and purely wish to further the advancement of our art-science, and not to gratify personal pique or wounded pride? I do not wish to impute such unworthy motives to anyone; but it does seem singular that the proposition should come from the Chairman of the North London Photographic Association almost simultaneously with the resignation of his seat at the council board of the Parent Society.

If, however, the motives are pure, honest, and earnest, I heartily approve of the suggestion as a step in the right direction, although I candidly admit that I would much rather see all the societies united in one, and fully believe that that would be the most advantageous arrangement that could possibly be made for all concerned.—I am, yours, &c ,

London, February 18th, 1867. UNION JACK (J. Werge).

UNION OF THE LONDON PHOTOGRAPHIC SOCIETIES.
To the Editors of the British Journal.

GENTLEMEN,—Perhaps I am in courtesy bound to answer the questions of your correspondents, Mr. Homersham and "Blue Pendant," but in self-justification I do not think it necessary, for it turns out that my suspicions of antagonism to the Parent Society were well founded; and, from their remarks, and the observations of your contributor "D.," I learn that the disaffection is more widely spread than I at first thought it was.

I may have been wrong in suspecting the Chairman of the

North London Photographic Association of unworthy motives; if so, I frankly beg that gentleman's pardon. But I am not wrong in suspecting that antagonism is mixed up with the movement.

Your contributor "D." chooses to construe my unwillingness to make a direct charge—my hope that there were no such unworthy motives—into timidity; but I beg to remind "D." that there is not much, if any, of that apparent in my putting the plain questions I did, which, by-the-bye, have not yet been very satisfactorily answered

I flatter myself that I know when and how to do battle, and when to sue for peace, as well as any in the service under whose flag I have the honour to sail; and I, as much as anyone, admire the man that can fight courageously when in the right, or apologise gracefully when in the wrong; but, as the object of this correspondence is neither to make recriminations, nor indulge in personal abuse, I return to the primary consideration of the subject, and endeavour to sift the motives of the movers of the proposition to unite the North and South London Societies, and ascertain, if possible, whether they have the good of those societies and the furtherance of photography really at heart or not.

Imprimis, then, let us consider the arguments of "D.," who cites the resignation of three gentlemen in proof of the management of the London Photographic Society being "out of joint." He might as well say, "because a man is sick, leave him and let him die." If there were anything they disliked in the government of the Society, or any evil to be corrected, their most manly course was to have held on, and fought the evils down. They all had seats at the Council board, and if they had wished well to the Society, they would not have resigned them, but battled for the right, and brought their grievances, real or imagined, before the members. A special meeting has been called before now to consider personal grievances which affected the honour of the Society, and I should think it could have been done again. I do not maintain that all is right in the Society, but I do think that they were wrong in resigning their seats because an article appeared in the Society's journal condemnatory of a process to which they happened to be devotedly attached.

It can scarcely be supposed that the cause of reform, or the general good of the country, would have been forwarded had Gladstone, Bright, and Earl Russell resigned their seats as members of either House because they could not carry their ministerial bill of last session. From this I argue that men who have the object they advocate, and the "best interests" of the Society, thoroughly at heart, will stick to it tenaciously, whether in or out of office, and, by their watchfulness, prevent bad becoming worse, in spite of captious opposition, fancied insults, or journalistic abuse.

The next paragraph by "D." on which I shall comment contains that bold insinuation of timidity, which I have already noticed as much as I intend to do. But I wish to discuss the question of "absorption" a little more fully. I cannot at all agree with the sentiments of "D." on that subject. Absorption is in many instances a direct and positive advantage to both the absorber and absorbed, as the absorption of Sicily by Italy, and Frankfort and Hanover by Prussia. Nitric acid absorbs silver, and how much more valuable and useful to the photographer is the product than either of the two in their isolated condition; and so, I hold, it would be with the Society were the two other Societies to join the old one, impart to it their chief characteristics, re-model the constitution, and elect the members of the Council by ballot. We should then have a society far more powerful and useful than could ever be obtained by the formation of a new one.

In the foregoing, I think I have also answered the question of Mr. Homersham, as well as that part of "Blue Pendant's" letter relating to the establishment of a *fourth* society. On that point my views harmonise with those of your contributor, "D."

On the subject of "members of Council," I do not agree with either "D." or your correspondent "Blue Pendant." The Council should be elected from and by the body of members, and the only qualifications necessary should be willingness and ability to do the work required. No consideration of class should ever be admitted. The members are all recommended by "personal knowledge," and elected by ballot, and that alone should be test sufficient on the score of respectability.

Concerning "papers written as puffs," I cordially agree with "Blue Pendant" as far as he goes; but I go further than that, and would insist on each paper being scrutinised, before it is read, by a committee appointed for the purpose, so as to prevent "trade advertisements" and such shamefully scurrilous papers as I have heard at the South London Photographic Society.

With reference to the questions put by "Blue Pendant," I beg to decline answering his second, it not being pertinent; but I shall reply to his first more particularly. He seems to have forgotten or overlooked the fact that I thought the advantages I enumerated would result from a union of the *three* societies—not from an alliance of the two only. That I still look upon suspiciously as antagonistic to the Parent Society; and "Blue Pendant's" antagonism is proved beyond doubt when he says it is "tottering to its fall," and he almost gloatingly looks forward to its dissolution coming, to use his own words, "sooner or later," and "perhaps the sooner the better." But I venture to think that "Blue Pendant" is not likely to be gratified by seeing the "aged Parent" decently laid in the ground in his time. There is too much "life in the old dog yet"—even since the secession—for that to come to pass. It cannot be denied that the Parent Society has amongst its members some of the best speakers, thinkers, writers, and workers in the whole photographic community.

While discussing this subject, allow me, gentlemen, to advert to an article in your contemporary of Friday last. In the "Echoes of the Month," by an Old Photographer, the writer thinks that the advantages I pointed out as likely to accrue from a union of the societies are a "pleasant prospect that will not bear the test of figures." It is a fact that "figures" are subject to the rules of addition as well as of subtraction, and I wish to show by figures that my ideas are not so impracticable as he imagines. In addition to the eight guineas a year paid by the North and South London Photographic Societies for rent, I notice in the report of the London Photographic Society, published last month, two items in the "liabilities" which are worth considering. One is "King's College, rent and refreshment, £42 4s. 6d.," which, I presume, is for one year. The other is "King's College *soiree* account, £20 15s. 6d.," part of which is undoubtedly for rent of rooms on that occasion. Now there is a clear showing of over £50 12s. 6d. paid in one year by the three societies for rent and refreshment, the latter not being absolutely necessary. I may be mistaken in my estimate of the value of central property; but I do think a sum exceeding £50 is sufficient to secure a room or chambers large enough for the purposes of meeting, and keeping a library, &c.; or, if not, would it not be worth while making a strain to pay a little more so as to secure the accommodation required? If the Coventry Street experiment were a failure from apathy or other causes, that is no proof that another attempt made by a more numerous, wealthy, and energetic body would also be abortive. In sea phraseology, "the old ship has made a long leg to-day!" but I hope, gentlemen, you will not grudge the space required for the full and careful consideration of this subject. The "developing dish" and the ordinary *modus operandi* of photography can well afford to stand aside for awhile to have this question discussed

to the end. I have not said all I can on the amalgamation project, and may return to it again with your kind permission, if necessary.—I am, yours, &c., UNION JACK (J. Werge).
London, March 4, 1867.

THE SOCIETY'S EXHIBITION.

IMPRESSIONS AND CONVICTIONS OF "LUX GRAPHICUS."

THE brief and all but impromptu Exhibition of the Photographic Society, recently held in the rooms of the Architectural Society, 9, Conduit Street, Regent Street, where the Society's meetings are to be held in future, was one of the pleasantest and most useful expositions in connection with photography that has been consummated for many years. In the first place the idea of an exhibition evening free from the formalities of a *soiree* was a happy one; the *locale* was happily chosen; and the whole arrangements most happily successful. Everybody seemed to be pleased; cordial expressions of agreeable surprise were freely exchanged; and there were abundance and variety enough of pictorial display to satisfy the most fastidious visitor.

As might have been expected, the works of M. Salomon, exhibited by Mr. Wharton Simpson, were the chief objects of attraction, and during the whole of the evening an anxious group surrounded the collection; and it was curious to remark with what eagerness these pictures were scrutinized, so as to ascertain whether they were examples of photography "pure and undefiled," or helped by artistic labour afterwards. That they are the very finest specimens of art-photography—both in the broad and masterly treatment of light and shade, pose, manipulation, tone of print, and after finish—that have ever been exhibited, is unquestionable; but to suppose that they are photographs unaided by art-labour afterwards is, I think, a mistake. All of the heads, hands, and portions of the drapery bear unmistakable proofs of after-touching. Some of them give evidence of most elaborate retouching on the hands and faces, on the surface of the print. I examined the pictures by daylight most minutely with the aid of a magnifying glass, and could detect the difference between the retouching on the negative, and, after printing, on the positive. The faces of nearly all the ladies present that appearance of dapple or "stipple" which nothing in the texture of natural flesh can give, unless the sitter were in the condition of "goose flesh" at the moment of sitting, which is a condition of things not at all likely. Again, hatching is distinctly visible, which is not the photographic reproduction of the hatch-like line of the cuticle. In support of that I have two forms of evidence: first, *comparison*, as the hatchings visible on the surface of the print are too long to be a reproduction of the hatch-like markings of the skin, even on the hands, which generally show that kind of nature's handiwork the most. Besides, the immense reduction would render that invisible even under a magnifying glass, no matter how delicate the deposit of silver might be on the negative; or even if it were so, the fibre of the paper would destroy the effect. Again, the hatchings visible are not the form of nature's hatchings, but all partake of that art-technical form called "sectional hatchings." I could name several of the prints that showed most conclusive evidence of what I say, but that is not necessary, because others saw these effects as well as I did. But I wish it to be distinctly understood that I have not been at the pains to make these examinations and observations with the view of lessening the artistic merit of these pictures. I unhesitatingly pronounce them the most beautiful achievements of the camera that have ever been obtained by combining artistic knowledge and skill with the mechanical aid of the camera and ability to handle the compounds of photographic chemistry. There is unmistakable evidence of the keenest appreciation of art, and all that is beautiful in it in the production of the negative; and if the artist see or think that he can perfect his work by the aid of the brush, he has a most undoubted right to do it. This question of pure and simple photography has been mooted all the summer, ever since the opening of the French Exhibition, and I am glad that I, as well as others, have had an opportunity of seeing these wonderful pictures, and judging for myself. Photography is truth embodied, and every question raised about the purity of its productions should be discussed as freely and settled as quickly as possible.

There was another picture in the exhibition very clever in its conception, but not so in its execution, and I am sorry to say I cannot endorse *all* the good that has been said of it. I allude to Mr. Robinson's picture of "Sleep." How that clever photographer, with such a keen eye to nature as he generally manifests in his composition pictures, should have committed such a mistake I am at a loss to know. His picture of "Sleep" is so strangely untrue to nature, that he must have been quite overcome by the "sleep that knits up the ravell'd sleeve of *care*" when he composed it. In the centre of the picture he shows a stream of light entering a window—a ghost of a window, for it is so unsubstantial as not to allow a shadow to be cast from its *seemingly* massive bars. Now, if the moon shone through a window at all, it would cast shadows of everything that stood before it, and the shadows of the bars of the window would be cast upon the coverlet of the bed in broken lines, rising and falling with the undulations of the folds of the covering, and the forms of the figures of the children. In representing moonlight, or sunlight either, there is no departing from this truth. If the direct ray of either stream through a closed window and fall upon the bed, so will the shadows of the intervening bars.

Any picture, either painted or photographed, that does not render those shadows is simply untrue to nature ; and if the difficulty could not have been overcome, the attempt should have been abandoned. Then the beams are not *sharp* enough for moonlight, and the shadows on the coverlet and children are not deep enough, and the reflections on the shadow side of the children's faces are much too strong. In short, I do not know when Mr. Robinson more signally failed to carry out his first intentions. Wanting in truth as the composition is, it proves another truth, and that is, the utter inability of photography to cope with such a subject. Mr. Robinson exhibited other pictures that would bear a very different kind of criticism ; but as they have been noticed at other times I shall not touch upon them here.

Herr Milster's picture bears the stamp of truth upon it, and is a beautiful little gem, convincing enough that the effect is perfectly natural.

Mr. Ayling's pictures of the Victoria Tower and a portion of Westminster Abbey are really wonderful, and the bit of aerial perspective " Across the Water " in the former picture is truly beautiful.

Mrs. Cameron persists in sticking to the out-of-the-way path she has chosen, but where it will lead her to at last is very difficult to determine. One of the heads of Henry Taylor which she exhibited was undoubtedly the best of her contributions.

The pictures of yachts and interiors exhibited by Mr. Jabez Hughes were quite equal to all that could be expected from the camera of that clever, earnest, and indefatigable photographer. The portrait enlargements exhibited by that gentleman were exquisite, and of a totally different character from any other exhibitor's.

Mr. England's dry plate pictures, by his modified albumen process, are undoubtedly the best of the kind that have been taken. They lack that appearance of the representation of *petrified* scenes that most, if not all, previous dry processes exhibited, and look as "juicy" as "humid nature" can well be rendered with the wet process.

Mr. Frank Howard exhibited four little gems that would be perfect but for the unnatural effect of the artificial skies he has introduced. The "Stranded Vessels" is nicely chosen, and one of the wood scenes is like a bit of Creswick uncoloured.

Messrs. Locke and Whitfield exhibited some very finely and sketchily coloured photographs, quite up to their usual standard of artistic excellence, with the new feature of being painted on a ground of carbon printed from the negative by the patent carbon process of Mr. J. W. Swan.

Mr. Adolphus Wing's cabinet pictures were very excellent specimens, and I think it a great pity that more of that very admirable style of portraiture was not exhibited.

Mr. Henry Dixon's copy of Landseer's dog "Pixie," from the original painting, was very carefully and beautifully rendered.

Mr. Faulkner's portraits, though of a very different character, were quite equal in artistic excellence to M. Salomon's.

Mr. Bedford's landscapes presented their usual charm, and the tone of his prints seemed to surpass the general beauty of his every-day work.

Mr. Blanchard also exhibited some excellent landscapes, and displayed his usual happy choice of subject and point of sight.

An immense number of photographs by amateurs, Mr. Brownrigg, Mr. Beasley, and others, were exhibited in folios and distributed about the walls, but it is impossible for me to describe or criticise more.

I have already drawn my yarn a good length, and shall conclude by repeating what I said at starting, that a pleasanter evening, or more useful and instructive exhibition, has never been got up by the Photographic Society of London, and it is to be hoped that the success and *eclat* attending it will encourage

them to go and do likewise next year, and every succeeding one of its natural life, which I doubt not will be long and prosperous, for the exhibition just closed has given unmistakable evidence of there being "life in the old dog yet."
Photographic News, Nov. 22nd, 1867.

THE USE OF CLOUDS IN LANDSCAPES.

THE subject of printing skies and cloud effects from separate negatives having been again revived by the reading of papers on that subject at the South London Photographic Society, I think it will not be out of place now to call attention to some points that have not been commented upon—or, at any rate, very imperfectly—by either the readers of the papers or by the speakers at the meetings, when the subject was under discussion.

The introduction of clouds in a landscape by an artist is not so much to fill up the blank space above the object represented on the lower part of the canvas or paper, as to assist in the composition of the picture, both as regards linear and aerial perspective, and in the arrangement of light and shade, so as to secure a just balance and harmony of the whole, according to artistic principles.

Clouds are sometimes employed to repeat certain lines in the landscape composition, so as to increase their strength and beauty, and to unite the terrestrial part of the picture with the celestial. At other times they are used to balance a composition, both in form and effect, to prevent the picture being divided into two distinct and diagonal portions, as evidenced in many of the pictures by Cuyp; on other occasions they are introduced solely for chiaroscuro effects, so as to enable the artist to place masses of dark upon light, and *vice versa*. Of that use I think the works of Turner will afford the most familiar and beautiful examples.

In the instances cited, I make no allusion to the employment of clouds as repeaters of colour, but merely confine my remarks to their use in assisting to carry out form and effect, either in linear composition, or in the arrangement of light and shade in simple monochrome, as evidenced in the engraved translations of the works of Rembrandt, Turner, Birket Foster, and others, the study of those works being most applicable to the practice of photography, and, therefore, offering the most valuable hints to both amateur and professional photographers in the management of their skies.

Before pursuing this part of my subject further, it may be as well, perhaps, to state my general opinions of the effects of so-called "natural skies," obtained by one exposure and one printing. Admitting that they are a vast improvement on the white-sky style of the early ages of photography, they fall far short of what they should be in artistic effect and arrangement. In nearly all the "natural skies" that I have seen, their office appears to be no other than to use up the white paper above the terrestrial portion of the picture. The masses of clouds, if there, seem always in the wrong place, and never made use of for breadth of chiaroscuro.

No better illustrations of this can be adduced than those large photographs of Swiss and Alpine scenery by Braun of Dornach, which nearly all contain "natural clouds;" but, on looking them over, it will be seen that few (if any) really exhibit that artistic use of clouds in the composition of the pictures which evidence artistic knowledge. The clouds are taken just as they happen to be, without reference to their employment to enhance the effects of any of the objects in the lower portion of the view, or as aids to the composition and general effect. For the most part, the clouds are small and spotty, ill-assorting with the grandeur of the landscapes, and never assisting the chiaroscuro in an artistic sense. The most noticeable example of the latter defect may be seen in the picture entitled "Le Mont Pilate," wherein a bald and almost white mountain is placed against a light sky, much to the injury of its form, effect, and grandeur; indeed, the mountain is barely saved from being lost in the sky, although it is the principal object in the picture. Had an artist attempted to paint such a subject, he would have relieved such a large mass of light against a dark cloud. An example of a different character is observable in another photograph, wherein a dark conical mount would have been much more artistically rendered had it been placed against a large mass of light clouds. There are two or three fleecy white clouds about the summit of the mountain, but, as far as pictorial effect goes, they would have been better away, for the mind is left in doubt whether they are really clouds, or the sulphurous puffs that float about the crater of a slumbering volcano. That photographs possessing all the effects required by the rules of art are difficult, and almost impossible to obtain at one exposure in the camera, I readily allow. I know full well that a man might wait for days and weeks before the clouds would arrange themselves so as to relieve his principal object most advantageously; and, even if the desirable effects of light and shade were obtained, the chances are that the forms would not harmonize with the leading lines of the landscape.

This being the case, then, it must be self-evident that the best mode of procedure will be to *print in skies* from separate negatives, either taken from nature or from drawings made for the purpose by an artist that thoroughly understands art in all its principles. By these means, especially the latter, skies may be introduced into the photographic picture that will not only be adapted to each individual scene, but will, in every instance where they are employed, increase the artistic merit and value of the composition. But to return to the subject chiefly under consideration.

Clouds in landscape pictures, like "man in his time," play many parts—"they have their exits and their entrances." And it is almost impossible to say enough in a short paper on a subject so important to all landscape photographers. I will, however, as briefly and lucidly as I can, endeavour to point out the chief uses of clouds in landscapes. Referring to their use for effects in light and shade, I wrote, at the commencement of this paper, that the engraved translations of Turner afford the most familiar and beautiful examples, which they undoubtedly do. But when I consider that Turner's skies are nearly all sunsets, the study of them will not be so readily turned to practical account by the photographer as the works of others,—Birket Foster, for instance. His works are almost equal to Turner's in light and shade; he has been largely employed in the illustration of books, and five shillings will procure more of his beautiful examples of sky effects than a guinea will of Turner's. Take, for example, Sampson Low and Son's five shilling edition of Bloomfield's "Farmer's Boy," or Gray's "Elegy in a Churchyard," profusely illustrated almost entirely by Birket Foster; and in them will be seen such a varied and marvellous collection of beautiful sky effects as seem almost impossible to be the work of one man, and all of them profitable studies for both artist and photographer in the varied uses made of clouds in landscapes. In those works it will be observed that where the lower part of the picture is rich in variety of subject the sky is either quiet or void of form, partaking of one tint only slightly broken up. Where the terrestrial part of the composition is tame, flat, and destitute of beautiful objects, the sky is full of beauty and grandeur, rich in form and masses of light and shade, and generally shedding a light on the insignificant object below, so as to invest it with interest in the picture, and connect it with the story being told.

From both of these examples the photographer may obtain a suggestion, and slightly tint the sky of his picture, rich in objects of interest, so as to resemble the tint produced by the "ruled lines" representing a clear blue sky in an engraving.

Hitherto that kind of tinting has generally been overdone, giving it more the appearance of a heavy fog lifting than a calm blue sky. The darkest part of the tint should just be a little lower than the highest light on the principal object. This tint may either be obtained in the negative itself at the time of exposure, or produced by "masking" during the process of printing. On the other hand, when the subject has little to recommend it in itself, it may be greatly increased in pictorial power and interest by a judicious introduction of beautiful cloud effects, either obtained from nature, or furnished by the skill of an artist. If the aid of an artist be resorted to, I would not recommend painting on the negative, but let the artist be furnished with a plain white-sky print; let him wash in a sky, in sepia or india ink, that will most harmonise, both in form and effect, with the subject represented, take a negative from that sky alone, and put it into each of the pictures by double printing. This may seem a great deal of trouble and expense, and not appear to the minds of some as altogether legitimate, but I strenuously maintain that any means employed to increase the artistic merit and value of a photograph is strictly legitimate; and that wherever and however art can be resorted to, without doing violence to the truthfulness of nature, the status of our art-science will be elevated, and its professional disciples will cease to be the scorn of men who take pleasure in deriding the, sometimes—may I say too often?—lame and inartistic productions of the camera.

THE USE OF CLOUDS AS BACKGROUNDS IN PORTRAITURE

There has long been in the world an aphorism that everything in Nature is beautiful. Collectively this is true, and so it is individually, so far as the adaptability and fitness of the object to its proper use are concerned; but there are many things which are truly beautiful in themselves, and in their natural uses, which cease to be so when they are pressed into services for which they are not intended by the great Creator of the universe. For example, what can be more beautiful than that compound modification of cloud forms commonly called a "mackerel sky," which is sometimes seen on a summer evening? What can be more lovely, or more admirably adapted to the purposes of reflecting and conducting the last flickering rays of the setting sun into the very zenith, filling half the visible heavens with a fretwork of gorgeous crimson, reflecting a warm, mysterious light on everything below, and filling the mind with wonder and admiration at the marvellous beauties which the heavens are showing? Yet, can anything be more unsuitable for forming the background to a portrait, where everything should be subdued, secondary, and subservient to the features of the individual represented—where everything should be lower in tone than the light on the face, where neither colour nor light should be introduced that would tend to distract the attention of the observer—where neither accessory nor effect should appear that does not help to concentrate the mind on the grand object of the picture—the likeness? Still, how often do we see a photographic portrait stuck against a sky as spotty, flickering, and unsuitable as the one just described! How seriously are the importance and brilliancy of the head interfered with by the introduction of such an unsuitable background! How often is the interest of the spectator divided between the portrait and the "overdone" sky, so elaborately got up by the injudicious background painter! Such backgrounds are all out of place, and ought to be abandoned—expelled from every studio

As the photographer does not possess the advantages of the painter, to produce his effects by contrast of colour, it behoves him to be much more particular in his treatment of light and shade; but most particularly in his choice of a background that will most harmonise with the dress, spirit, style, and condition in life of his sitter. It is always possible for a member of any class of the community to be surrounded or relieved by a plain, quiet background; but it is not possible, in nine cases out of ten, for some individuals who sit for their portraits ever to be dwellers in marble halls, loungers in the most gorgeous conservatories, or strollers in such delightful gardens. In addition to the unfitness of such scenes to the character and every-day life of the sitter, they are the most unsuitable for pictorial effect that can possibly be employed. For, instead of directing attention to the principal object, they disturb the mind, and set it wandering all over the picture, and interfere most seriously with that quiet contemplation of the features which is so necessary to enable the beholder to discover all the characteristic points in the portrait. When the likeness is a very bad one, this may be advantageous, on the principle of putting an ornamental border round a bad picture with the view of distracting the attention of the observer, and preventing the eye from resting long enough on any one spot to discover the defects.

When clouds are introduced as backgrounds to portraits, they should not be of that small, flickering character previously alluded to, but broad, dark, and "massy," so as to impart by contrast more strength of light to the head; and the lighter parts of the clouds should be judiciously placed either above or below the head, so as to carry the light into other parts of the picture, and prevent the strongly-lighted head appearing a spot. The best examples of that character will be found in the engraved portraits by Reynolds, Lawrence, Gainsborough, and others, many of which are easily obtained at the old print shops; some have appeared in the *Art Journal*.

As guides for introducing cloud effects, accessories, and landscape bits into the backgrounds of carte-de-visite and cabinet pictures, no better examples can be cited than those exquisite little figure subjects by R. Westall, R.A., illustrating

Sharpe's Editions of the Old Poets. The engravings are about the size of cartes-de-visite, and are in themselves beautiful examples of composition, light, and shade, and appropriateness of accessory to the condition and situation of the figures, affording invaluable suggestions to the photographer in the arrangement of his sitter, or groups, and in the choice of suitable accessories and backgrounds. Such examples are easily obtained. Almost any old bookstall in London possesses one or more of those works, and each little volume contains at least half-a-dozen of these exquisite little gems of art.

Looking at those beautiful photographic cartes-de-visite by Mr. Edge, I am very strongly impressed with the idea that they were suggested by some such artistic little pictures as Westall's Illustrations of the Poets. They are really charming little photographs, and show most admirably how much the interest and artistic merit of a photograph can be enhanced by the skilful and judicious introduction of a suitable background. I may as well observe, *en passant*, that I have examined these pictures very carefully, and have come to the conclusion that the effects are not produced by means of any of the ingeniously contrived appliances for poly-printing recently invented and suggested, but that the effects are produced simply by double-printing, manipulated with consummate care and judgment, the figure or figures being produced on a plain or graduated middle tint background in one negative, and the landscape effect printed on from another negative after the first print has been taken out of the printing frame; the figures protected by a mask nicely adjusted. My impressions on this subject are strengthened almost to conviction when I look at one of Mr. Edge's photographs, in particular a group of two ladies, the sitting figure sketching. In this picture, the lower part of the added landscape—trees—being darker than the normal tint of the ground, shows a *line* round the black dress of the lady, as if the mask had overlapped it just a hair's breadth during the process of secondary printing. Be that as it may, they are lovely little pictures, and afford ample evidence of what may be done by skill and taste to vary the modes of treating photography more artistically, by introducing natural scenery sufficiently subdued to harmonise with the portrait or group; and, by similar means, backgrounds of clouds and interiors may be added to a plain photograph, which would enrich its pictorial effect, and enable the photographer to impart to his work a greater interest and beauty, and, at the same time, be made the means of giving apparent occupation to his sitter. This mode of treatment would enable him, in a great measure, to carry out the practice of nearly all the most celebrated portrait painters, viz., that of considering the form, light, shade, and character of the background *after* the portrait was finished, by adapting the light, shade, and composition of his background to the pose and condition of life of his sitter.

I shall now conclude my remarks with a quotation from Du Fresnoy's "Art of Painting," bearing directly on my subject and that of light and shade :—

> "Permit not two conspicuous lights to shine
> With rival radiance in the same design ;
> But yield to one alone the power to blaze,
> And spread th' extensive vigour of its rays ;
> There where the noblest figures are displayed,
> Thence gild the distant parts and lessening fade ·
> As fade the beams which Phœbus from the east
> Flings vivid forth to light the distant West,
> Gradual those vivid beams forget to shine,
> So gradual let thy pictured lights decline."

"LUX GRAPHICUS" ON THE WING.

Dear Mr. Editor,—I have often troubled you with some of my ideas and opinions concerning the progress and status of photography, and you have pretty often transferred the same to the columns of the *Photographic News*, and troubled your readers in much the same manner. This time, however, I am going to tell you a secret—a family secret. They are always more curious, interesting, and important than other secrets, state secrets and Mr. McLachlan's photographic secret not excepted. But to my subject: "*The* Secret." Well, dear Mr. Editor, you know that my vocations have been rather arduous for some time past, and I feel that a little relaxation from pressing cares and anxieties would be a great boon to me. You know, also, that I am a great lover of nature, almost a stickler for it, to the exclusion of *prejudicial art*. And now that the spring has come and winter has fled on the wings of the fieldfares and woodcocks —that's Thomas Hood's sentiment made seasonable—I fain would leave the pent-up city, where the colour of the sky can seldom be seen for the veil of yellow smoke which so constantly obscures it, and betake myself to the country, and inhale the fresh breezes of early spring; gladden my heart and eyes with a sight of the bright blue sky, the glistening snowdrops and glowing yellow crocuses, and regale my ears and soul with the rich notes of the thrush and blackbird, and the earliest song of the lark at the gates of heaven.

It is a pleasant thing to be able to shake off the mud and gloom of a winter's sojourn in a town, in the bright, fresh fields of the country, and bathe your fevered and enfeebled body in the cool airs of spring, as they come gushing down from the hills, or across the rippling lake, or dancing sea. I always had such a keen relish for the country at all seasons of the year, it is often a matter of wonder to me that I ever could bring my mind to the necessity of living in a town. But bread and butter do not grow in hedgerows, though "bread and cheese" do; still the latter will not support animal life of a higher order than grub or caterpillars "There's the rub." The mind is, after all, the slave of the body, for the mind must bend to the requirements of the body; and, as a man cannot live by gazing at a "colt's foot," and if he have no appetite for horseflesh, he is obliged to succumb to his fate, and abide in a dingy, foggy, slushy, and bewildering world of mud, bricks, and mortar, instead of revelling in the bright fields, fresh air, and gushing melodies which God created for man, and gave man senses to enjoy his glorious works.

But, Mr. Editor, I am mentally wandering among "cowslips," daises, buttercups, and wild strawberry blossoms, and forgetting the stern necessity of confining my observations to a subject coming reasonably within the range of a class journal which you so ably conduct; but it is pardonable and advantageous to allow mind to run before matter sometimes, for the latter is more frequently inert than the former, and when the mind has gone *ahead*, the body is sure to follow. Melancholy instances of that present themselves to our notice too frequently. For example, when a poor lady's or gentleman's wits are gone, *lettres des cachets*, and some kind or *un*kind friends, send the witless body to some retreat where the wits of all the inmates are gone. I must, however, in all sober earnestness, return to my subject, or I fear you will say "He is going to Hanwell." Well, perhaps I am, for I know that photography is practised at that admirable institution; and now that I have struck a professional chord, I may as well play on it.

Lenses and cameras, like birds and flowers, reappear in spring, and, as the season advances and the sun attains a higher altitude, amateurs and professionals are quickened into a surprising activity. Renewed life is imparted to them, and the gregarious habits of man are developed in another form, and somewhat in the manner that the swallows return to their old haunts. At first, a solitary scout or reconnoitering party makes his appearance, then another, and another, until a complete flock of amateur and professional photographers are abroad, seeking what food they can devour: some preferring the first green "bits of foliage" that begin to gem the woods with emeralds, others waiting till the leaf is fully out, and the trees are thickly clothed in their early summer loveliness: while others prefer a more advanced state of beauty, and like to depict nature in her russet hues, when the trees " are in their yellow leaf." Some are contented with the old-fashioned homesteads and sweet green lanes of England for their subjects; others prefer the ruined abbeys and castles of the feudal ages, with their deeply interesting associations; others choose the more mythical monuments of superstition and the dark ages, such as King Arthur's round tables, druidical circles, and remains of their rude temples of stone. Some delight in pictorializing the lakes and mountains of the north, while others are not satisfied with anything short of the sublime beauty and terrific grandeur of the Alps and Pyrennees. Truly, sir, I think it may be safely stated that photographers are lovers of nature, and, I think, they are also lovers of art. If some of them do not possess that art knowledge which is so necessary for them to pursue advantageously either branch of their profession, it is much to be regretted; but there is now no reason why they should continue in darkness any longer. I know that it requires years of study and practice to become an artist, but it does not require a very great amount of mental labour or sacrifice of time to become an artistic photographer. A little hard study of the subject as it appears in the columns of your journal and those of your contemporaries—for I notice that they have *all* suddenly become alive to the necessity of imparting to photographers a knowledge of art principles—will soon take the scales off the eyes of a man that is blind in art, and enable him to comprehend the mysteries of lines, unity, and light and shade, and give him the power to compose his subject as readily as he could give a composing draught to an infant, and teach him to determine at a glance the light, shade, and atmospheric effects that would most harmonize with the scene to be represented. Supposing that he is master of the mechanical manipulations of photography, he has acquired half the skill of the artist; and by studying and applying the rules of composition and light and shade to his mechanical skill, he is then equal to the artist in the treatment of his subject, so far as the means he employs will or can enable him to give an art rendering of nature, fixed and immovable.

I do not profess to be a teacher, but I do think it is much more genial in spirit, and becoming the dignity of a man, to impart what little knowledge he has to others, than to scoff at those who do not know so much. If, therefore, Mr. Editor, in the course of my peregrinations, I see an opportunity of calling your attention, and, through you, the attention of others, to any glaring defects or absurdities in the practice of our dearly beloved art, I shall not hesitate to do so; not, however, with any desire to carp and cavil at them for cavilling's sake, but with the more laudable desire of pointing them out, that they may be avoided. During the coming summer I shall have, or hope to have, many opportunities of seeing and judging, and will endeavour to keep you duly advised of what is passing before me.

My letters may come from all parts—N., E., W., and S.—so that they will, in that sense at least, harmonize with the nomenclature of your periodical. Where I may be at the date of my writing, the post-mark will reveal to you. And now I must consider my signature: much is in a name, you know. I can hardly call myself your "Special Correspondent"—that would be too much *a la Sala;* nor can I subscribe myself an "Old Photographer," for that would be taking possession of another man's property, and might lead to confusion, if not to difficulties; neither can I style myself a "Peripatetic Photographer"—though I am one—for that name sometimes appears in the columns of a contemporary; and my own name is such a long one, consisting of nearly half the letters of the alphabet. Well, I think, all things considered, I cannot do better than retain my old *nom de plume.* And with many apologies for this

long, round-about paper, and every expression of regard, I beg to subscribe myself your obliged and humble servant,
  March 27th, 1868. Lux Graphicus (J. Werge).

"LUX GRAPHICUS" ON THE WING.
Oxford and Cambridge—Cabinet Portraits—Mr. McLachlan's Secret.

Dear Mr. Editor,—Do not let the above heading alarm you. I have no desire to convert the columns of your valuable journal into a kind of photographic *Bell's Life* or *Sporting Chronicle*. Although the great University boat race has just been decided for the eighth consecutive time in favour of Oxford, it is not of that aquatic struggle that I am going to write, but of another matter in which the Cantabs seem to be behind the Oxonians in the race of life, or the pursuit of novelties. Not only are the Cantabs short in their stroke with the oars, and unable to obtain the first place in the contests on the Thames, they are also slow in giving their orders for a certain article of commerce which is of very great importance to professional photographers, especially those in the neighbourhood of the University of Cambridge. It is a remarkable fact, that while Oxford has gone in with a rush for those very charming portraits technically named "cabinets," Cambridge holds aloof. How is this, I wonder. There are as good photographers in Cambridge—Mr. Mayland, to wit, whose work is all of the first class—as in Oxford; the sun shines as brightly in the region of the Cam as he does in that of the Isis. Have the Cantabs made up their minds not to be *cabinet* men in opposition to Oxford? or is the fact due to the lukewarmness of the Cambridge photographers themselves? It seems somewhat strange that two places likely to be so similar in tastes and a refined appreciation of the beautiful should so differ in this respect. Are the men of the two great seats of learning in this country opposed in matters of photographic proportion as they are in other matters of minor importance—as in the proper pronunciation of either and neither, for instance? Not having graduated at either, I do not know which is correct, neither do I care; but I am concerned in this question of photography. While at Oxford the cabinet picture has taken deep root, and has grown into a strong and vigorous article of demand, it is a well-known fact that at Cambridge it is "sicklied o'er with the pale cast of thought," and languishes on in a state trembling between life and death. Whether the producers or consumers are to blame for this langour in the demand for an article that is certainly worth being cultivated, is more than I can say. I know that the discrepancy exists, and the rest I leave to those most immediately interested. It cannot, however, be supposed that a demand for any particular size or style can spring up spontaneously; that must be created by the producer, by popularising the style in some attractive and judicious manner, and the cabinet size is well deserving of a very strenuous effort being made in its favour.

Of all the photographic sizes that have been introduced to the public, the cabinet is the most artistic in its proportions. As nearly as possible it falls under that art rule of producing an oblong or parallelogram of the most agreeable proportions, which is as the diagonal is to the square. The size of the cabinet is $5\frac{1}{2}$ by 4, and if you measure the diagonal of the square of 4 inches, you will find that the length of the cabinet, $5\frac{1}{2}$ inches, is as near that as possible. Doubtless Mr Window had this in view when he introduced the size, and whether for upright or horizontal pictures, such proportions are decidedly the best. Many of the sizes already in use are too long, others are too short and square. In addition to the beautiful proportions of the cabinet size, it gives the portrait photographer more room and opportunities to introduce harmonious forms and effects in the posing and arrangements of portraits and groups, and I have seen some very charming views on the cabinet size, $5\frac{1}{2}$ by 4 inches horizontally; as well as some very beautiful interiors of Westminster Abbey, by Mr. V. Blanchard, on the cabinet cards vertical, which proves pretty conclusively that the proportions of the diagonal to the square of any size will suit both vertical and horizontal pictures. I have not the least doubt but a much greater demand for those cabinet pictures, both portrait and landscape, could be created, if photographers would set about introducing them with a will: depend upon it if they will but put their heart into the matter, they would put money into their pockets. I know how much has been done by launching them fearlessly on the sea of public patronage in several localities, and I feel certain the demand would be much more general if the cabinet picture were judiciously introduced. Mr. H. P. Robinson and Mr. Nelson K. Cherrill, having entered into partnership, are on the point of opening a photographic establishment at Tunbridge Wells, where they intend to incur considerable expense to introduce the cabinet portrait, and give it that prominence it so justly merits.

Since writing you last, I learn from a friend who is intimate with Mr. McLachlan that there is every possibility of his secret being revealed ere long. That this secret formula will be an immense boon to all photographers, there can be little doubt. If an absolute immunity from streaks in the direction of the dip, brain-markings, and pinholes—which are the advantages said to be derived from the process—can be guaranteed, then will the manipulatory part of photography be at once made easy; and Mr McLachlan will have conferred a personal obligation on every photographic manipulator. Not only will photographers be benefitted by Mr. McLachlan's generous conduct, the whole world will participate in the advantages he intends to place as a gift in the hands of photographers; and even *art*, that is so afraid of a photographic amalgamation, will be *honoured* by the revelation. But once let the mind of the operator be for ever free from the cares and anxieties of his negative being clean, spotless, and excellent in quality, he will then have more time and inclination to put his art knowledge, if he have any, into practice, by paying more attention to the pose of his sitters and the artistic choice and arrangement of accessories. If he be without art knowledge he will be obliged to acquire it and put it into practice, or be driven out of his field of operations. For, if the chemical difficulties and uncertainties are to be so summarily disposed of, and all the manipulations reduced to a certainty and dead level, a pre-eminence in the profession can only be maintained by him who exhibits a taste, feeling, and love for his labours superior to the desire to palm upon the public, for mere gain, works that are a disgrace and a scandal to the profession of which he is a member. That such a condition of things photographic may be quickly brought about is much to be desired, and if such be the result of Mr. McLachlan's very noble willingness to give to the photographic community experiences that have cost him much time and money in acquiring by close observation and experiment, he will, at the least, be entitled to the sincere and hearty acknowledgments of all well-wishers and lovers of our art-science.

Apropos of clean and easy development, I should like to know if any of your numerous readers have tried the effect of sulphate of zinc with the iron developer. I understand its use obviates the necessity of using acetic acid as a retardant; that the deposit of silver is much more delicate than that produced by iron alone; that the control over it is very great; that any amount of intensity can be obtained by one or more applications, without the aid of pyrogallic acid, and without producing harshness or hardness. With such recommendations it is certainly worth a trial. I have had no time to try it myself, but think it is of sufficient importance to give your readers an opportunity of experimenting with it, and judging for themselves.

Photographic News, April 10th, 1868.

"LUX GRAPHICUS" ON THE WING.

THE LATE LORD BROUGHAM—NEW FIELDS FOR PHOTOGRAPHY—
NATURAL OBJECTS COLOURED—THE MONOCHROME AND AUTO-
TYPE—MR. MCLACHLAN AGAIN.

DEATH has just swept away one of the most gigantic intellects of the nineteenth century. For me to state what the late Lord Brougham was, or attempt to enumerate his vast attainments, or measure the strength of his colossal mind, would be a piece of intolerable presumption; but I think I may safely say that he was an enthusiastic admirer of photography. Years ago, in the midst of his parliamentary and other pressing duties, whenever he could find time to enjoy the quiet of Brougham Hall, near Penrith, his giant mind was not above indulging in the delightful relaxation it afforded; and many a pleasant hour he used to spend chatting with Mr. Jacob Thompson, an artist of great ability, and also a very early amateur photographer, on the wonderful results obtained by the new art. The late Lord Brougham began his literary career by publishing a treatise on "Light," before photography was known or thought to be practicable; in after life he interested himself in its marvellous productions, and his last literary labour was also about light. Not only did the great statesman "know a little of everything," he did a little in everything. The deceased lord took a lively interest in the progress of photography during his lifetime, from its earliest introduction to within a short period of his death; and it would have been a graceful and fitting compliment to the memory of the great man of law, politics, literature, and science, if the English newspapers had embellished their memoirs of the late Lord Brougham with a photographic portrait of his lordship. Such a thing is quite practicable, and has been done successfully by our more enterprising confrères in Canada and the United States. The *Montreal Weekly Herald* of April 18th illustrates its memoir of the late Mr. T. d'Arcy McGee with a very excellent carte-de-visite portrait of the lamented and unfortunate Canadian Minister, mounted on the upper corner of the front page, surrounded with a deep black border What an appropriate accompaniment such a presentation would have been to the able articles and memoirs which appeared in the daily press on Monday, May 11th, 1868! How much more interesting and valuable those clever biographical sketches of great men, as they pass away to their rest, which appear in the *Daily Telegraph* and other daily and weekly papers, would appear if illustrated with a photograph from life! That it can be done the *Montreal Weekly Herald* has recently and satisfactorily shown ; and surely there is enterprise, spirit, and wealth enough among the British newspaper proprietors to follow the very laudable example of our transatlantic cousins. Negatives of great men are always attainable, and there need be no commercial difficulty between the photographer and newspaper proprietor on the score of supply. A multiplication of negatives or Woodbury's process, would afford all the necessary facilities for producing the prints in large numbers.

Many new fields for the good of photography are opening up. Pathological works have been photographically illustrated with some amount of success. But far pleasanter fields are open to enterprising photographers in the faithful representation of natural objects, such as flowers, fruits, ferns, grasses, shrubs, trees, shells, seaweeds, birds, butterflies, moths, and every variety of animal life, from the lowest orders to the highest. I believe the time is not far distant when the best works on all the physical sciences will be illustrated by coloured photographs. Those very beautiful German photographs of flowers recently introduced show most conclusively of what photography is capable as a help to a study of the natural sciences The flowers are not only photographed from nature, but exquisitely coloured after the same fountain of truth ; and the sense of reality, roundness, and relief which they convey is truly wonderful.

Hitherto the colouring of natural objects photographed from nature has been a very difficult thing to accomplish; but now it is done, and with a marvellous success.

The monochromatic process is also making great strides in advance. Those very beautiful transparencies, cabinet size, of the Queen and Royal Family are now to be seen in most of the photographic picture shop-windows in town and country. These transparencies are the productions of the Disderi Company, by Woodbury's photo-relief process, and the results now obtained are really beautiful, both in effect and colour, and sold at a very low price. But the *chef d'œuvre* of all monochromatic effects has just been achieved by the triple labours of Mr. Macnee, the artist, and Mr. Annan, the photographer, of Glasgow, and Mr. J. W. Swan, of Newcastle. The subject in question is a work of art in every respect. The original is a full-length portrait of Lord Belhaven, painted by Daniel Macnee, and now in the Royal Academy Exhibition. A photograph taken from the painting by Mr. Annan was worked up in monochrome by the eminent artist, from which another negative was taken by the same skilful photographer, and placed in the hands of Mr. J. W. Swan to be printed in carbon, which the latter gentleman has done in the most admirable manner. Altogether, the result is the most satisfactory reproduction by photography that has ever been placed before the public, and is less like a photograph and more like a fine mezzotint engraving than anything I ever saw. Mr. Annan is now publishing the work on his own responsibility, and a specimen of it can be seen at the offices of "The Autotype Printing and Publishing Co.," 5, Haymarket, London. Mr. Hill, of Edinburgh, is also about to publish, in carbon, a photograph of that beautifully painted picture entitled "A Fairy Raid," which was exhibited last year in the rooms of the Royal Academy by Sir Noel Paton. As in the former case, Mr. Annan copied the painting, Sir Noel worked on a print in monochrome, which was again photographed by Mr. Annan, and the negative passed to Mr. J. W. Swan to be printed in carbon. I understand that Poynter's celebrated picture of "Israel in Egypt" is about to be published, in a similar manner, by the Autotype Company. It is therefore quite evident that photography is becoming, in reality, more and more "a foe to graphic art," and eclipsing the lights and deepening the shadows of the *unluxy* engraver.

Mr. McLachlan has again spoken without giving any very materially new facts, or throwing much more light on his mysterious mode of working. The great point is, to throw light on the concentrated solution of nitrate of silver; and until that has been done it will be impossible for any one to say from experience and practice that there is nothing in the principle. Mr. McLachlan attributes a chemical property to the action of light on the bath that has never been thought of before, and he seems to believe it so sincerely himself, and expresses his convictions so earnestly, that I think photographers are somewhat bound to wait patiently till time and light will enable them to comply with all the conditions he lays down, and make a series of careful experiments, before they can say whether they are under obligations to him or not. At any rate, natural justice suggests that they should not render a foregone verdict.

May 17th, 1868.

THE EXHIBITION OF NATIONAL PORTRAITS—THE TINTYPE OF AMERICA—THE SPIRIT OF PHOTOGRAPHY IN CANADA—THE "WISE WEEK," AND THE TOTAL ECLIPSE OF THE SUN.

DEAR MR. EDITOR,—From various causes I have been absent from your columns as a contributor for some time, but not as a reader. The chief reason for this was the weather, which of late has been so hot and prostrating as to dry up both my ink and my energies. Now that the atmosphere is more cool, moist, and pleasant, my ink and my thoughts may flow together, and the resulting epistle may find a place on some page of the PHOTOGRAPIC NEWS; if not, I shall not be angry. I know that the world—and photography is my world—is not always mindful of its atoms. The great and immortal Cicero discovered that even he could be absent from Rome, and all Rome not know it. How much easier, then, for your readers not to discover my absence from your pages. But my inability to write and attend to other duties entailed more serious losses to myself. Amongst others I missed seeing the Royal Academy Exhibition, but found a compensating pleasure in going to see the Exhibition of National Portraits at South Kensington. What a school it is for photographers! What a variety of pose, arrangement, management of light and shade, is to be seen in that glorious collection of Vandykes, Hogarths, Gainsboroughs, Reynolds, Opies, Wilkies, Raeburns, Northcotes, Lawrences, Phillips, Shees, Richmonds, Grants, and many others of the present day! I hope many photographers have seen the collection. None ought to have missed the opportunity. All that saw must have profited by the sight. Portraits of great men that have been familiar to me in black and white for years were there before me in the rich mellow colouring of Vandyke, Reynolds, Wilkie, and Lawrence, and the mind seemed carried back into the past while looking at the works of those great artists.

The exhibition will soon close, and all that have not seen it should endeavour to do so at once. There may never again be seen such a gathering together of the great of England, painted by England's greatest portrait painters. The Manchester Art Treasures Exhibition was a great assemblage of the glory of England, but it was not so complete, nor so instructive, nor so comfortable to view as that now open at South Kensington. In addition to the paintings there is a large and valuable collection of rare engravings, both in mezzotints and in line. The latter collection alone would make a visit highly pleasing, and, in a sense, remunerative to every photographer. Art is beginning to take root in the minds of those who follow photography, either professionally or for amusement, and those exhibitions are the salt that "savoureth the earth," which in due time will bring forth rich fruits

The "Tintype" is now being largely practised in America, and is fitted into an envelope or slip, carte-de-visite size. The slip is formed of paper, with an aperture to show the picture, and a flap to fall over it as a protector. I had some of these shown to me a short time ago. The tintype is only another name for the ferrotype or melainotype, which is a collodion positive picture taken on a piece of tin or iron, coated with black japan on the front, and a varnish on the back, to prevent the metal from acting on the bath. The carte-de-visite form of the tintype fitted in the envelope or holder is a very good and ready way of supplying all portraits wanted in a hurry, and its adoption might be found very serviceable to many photographers in England. The American examples that I have seen are very brilliant and beautiful, and, to my mind, next in delicacy of detail and richness of colour to the long discarded but ever beautiful Daguerreotype. I must admit, *en passant*, that the Americans always excelled in producing fine, brilliant Daguerreotypes, and it is much the same with them in the production of glass positives, ferrotypes, or tintypes

The spirit of photography in America and Canada is admirable. Mr. Notman, of Montreal, has long been doing some excellent cabinet pictures representing out of-door-life, pleasures, and pastimes. Now Mr. Inglis, of Montreal, also produces most beautiful carte-de-visite and cabinet pictures of indoor and out-of-door scenes, such as drawing-rooms, libraries, &c., with suitably arranged and occupied figures in the former, and boating, bathing, and fishing parties in the latter Some of these pictures have recently been shown to me. They are all very fine examples of photography. The tone and quality of some are beautiful. Many of them are admirably arranged, and exhibit considerable knowledge of composition; but some of them, particularly the interiors, are sadly at fault in their chiaroscuro. They possess no dominant light, or, if they do, it is in the wrong place, leading the eye away from the principal object. In most cases the lights are too scattered, giving a spotty and flickering effect to the picture, which is painful to look at. With his out-of-door scenes Mr. Inglis is more happy, and probably, from his antecedents, more at home. For example, the "Boating Party" is very happily composed, embracing the double form of angular composition—the triangle and the lozenge—and just a little more skill or care would have made it perfect in its lines. The whole scene is well lighted and got up. The boat, foreground of pebbles, stones, shrubs, and trees are all real; the water is represented by tin-foil, wet black oilcloth, or something of the kind, which reflects the forms and colours of objects placed upon or above it. The reflections seem too sharp to be those of water. The plan adopted by Mr. Ross, of Edinburgh, is the best. That gentleman has a large shallow trough fitted up in his studio with water in it.

Surely such pictures of groups of friends and families would take in London and the provinces if people only knew where to get them. At present I know there is not a place in London where photographic pictures possessing such a variety and interest can be obtained. Mr. Faulkner is the only photographer that has yet attempted to produce such rural subjects in London, but I am not aware that he has yet introduced "the boat" into his studio.

This is the "Wise Week," and it is to be hoped that the gathering together of the wisdom of the world at Norwich will in some way be beneficial to photography. You, Mr. Editor, I presume, will attend the meetings, and I shall look forward with considerable interest to your gleanings from the harvest of science that will this year be garnered in the transactions of the British Association.

As I think of the date to affix to my letter, I am reminded that this is the day of the great total eclipse, visible in India, and that several expeditions are engaged in taking observations. The photographic arrangements, I notice, are more than usually complete, and I most sincerely hope that the astronomical photographers are favoured with bright and calm weather, so that they may succeed in obtaining the best photographic representations of the phenomenon. In this I am not influenced by the mere photographic idea of getting a picture, but rather with the hope that photography may be the legitimate and honourable handmaiden to the savants, astronomers, and mathematicians in enabling them to ascertain the constitutional condition, mode of sustenance, and interminable length of life of the great source of all our labours and achievements. Then would the sun write his autobiography, and his amanuensis would be his favoured child, photography.

August 18*th*, 1868

THE HARVEST IS OVER, THE GRANARIES ARE FULL, YET FAMINE IS IN OUR MIDST—PHOTOGRAPHERS' BENEVOLENT AND PROVIDENT SOCIETIES—PHOTOGRAPHY ENNOBLED—REVIVAL OF THE EBURNEUM PROCESS—THE SOCIETIES AND THE COMING SESSION—PHOTOGRAPHIC APPARATUS *v* PERSONAL LUGGAGE.

DEAR MR. EDITOR,—My quill is as restless as my wing, and, as I skim about like the swallows, many things fall under my observation that would otherwise not do so, some of which are noteworthy and of interest to the photographic profession, many are not; but harvest time is interesting to everyone, and it is of this I am going to make a few remarks. It is always a subject of grave importance and anxiety to a nation like ours, with a very limited area of cereal land, until it is known whether the harvest has been abundant or otherwise. It is also equally important that the harvest, however plentiful, should be carefully reaped and garnered, so that famine may not fall upon the people before another season of plenty shall come in its course. The cereal harvest is over, and has been wonderfully abundant, in spite of the unusually long, dry, and hot summer. The stack-yards are full, and the granaries are teeming with plenty, and there is bread enough for all that can afford to buy. There, that is the qualification that brings to my mind the most serious part of this subject. Although the season has been wonderfully fine and favourable for a rich harvest of all things, "famine is in our midst." A cry of woe is mingled with our mirth. A glorious summer and autumn have, on the whole, yielded a rich reward to the labourers in the pleasant and profitable fields of photography; yet there is want among some of the workers. In the columns of your contemporary I observe a letter "begging alms" on behalf of a poor widow and her little orphans. It is a case of pure charity, and far be it from me to say to anyone, "Do not help her;" "They have no claim on the sympathies of the photographic public;" "Neither she nor her late husband did anything to forward the progress of the art nor advance the interests of photographers in general." I grant the latter hypothesis, and say, "He that giveth to the poor lendeth to the Lord." Nevertheless, I cannot refrain from expressing my opinion that such painful appeals should not be allowed to appear in the columns of the photographic journals; all such private cases could and should be provided for by any of the provident organisations so common to other trades. The subject has been frequently mooted in your own columns, but no action has been taken. Very recently a lady correspondent called attention to the subject again, and now, in the pages of your contemporary, I notice an elaborate plan is laid down as the ground-work of a Photographers' Provident and Benevolent Society. That plan is open to some objections, but it is certainly desirable that such a society should be formed. It is rather late in the season for photographers to make any provision for cases 1 and 2, as the correspondent in your contemporary suggests—this year, at least; but I think his other plan of making a provision, however small, for widows and orphans is highly to be commended, and, if only carried into effect, would undoubtedly mitigate the anguish and lessen the fear of want in the minds of many deserving women, and might prevent the recurrence of those painful appeals to which I have just alluded. It is just as important and imperative a duty for every man to make some sort of provision for those dependent upon him as it is for the husbandman to reap and carefully house his harvest. Knowing the interest which you, Mr. Editor, personally take in this subject, I trust that you will exert your influence, and see if it be possible to found a society *at once* that will grow in after years to be a monument to photography and to the goodness and forethought of the photographers of the present generation.

Photography, like the fine arts, is honoured with a title of nobility. A baronetcy has recently fallen to the lot of one who for years has followed photography as a profession, taking cartes-de-visite and other photographs in the usual business-like manner. Of all the styles of distinction that are conferred upon men, I think baronetcies have been subject to the greatest number of vicissitudes, and spiced with the greatest amount of romance, from the romantic succession of Sir Robert Innes to Sir William Don, "a poor player;" and now the photographic profession includes among its members one of the baronets of England.

Your description of the Eburneum process, given recently in your "Visits to Noteworthy Studios," has awakened quite a new interest in that beautiful form of photograph, introduced a few years ago by Mr. Burgess. Several photographers whom I know have set about producing them. The specimens which I have seen are very beautiful as cards, but they are particularly suitable for lockets, brooches, studs, pins, rings, &c., being sharp, clear, and delicate, and easily cut to fit any size or shape.

Next month some of the London photographic societies will commence the session of 1868-9, and it might be asked, What are their prospects? It is to be hoped that the North London will do better than it did last session. There was more than one *nil* meeting. The South London will doubtless keep up its character, and exhibit its usual vitality. The personal interest taken in the meetings by their kind, genial, and courteous President is almost sure to develop all the latent force of the members. It is also to be hoped that *the* Society will make as brilliant a start as it did at the commencement of the session last November. Such an exhibition as that in Conduit Street may easily be repeated, though it may not be such a startling one.

The question raised, whether photographic apparatus be or be not considered "personal luggage" by the railway companies, is one of very great importance to photographers, but particularly to amateurs, for if decided against them it will cause no end of inconvenience, vexation, and expense by delays and extra charges. On the other hand, it must be admitted that the view taken by the railway authorities is technically correct. The very word "personal" shows that they mean such articles as are really and absolutely necessary for the personal comfort and convenience of travellers, which can only rightly include wearing apparel, changes of linen, dressing-cases, ladies' work boxes, and writing desks. These are absolutely indispensable for the comfort and convenience of travellers. Photographic apparatus, and particularly chemicals, do not come under that classification, and I think it is of great consequence to the railway companies and their passengers to know what should, or should not, be put into the "luggage van." I know a case where an amateur photographer was travelling by rail with a 12 by 10 bath full of nitrate of silver solution packed among his clothes in a box in the luggage van. The bath leaked, the solution spoiled all his shirts, and he was driven to the shift of papering the fronts. Now, supposing the box containing the leaky bath had stood upon someone else's box—say a lady's—it might have run through and spoiled some valuable dresses; at the least, it would have spoiled the appearance of the box, to the great annoyance of the lady passenger, and the probable claim on the company for compensation. There are always two sides to a question, and though few men have travelled more with photographic apparatus in the luggage van than myself, I think, in this case, the best of the argument may be fairly ceded to the railway companies.

September 18*th*, 1868.

"LUX GRAPHICUS" ON THE WING.
His Flight to and from the Exhibition of the Photographic Society.

Dear Mr. Editor,—On Tuesday night last I took the liberty of looking into the rooms of the Architectural Society, to see the photographs, and listen to the gossip of the visitors at the *conversazione* of the Photographic Society. To hear the complimentary remarks and the exclamations of pleasure was as delightful to my ear as the first song of the lark in spring.

The assemblage—not brilliant, but genial, pleasant, and happy—was as refreshing to the eye as the first glimpse of the vernal flowers; and the pictures hung upon the walls and screens, and laid upon the tables, were, in more senses than one, a feast to the mind almost without alloy. For my own part, I felt so joyful, I could not help fluttering my wings, shaking my feathers, and flitting about from one place to another, chirping, chatting, and pecking lovingly about this pretty thing, and at that old friend, till long after my usual time of going to roost. And when I did at last tear myself away and fly home, I could not help exclaiming, Well, there never was a pleasanter evening nor a nicer exhibition in the whole history of the Society! But

I could not sleep; I put my head under my wing, shook my feathers, and tried to settle into the most comfortable and cosy positions, but it was no use. The pretty landscapes and pleasing portraits I had seen shone brighter and brighter before me; I was compelled to mentally review them; and here follows the result of my incubations. My first thoughts were to work the pleasures of the evening by a kind of rule-of-three process, by considering the value of the landscapes and portraits exhibited, to arrive at the worth of the exhibition; but not so much in a money point of view, as in the merits of the works, and their probable influences on the workers.

Taking the landscape portion of the exhibition as first in the order into which I had mentally catalogued the pictures, it was an easy and delightful thing to skim over such a vast extent of this world's surface that evening. To journey to and from the glens of Scotland, the dales of England and Wales, the lakes of Ireland, the mountains of the Tyrol, to Abyssinia and the famous heights of Magdala, was but the work of a few minutes, thanks to the purveyors of that mental banquet. But to do full justice to the exhibitors I must endeavour to enumerate their principal works, and comment thereon with the utmost impartiality. Most unquestionably the gems of the landscape portion of the exhibition were eight exquisite little pictures by Mr. Russell Manners Gordon, affording unmistakable proof of what the gum-gallico dry process is capable of yielding in his hands. It is almost, if not quite, equal to the wet process for detail and delicacy. This is particularly noticeable in the view of Carnarvon Castle. Indeed, Mr. Bedford's picture of the same subject—which, I presume, is by the wet process—on the other side of the screen, contrasts rather unfavourably with it. Mr. Gordon's selection of his point of sight, and general treatment of that subject alone, are unmistakable proofs of his refined taste and feeling for the art capabilities of landscape photography. The wet-collodion pictures by Mr. Gordon are also beautiful examples of the art. His cottages with sheep browsing in the foreground, which is an instantaneous picture, is remarkable for its beauty and arrangement. These pictures are beautifully printed, and possess a tone which harmonizes charmingly with the subjects. Amongst the other landscaape photographers Mr. England and Mr. Bedford stand unrivalled in their peculiar branches. The views in the Tyrol, lately taken by Mr. England, are so excellent that they cannot but add to that gentleman's high reputation.

Mr. Bedford's views are also quite equal, if not superior, to his previously-exhibited works. Some pretty views of the Lakes of Killarney by Mr. Archibald Irvine were well worthy of notice. Mr. F. Beasley, Junr., exhibited some very excellent examples of the Fothergill process; some printed in silver, and others in carbon, from the same negatives. I think the carbon prints were superior in colour, but the silver prints possess most detail and depth. Views of Wimbledon and other places by Mr. Vernon Heath were also good examples of that gentleman's photography. Some beautiful cloud effects by Messrs. Robinson and Cherrill, of Tunbridge Wells, and Mr. Fox, of Brighton, attracted considerable attention, and elicited great praise. The large composition picture, "Returning Home," by Mr. Robinson, was greatly admired by nearly everyone that looked at it. One or two ill-natured or ignorant remarks were made about that picture, but I candidly think it is the very best picture that Mr. Robinson has produced. The sunshine on the one side, and the rain storm sweeping over the other, are both cleverly and artistically managed. I am sorry I cannot say the same of the group of children which hung near the latter. The group, though perfect in its photographic details and tone, is too suggestive of scissors and paste to be a good picture, in my estimation.

Mr. Wardley's large Taupenot pictures were very excellent. The very interesting pictures of Abyssinia by the 10th Company of Engineers were very attractive. Groups of the captives—political, religious, and artisan, with their families—and the officers of the Expedition, formed interesting pictures The views of Magdala, Theodore's house, the mushroom fortifications, and other flimsy defences, as revealed by the truth-telling camera, seemed to lessen considerably the glory of the capture of Magdala.

Having dismissed the landscape portion of the exhibition without mentioning all the many excellent contributions thereto, I next turn my thoughts again to the contributions of portraits. The examples of that branch of photography were nearly all of first-rate excellence, a large number of them being à la Salomon, M. Adam-Salomon himself contributing no less than fifteen. With one or two remarkable exceptions, these pictures were not equal to those exhibited last year, and a general feeling prevailed that they were neither his later works, nor the best of his former; still, they were a very effective display, and attracted great and deserved attention. As I have, on a former occasion, expressed my opinion on the great excellence of M. Salomon's works, I shall not comment further thereon at present, but proceed to notice those which most nearly approached them in photographic and artistic essentials. Undoubtedly Mr. Valentine Blanchard's contributions, both in number and quality, come nearer to M. Salomon's works than any other contributor's. Mr. Blanchard exhibited ten portraits à la Salomon, some of which are quite equal to the French artist's best works, without the elaborate working-up which the latter exhibit. Mr. Blanchard has not been at all times fortunate in his sitters, which is very much to be regretted, for we all know how much a beautiful subject helps a good photograph. Hitherto, Mr. Blanchard has been an exhibitor chiefly as a landscape and figure-study photographer. Now that he has taken more kindly to portraiture, and exhibits such capabilities for its successful practice, I hope he will find it sufficiently remunerative to induce him to be a steady and persevering disciple of M. Salomon. Messrs Robinson and Cherrill also exhibited two beautiful and Salomon-like portraits: one of M. Salomon himself, and one of Mr. Hain Friswell; the latter, I think, is decidedly the best. Mr. Mayland, of Cambridge, sent six very excellent portraits in Salomon's style, all very good but one; a gentleman in a velvet coat was particularly successful.

The pictures exhibited by Mr. Briggs, of Leamington, though extremely forcible and beautiful, were not exactly an imitation of the style of M. Salomon.

Mr. Leake, of Cornhill, had a frame containing six very capital portraits in the style of the eminent French photographer, but a little over-done in after-touching—too much elaborated. In this respect he far outdid his great prototype. Messrs Fradelle and Leach also exhibited a number of whole-plate pictures *à la Salomon*, which were very good indeed. Messrs. Slingsby, Burgess, Ashdown, Dunmore, and S. Fry, were also exhibitors of the same style of portraits, 10 by 8 size; but it is a pity the latter did himself the injustice of exhibiting so many, for there was only one—an old gentleman with a grey beard—that was really worthy of him. Never did any man's joke recoil more forcibly on himself than that of Mr. Fry's. The faces of some of his female portraits—one in particular—were, in my estimation, as flat, white, and shadowless as a piece or knob of sal-ammoniac itself; but I must say that the portrait of the gentleman above referred to was all that could be desired as an artistic photograph.

Amongst the cabinet pictures exhibited by English photographers, I think those by Mr. Hubbard were decidedly the finest. One entitled " The Toilet," and another of a lady seated at a window, which might be named "A Sultry Day in Town," are charmingly artistic photographs. A composition picture by the same artist was also very skilfully treated; indeed, it was mistaken by many to be a copy of a picture, and might easily have been taken for a copy of a painting by T. Faed. Mr. Briggs, Mr. Godbold (of Hastings), Mr. Gillo, Messrs. Lucas and Box, also exhibited some beautiful cabinet pictures.

Cartes-de-visite in their ordinary form were somewhat scarce, but Dr. Wallich, Mr. Charles Heath, Mr. Bateman, and others, made a good show of vignettes.

Mrs. Cameron exhibited some large pictures in her peculiar style; but my own opinion and that of others was, that she is improving.

Mr. Ernest Edwards exhibited a large collection of carbon pictures, in black and other colours; some mounted on chromo-tinted paper, and some excellent enlargements in carbon. The Autotype Company exhibited a fine copy of Lord Belhaven, which I noticed some time ago; also a very valuable and beautiful collection of copies from drawings by old masters, all bound together, making a handsome and very interesting collection.

Mr. Rejlander had a large collection of his art photographs on view, all of which were clever, some facetious, and many very beautiful conceptions.

A frame of coloured enamels by Mr. Bailey, and some in black-and-white by Mr. Henderson and Mr. Barnes, also attracted considerable notice.

The eburneumtypes by Mr. Burgess, a coloured collodio-chloride portrait on ivory by Mr. J. Edwards, and other collodio-chloride and opalotype pictures, were very much admired. The cabinet vignettes by Reutlinger, and the cabinet pictures by Wenderoth, were both in request at the table, on account of their beauty and interest.

I must not forget to mention a very interesting series of twenty-four stereoscopic pictures by Mr. Alfieri, illustrative of "The Potter's Art."

Mr. Jabez Hughes and Mr. Meagher were both exhibitors of very excellent and useful apparatus—cameras, camera-stands, and rolling presses.

Now I think such an exhibition as I have but partially described cannot fail to have produced a pleasing and beneficial effect on the minds of all who saw it, and ought, on the whole, to have given infinite pleasure and satisfaction to both exhibitors and visitors. Yet I think I heard one or two growls of discontent about the hanging from some one whose pictures or whose friend's pictures were not on the line; but I think I may safely say there never was a case of hanging yet that was not objected to by one individual at least. Even the hangers of the Royal Academy do not escape censure, and they are supposed to have far more skill, taste, and experience in hanging than the volunteer hangers of the late photographic exhibition. I think, however, that the hangers performed their duties both conscientiously and creditably, especially when it is considered in how very short a time the work had to be done. Anyone who felt aggrieved, and expressed himself churlishly on that point, must surely have been in that unenviable state which the French very adroitly designate *Etre marqué au B.*

After these reflections I felt too drowsy to reflect any more, and was barely awake enough to subscribe myself—Yours very truly.

November 10*th*, 1868.

THE REFUNDING OF THE BALANCE OF THE GODDARD FUND—THE PHOTOGRAPHERS' PROVIDENT SOCIETY—A FEROCIOUS DOORSMAN—THE SOUTH LONDON DINNER—A CHRISTMAS CAROL.

MY DEAR SIR,—Now that the balance of the Goddard Fund is returned to the contributors, and all the trials and vexations the administration of the fund brought upon the chief promoters are known, I think the very best thanks of the whole body of subscribers to that fund are due to the committee for their firm and sensible determination to provide for the wants of the poor imbecile recipient in the manner they did, and for their withstanding the attempt made by a person who was not in the least related to the late Mr. Goddard to obtain possession of the balance in hand. I, for one, a subscriber to the fund, return them my most hearty acknowledgments, not for the money returned to me, but for the straightforwardness of their report, and the wise and judicious manner in which they dispensed the funds. While congratulating myself and confrères on seeing the money not required for the relief of the late Mr. Goddard returned to the subscribers instead of going into the possession of a person for whom it never was intended, I think it is to be regretted that no responsible party had foreseen that much of this returned money would have been gladly placed to the credit of some benevolent or provident institution connected with photography. The whole amount, or even the half of it, would have made a very handsome nucleus for the commencement of such a fund. I have heard several wishes to that effect expressed during the last few days. Doubtless the committee did the very best thing they could have done for their own credit and the entire satisfaction of the whole of the subscribers; but I am afraid an opportunity has been lost in the interest of the incipient relief fund by not having had a receiver for these stray and unexpected sums appointed. The praiseworthy act of Messrs. Ross and Pringle, as noticed in another journal, confirms this impression.

While the subject of a photographers' provident or relief fund is before me, I may mention that in the Report of the Friendly Societies recently issued by Mr Tidd Pratt, he speaks in the highest terms of those societies which are managed by the members themselves without salaries, and condemns the extravagance exhibited by the societies of a similar nature which are conducted by salaried officials. Now, as it is a friendly society pure and simple that sick or needy photographers ought to look to for future help, in my opinion the former is the kind of society that should be established. The movement is not to be started as a business speculation, and there should be no salaries attached to any of the offices. Each member joining the provident society should be prepared to submit to the tax on his time and energies, if elected to office, as part and parcel of the amount he subscribes for the general welfare of the body and relief of individual members. For my part, I object to the contemplated society taking the form of a relief fund depending upon donations, collections at dinners, &c., for its support. Such means for raising the necessary funds to start the society may be allowable; but after it is commenced, every individual connected with it should be a subscribing member, and not allowed to receive any benefit, except under the most urgent necessities, until he has paid a certain number of subscriptions.

During one of my peregrinations about town lately I stumbled upon a very ferocious doorsman. My attention was suddenly arrested, while passing one of those photographic establishments which keep a kind of two-legged hyena prowling up and down before their doors, by hearing the somewhat startling and cannibalistic exclamation of "I'll eat yer!" Looking round, I saw that one of those prowling bipeds had fastened upon two quiet-looking young gentlemen, evidently strangers in town and to town ways, and had so importuned them to sit for "a correct likeness," until they turned upon him, and threatened to give him in charge if he did not desist; when he retaliated by threatening to eat them, and used a great deal of sanguinary and abusive language as a substitute for more palatable suavity. Is such an "outsider" or hanger-on a fit and proper person to join a photographers' provident society, or be the recipient of a benevolent relief fund?

The South London Photographic Society's annual dinner came off on Saturday evening last at the "Salutation Tavern," Newgate Street. Twenty-three members and friends, all told, sat down to dinner, and enjoyed a thoroughly English repast. After the cloth was removed, the pleasantest part of the evening commenced. The worthy and honoured president, the Rev. F. F. Statham, M.A., who occupied the chair, was all geniality, and gave the toast of the evening—" The South London Photographic Society "—in his usually felicitous style. To Mr. Jabez Hughes was allotted the task of proposing the next important toast— " Photography "—which he did in the most glowing and eloquent terms, dwelling on the rise and progress of the art in England, its position in a competitive point of view at the Paris Exhibition, interspersed with some racy and facetious remarks on the different modes and kinds of rewards, from the bronze, silver, and gold medals, to the paper certificates, which he considered the most honourable mentions that could be given by a discerning public. From that he soared into the higher aspirations of photographers and sublime regions of photography, giving, with thrilling effect, a description of the social joys, scientific pursuits, and human ameliorations to which photography administers. Mr. Baynham Jones, being the oldest photographer present, had the honour of replying on behalf of the art. Mr. G. Wharton Simpson, in very appropriate terms, gave the toast, " Art Photography," which was responded to by Mr. O. G. Rejlander. Mr. Johnson, of the Autotype Company, had the honour of proposing the toast " Professional Photography," which was responded to by Mr. Valentine Blanchard, who occupied the vice-chair. Other toasts of a professional and semi-professional character were given and responded to. The intervals were filled up with part and instrumental music by members of the Society. Mr. Cooper contributed greatly to the evening's enjoyment by giving two charming performances on the cornet-a-piston, which were admirably accompanied by Mr. Henry Cooper on the piano. Taking it all in all, it was one of the pleasantest and merriest evenings I have ever enjoyed at the convivial meetings of the South London Photographic Society, and formed a delightful introduction to the season of universal festivity which is close at hand.

Christmas, all over the civilized world, is not only a period of festive reunion, but, according to the only rational interpretation of the word, a time of good will towards men, and peace upon earth. Photographers, like other men, have had their little differences of opinion, which have produced partial estrangements during a portion of the year which will so soon expire; but let the approaching season, which is held in commemoration of the birth of the greatest Peacemaker that ever came among men, be looked upon by all as the fittest time to forget and forgive all slights, injuries, or insults, real or imaginary; and let not the great festival of our common faith be clouded or eclipsed by an angry thought, nor the immeasurable charity of true Christianity be dimmed by one unforgiving feeling. The light of the Christian faith is a light that should penetrate to the dark cells of our hearts, and dispel all the gloomy and corrosive accumulations of controversy that may have lodged there, and unconsciously eaten away any part of our better nature. Few of us—none but the most presumptuous—can lay his hand upon his heart and say, "Mine is immaculate!" None of us are without sin, and charity and forgiveness are the greatest of the Christian virtues; and they should be the more carefully studied and practised by all who live in and by the Light of the world.

December 15th, 1868.

PHOTOGRAPHY AND THE IMMURED POMPEIIANS.

EVERY one must be sensible of the many and varied applications of photography. Even photographers themselves, familiar as they are with the capabilities of the art they practise, must necessarily have their wonder excited occasionally at the scope of their art-science, especially when they consider that the process, as practised at the present day, is not more than seventeen years old. That it should be the historian of the life and manners of the present period more fully and faithfully than any written account, is not so much a matter of surprise. Appealing, as it does, to the vanity and affections of the people, it is at once a recorder of the changes of fashion, a registrar of marriages, births, and deaths, and a truthful illustrator of the times in which we live; but that it should be brought to bear upon the past, and make the inhabitants of the world in the nineteenth century familiar with the forms, fashions, manners, life, and death of the people of the first century of the Christian Era, is something to be marvelled at, and at first seems an impossibility. Yet such is the fact; and photography has been made the cheap and easy means of informing the present generation of the manner in which the ancients behaved, suffered, and died in the midst of one of the most appalling catastrophes that ever overtook the inhabitants of any part of the world, ancient or modern, as vividly and undeniably as if the calamity had occurred but yesterday.

The foregoing reflections were excited by seeing very recently some photographs from plaster casts of the forms of human beings as they had fallen and died when Pompeii and Herculaneum were destroyed by the first known and terrible eruption of Mount Vesuvius. The photographs alluded to reveal with a fearful fidelity the dreadful agonies of some of those who perished at Pompeii, and, while looking at the pictures, it is very difficult to divest the mind of the idea that they are not the works of some ancient photographer who plied his lens and camera immediately after the eruption had ceased, so forcibly do they carry the mind back to the time and place of the awful immurement of both a town and its people.

That these photographs were not obtained from the lifeless forms of the Pompeiians the reader will readily understand, for their bodies have not been preserved entire from that day to this. The question then naturally arises, "How could plaster casts be obtained from which the photographs were produced?"

To answer that question I must briefly explain that Pompeii was not, as is generally understood, destroyed by an overflow of red hot lava, which would have burnt up every particle of human flesh with which it came in contact almost instantly, without leaving a mould or impress of the form which it surrounded. The *black mud* which flowed from Vesuvius into the doomed town of Pompeii entombed the houses and inhabitants—covered them up and formed a thick crust over them, which gradually hardened, and as the bodies crumbled away to dust a mould or matrix was left, from which plaster casts of great beauty and finish might have been obtained of almost everything that was destroyed. Unfortunately, this was not discovered until very recently, after many of the beautiful moulds had been destroyed by the process of hurried, thoughtless, and unsystematic excavation. It was only a short time ago, since Naples was united to Italy, that careful and intelligent excavation secured to future generations impressions from those matrices made by the most terrible process of natural mould making.

Sig. Fiorelli, who was appointed superintendent of excavations at Pompeii, happily thought of obtaining casts from these natural moulds by pouring in soft plaster of Paris, and thus secure more useful mementos than by preserving the moulds themselves. Amongst the first casts thus obtained were the forms of four human beings, described as follows in the *Quarterly Review* for 1864:—

"These four persons had perished in the streets. Driven from their homes, they sought to flee when it was too late. These victims of the eruption were not found together, and they do not appear to have belonged to the same family or household. The most interesting of the casts is that of two women, probably mother and daughter, lying feet to feet; they appear from their garb to have been people of poor condition. The elder seems to lie tranquilly on her side, overcome by the noxious gases. She probably fell and died without a struggle. Her limbs are extended, and her left arm drops loosely. On one finger is still seen her coarse iron ring. Her child was a girl of fifteen; she seems, poor thing, to have struggled hard for life. Her legs are drawn up convulsively. Her little hands are clenched in agony. In one she holds her veil, or part of her dress with which she had covered her head, burying her face in her arms to shield herself from the falling ashes and from the foul, sulphurous smoke. The form of her head is perfectly preserved. The texture of her coarse linen garments may be traced, and even the fashion of her dress, with its long sleeves reaching to her wrists. Here and there it is torn, and the smooth young skin appears in the plaster like polished marble. On her tiny feet may still be seen her embroidered sandals. At some distance from this group lay a third woman, apparently about the age of twenty-five, and belonging to a better class. Silver rings were on her fingers. She lay on her side, and had died in great agony. Her garments had been gathered up on one side, leaving exposed a limb of the most beautiful form. She had fled with her little treasure, two silver cups, a few jewels, and some silver coins, and her keys, like a careful matron. The fourth cast is that of a man of the people, perhaps a common soldier. He is almost of colossal size. He lies on his back, his arms extended by his side, and his feet stretched out, as if, finding escape impossible, he had laid himself down to meet death like a brave man. His dress consists of a short coat or jerkin, and tight-fitting breeches of some coarse stuff, perhaps leather; heavy sandals, with soles studded with nails, are laced tightly round his ankles. On one finger is seen his iron ring. His features are strongly marked, his mouth open, as in death. Some of his teeth still remain, and even part of the moustache adheres to the plaster."

Such is the description of the plaster casts; and the photographs which I possess of those casts convey to the mind at one glance all that is there written. Wonderful photography!

How eloquent in their silence are thy pictures! To what more dignified and sublime uses could any art be put? Only a few can look upon those casts of the dead Pompeiians in the Museum of Naples, but the whole world may view the photographs taken from them, and look upon the Pompeiians in their forms and habits as they died, and read a page from the unwritten histories of those terrible death-struggles, when the strong man, the tender, placid mother, and the young and delicate maiden were all entombed in that fearful sea of mud, amidst darkness and horrors that can never be adequately described.

Such an awful catastrophe will never cease to interest the student of ancient history, and photography will now be the means of deepening his interest, and revealing to his mind with greater force and lucidity many scenes that actually occurred at the very moment of the appalling destruction of Pompeii, on the 24th of August, A.D. 79.

A SIMPLE MODE OF INTENSIFYING NEGATIVES.

UNDOUBTEDLY the best possible practice of photography is that which requires no after intensification in the production of a first-class negative. This, however, though a "consummation devoutly to be wished," is not always attained, even by the most experienced photographer. Every operator knows that there is sometimes a condition of things that renders a simple and efficient process of intensifying afterwards indispensable.

Of all the modes of intensifying—and their name is legion—I think the readiest and most generally useful has been much neglected. The persulphate of uranium and ferridcyanide of potassium process gave wonderfully charming results. But what of that? It was completely impracticable, and a failure, in consequence of its tendency to go on increasing in intensity in the hands of the printer.

The bichloride of mercury and iodine processes, unlimited in number, also went on increasing in an unlimited degree, and no amount of "roasting" could reduce the negatives so treated to the desirable degree of transparency that would enable any printer to obtain good impressions. There is, however, one of the bichloride of mercury processes, published some years ago, which I modified so as to give the most satisfactory results. It rendered the negative sufficiently intense, and preserved the most exquisite modelling, without changing afterwards; but the process was very troublsome, and not very agreeable.

The simplest, cheapest, and most reliable process of intensifying negatives that I know of is with sulphuret of potassium (liver of sulphur) used in the following manner :—

Make a very dilute solution of sulphuret of potassium, put it into any old gutta-percha or porcelain bath; and, after the negative is developed as far as is desirable with the ordinary iron developer, fixed, and washed in the usual way, immerse the plate in that state at once into the solution of sulphuret of potassium, in the same manner as in sensitising the plate in the nitrate bath, by using a dipper, and leave it there until sufficiently intense, which is generally in about the time required for coating and sensitising another plate, so that, if the operator be working single-handed, very little, if any, time is lost in the process of intensifying.

The solution may also be flooded over the plate in the same manner as the developer, after fixing and washing as before.

When sufficiently intense, rinse the plate with water, dry, and varnish in the ordinary way. But it is best to use the intensifier in the manner first described, which is by far the most cleanly and economical plan, both in the saving of time and solution. By using it with the "bath and dipper," it is not offensive, on account of its extreme dilution, and not being disturbed so much, or immediately under the olfactory nerves of the operator, it may be worked in the ordinary dark room with the greatest safety and convenience.

A STRING OF OLD BEADS.

He is a rash man who announces "something new" in these days. I believe there is nothing new under the sun, and in photography especially. If any man be rash enough to rush into print with what he considers a new idea, some other man rushes into print also and says the idea is old, exploded, useless, worthless, or worse.

I lay no claim to originality. I have lived so long in the atmosphere of photography, I don't know where or how I picked up my knowledge—such as it is. Some of it I may have stumbled on, some of it I may have found, and some of it I may have stolen. If the latter, I forget from whom, when, or where, and in all such cases a bad memory is a good and convenient thing. But I will endeavour to atone for such sins by publicly restoring all I may have filched from other men's brains for the benefit of all whom it may concern. I shall not count the beads; that would be like running over a rosary, and I object to *sub rosa* revelations; neither shall I attend to the order of stringing the beads, but will put them on record just as they come to hand; and the first is—

How to Make Vignette Papers.—Take a piece of sensitized paper, lay it under a piece of glass and let it blacken. Then take a camels'-hair pencil dipped in a weak solution of cyanide of potassium, and paint the extreme size and shape of the desired aperture. Let it dry, and with a little stronger solution of cyanide paint *within* the size and shape, and then with a stronger solution paint the centre, which will be perfectly white and semi-transparent. The object of using the three strengths of solution and painting three separate times is to obtain gradation, and the edges will be yellow and softened like a vignette glass. These vignette papers can be attached to the back of the negative or to the outside of the printing-press, and can be used either in shade or sunshine without materially prolonging the time of printing. The cost of production is trifling, as any waste piece of paper and spare time can be employed in making them, and they do not occupy much time in making; in fact, one can be made in less time than will be spent in reading this description. I need not expatiate on the advantages of being able to make a special vignette quickly. Every photographer must have experienced the difficulty of purchasing a special size and shape to suit a particular subject.

How to Point a Pencil.—Rub the pencil to a point in the groove of a corundum file. This is a better and cheaper pointer than a Yankee pencil-sharpener, and it puts a finer point to a blacklead pencil than anything else I know. Retouchers, try it.

How to Ease a Tight Stopper.—There is nothing more annoying in the practice of photography than to take up a bottle and find the stopper *fixed*. In many instances the bottle is broken and time wasted in trying to remove the fixed stopper. When such an obstinate stopper gets into your hands, run a little glycerine round the top of the bottle. Set the bottle down, and in a few minutes the stopper will be free. Prevention is better than cure. Keep a little glycerine on all your stoppers. Glycerine agrees with every chemical in photographic use, and prevents stoppers and bottles coming to grief. In a thousand and one ways a little glycerine is beyond all price.

How to Prepare Albumenized Prints for Colouring.—Pour over them a little matt varnish. This removes the greasiness, and gives a fine tooth and ivory-like surface for the artist to work upon.

How to Remove Silver Stains from the White Ground of a Vignette—Touch it with a solution of cyanide of potassium, and wash off immediately. The other parts of the picture will not be injured.

How to Stipple a Window White or Yellow.—For white, mix a little dextrine and kaolin in water. Dab the mixture on the glass with a piece of cotton. For the purpose of obscuration that is quite enough; but if sightliness be essential, finish by stippling with the ends of a hog's-hair brush. For yellow, mix a little dextrine and deep orange chrome in powder together in water, and apply it to the window in the same manner. Dabbing once or twice with a piece of cotton will exclude white light and make a luminous dark room. The same mixture makes an excellent backing for dry plates to prevent halation

LIGHTS AND LIGHTING.

A GREAT deal has been written and said about lights and lighting —a great deal too much; yet more must be said and written.

Light is to the photographer what the sickle is to the shearer —a good reaper can cut well with an indifferent sickle, but an indifferent reaper never gets a good sickle in his hand. A good photographer, who also understands light and shade, can produce good pictures in an ordinary studio. It is the indifferent photographer who runs after "fancy lights," and is, like a benighted traveller in pursuit of a will-o'-the-wisp, eventually left floundering in a bog. It is folly to construct powerful concentrators if powerful reflectors have to be employed to counteract their defects. If a limited amount of 'diffused' light be absolutely necessary it is best to retain it and use it in its simplest and least expensive form.

When I commenced photography glass houses were scarcer in England than comets in the heavens, and the few that were in existence were all constructed on false principles. It was not until I visited America that I saw a *properly*-constructed studio. The Americans were, and are, prone to give stupid names to sensible things; and the names they gave to their studios were no exceptions. This, that, and the other photographer advertised his "mammoth skylight." I went to sit, see, and be satisfied that their mode of lighting was very superior to ours. I was convinced *instanter* that the perpendicular sides and sloping roofs of our miserable little hothouses were mistakes and things to be abhorred, while their spacious rooms and "mammoth skylights" were things to be admired and adopted

In one of these rooms, and almost without blinds or reflectors, the sitter could be "worked" on a semi-circle or half oval, and "lighted" either in front or on either side at pleasure, and with the greatest facility. I determined, there and then, to build my next studio on similar principles ; but until recently I have had no opportunity of carrying out my intentions. To get what I required and to make the best of my situation I had to "fence and fiddle" the district surveyor: but I gained my point, and the victory was worth the foils and the fiddlestick.

My studio can be lighted from either side; but the "light of lights" is the north one, and that is a large fixed window 11 by 9 feet with a single slope of two and a-half feet in the height; that is, two and a-half feet out of the perpendicular at the top, with no other top light and no perpendicular side light. With this light I do all ordinary work. I can work round the light from one side of the room to the other, as under a mammoth skylight, without using either blind or reflector. If I want Rembrandt effects I have only to open a shutter on the south side, and let in subdued sunlight. That at once becomes the dominant light, and the north light illumines the shadows. The bottom of the north light is three feet from the floor.

The advantages of this form of studio are these. It is cool, because no more light is admitted than is absolutely necessary. It is neat, because no rag-like curtains are hanging about. It is clean, because there is nothing to collect dirt. It is dry, because the pitch of the roof renders leakage impossible. It is pleasant to the sitter, because of these desirabilities, and that the light is not distressing. It is agreeable to the operator, because the work is easy and everything is comfortable.

BIBLIOLIFE

Old Books Deserve a New Life
www.bibliolife.com

Did you know that you can get most of our titles in our trademark **EasyScript**™ print format? **EasyScript**™ provides readers with a larger than average typeface, for a reading experience that's easier on the eyes.

Did you know that we have an ever-growing collection of books in many languages?

Order online:
www.bibliolife.com/store

Or to exclusively browse our **EasyScript**™ collection:
www.bibliogrande.com

At BiblioLife, we aim to make knowledge more accessible by making thousands of titles available to you – quickly and affordably.

Contact us:
BiblioLife
PO Box 21206
Charleston, SC 29413

Printed in Great Britain by
Amazon.co.uk, Ltd.,
Marston Gate.